An Hachette UK Company
www.hachette.co.uk

Summersdale Publishers Ltd
Part of Octopus Publishing Group Limited
Carmelite House
50 Victoria Embankment
LONDON
EC4Y 0DZ
UK

www.summersdale.com

Printed and bound in the Czech Republic

ISBN: 978-1-78685-536-7

2019

Substantial discounts on bulk quantities of Summersdale books are available to corporations, professional associations and other organisations.
For details contact general enquiries: telephone: +44 (0) 1243 771107 or email: enquiries@summersdale.com.

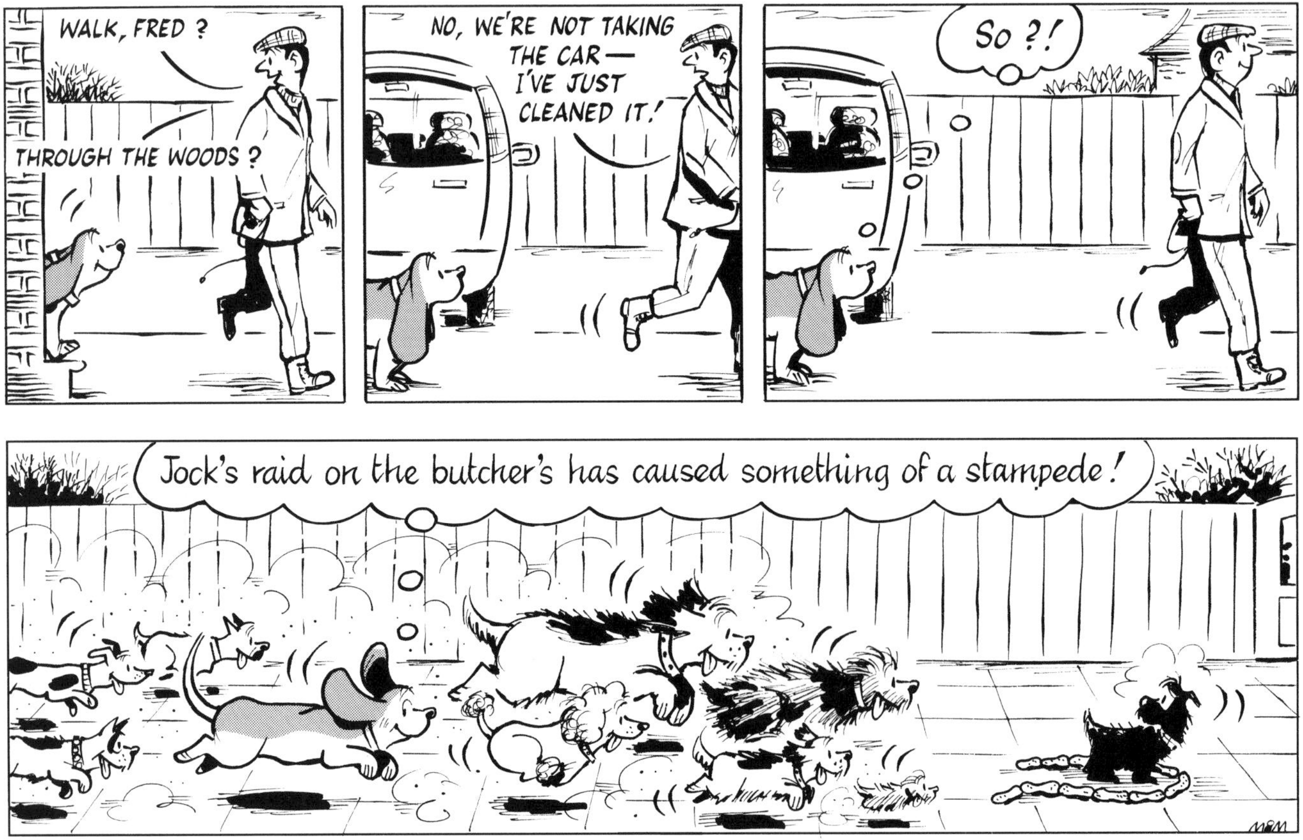
WALK, FRED ?
THROUGH THE WOODS ?
NO, WE'RE NOT TAKING THE CAR— I'VE JUST CLEANED IT!
So ?!
Jock's raid on the butcher's has caused something of a stampede!

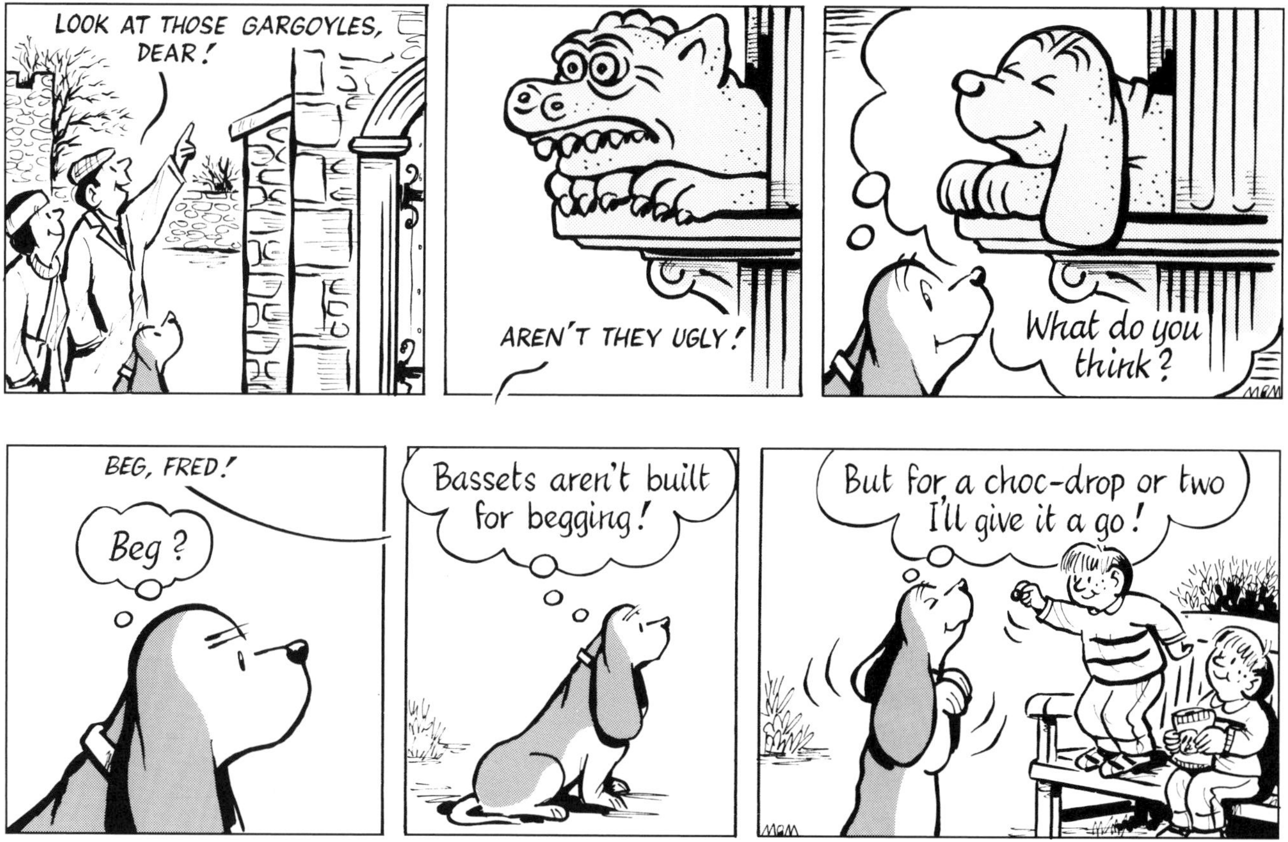
LOOK AT THOSE GARGOYLES, DEAR!
AREN'T THEY UGLY!
What do you think?
BEG, FRED!
Beg?
Bassets aren't built for begging!
But for a choc-drop or two I'll give it a go!

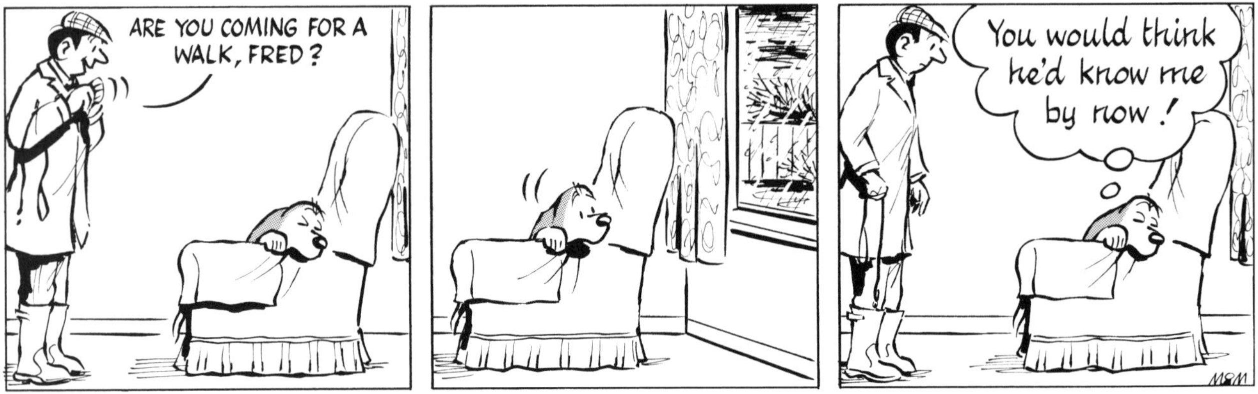
ARE YOU COMING FOR A WALK, FRED?
You would think he'd know me by now!

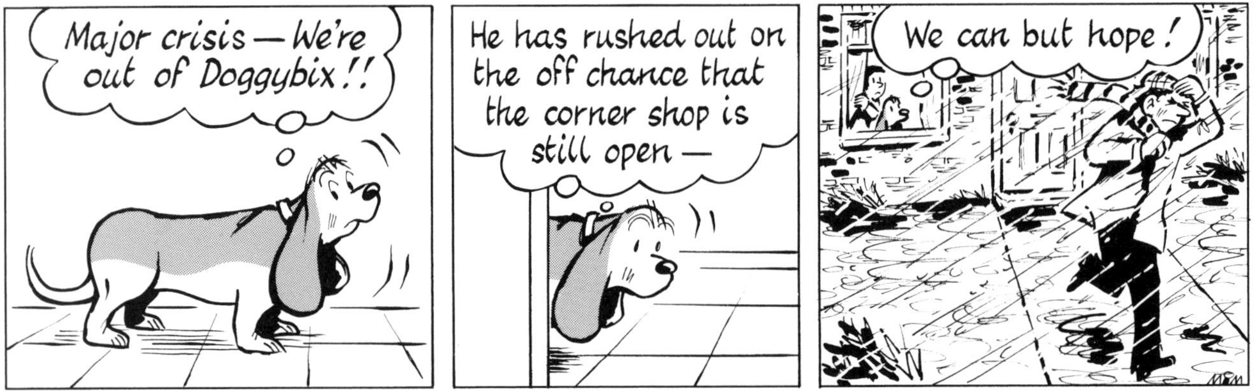
Major crisis — We're out of Doggybix!!
He has rushed out on the off chance that the corner shop is still open —
We can but hope!

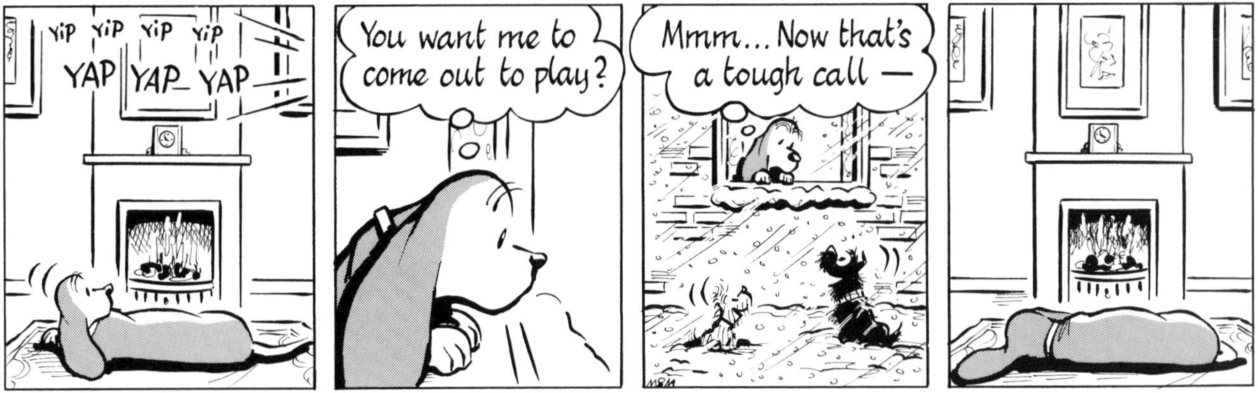
YIP YIP YIP YIP
YAP YAP_ YAP
You want me to come out to play?
Mmm... Now that's a tough call —

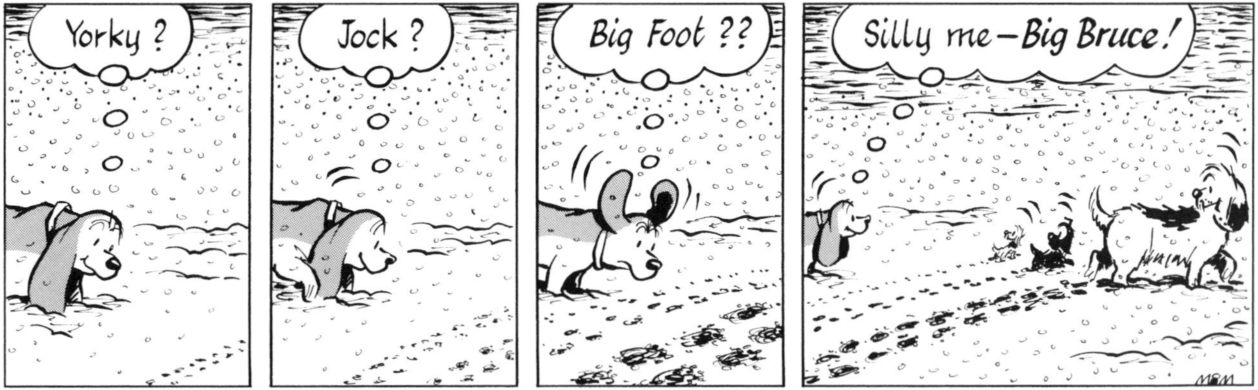
Yorky ?
Jock ?
Big Foot ??
Silly me—*Big Bruce!*

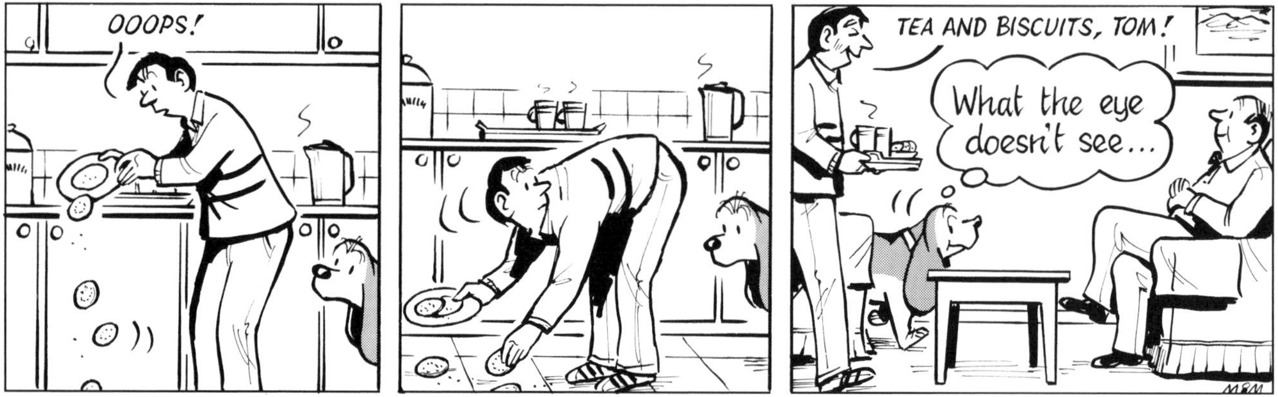
OOOPS!
TEA AND BISCUITS, TOM!
What the eye doesn't see...
M&M

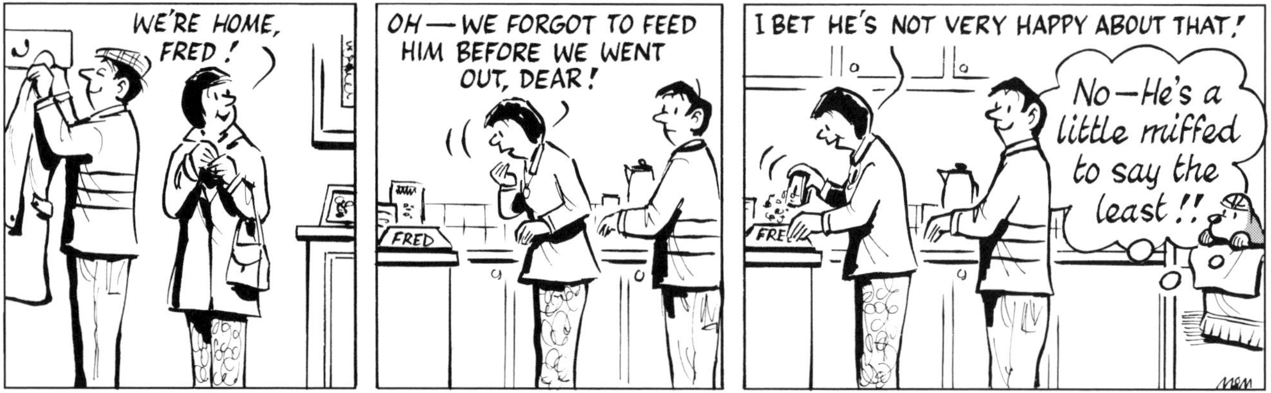
WE'RE HOME, FRED!
OH — WE FORGOT TO FEED HIM BEFORE WE WENT OUT, DEAR!
FRED
I BET HE'S NOT VERY HAPPY ABOUT THAT!
No — He's a little miffed to say the least!!
M&M

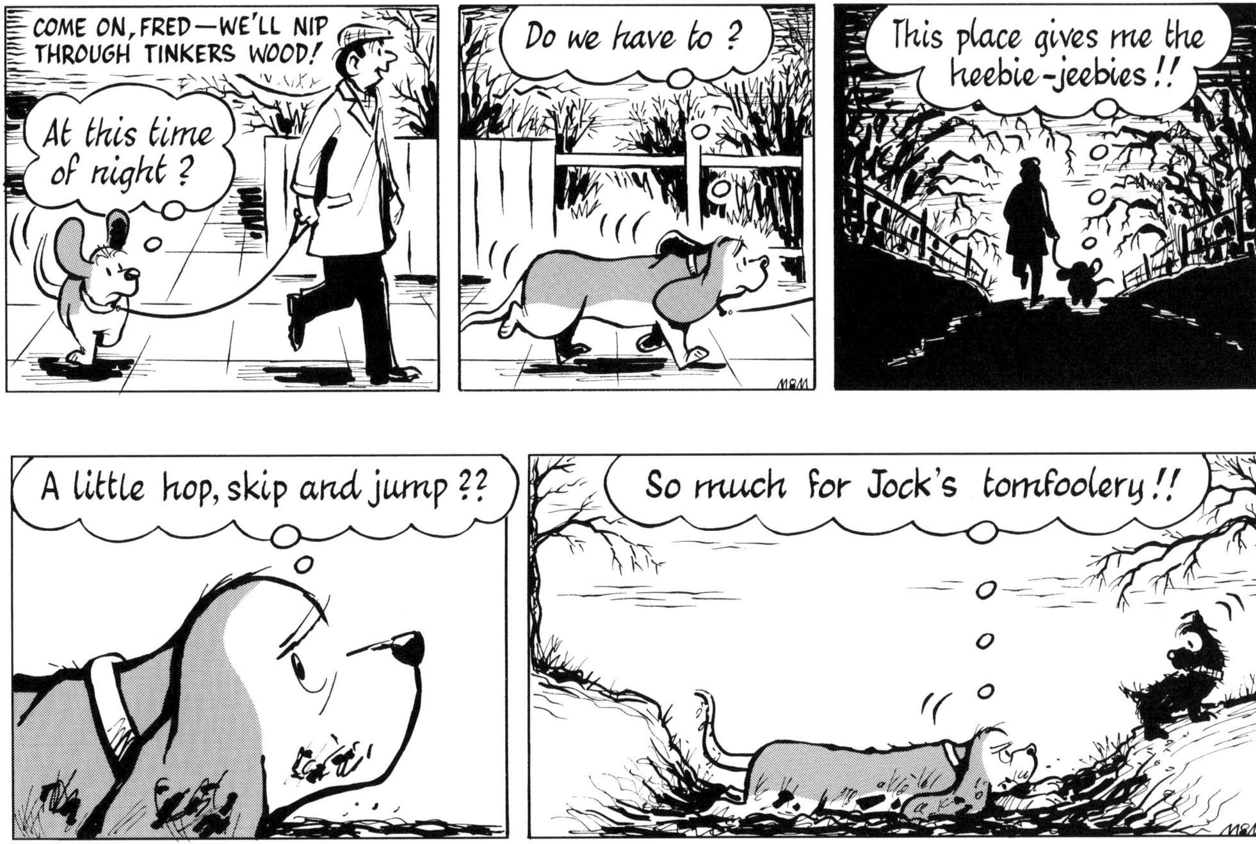

COME ON, FRED—WE'LL NIP THROUGH TINKERS WOOD!
At this time of night?
Do we have to?
This place gives me the heebie-jeebies!!
A little hop, skip and jump??
So much for Jock's tomfoolery!!

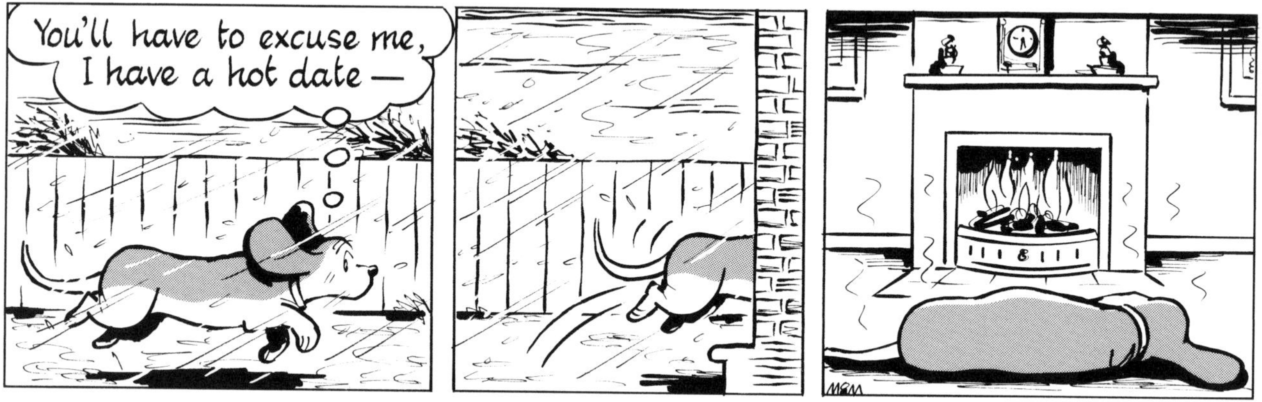
You'll have to excuse me, I have a hot date —

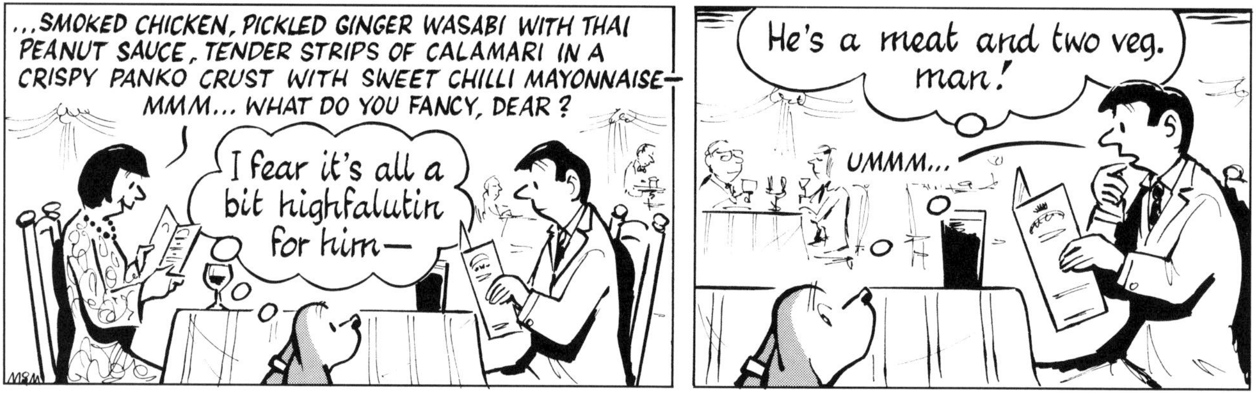
...SMOKED CHICKEN, PICKLED GINGER WASABI WITH THAI PEANUT SAUCE, TENDER STRIPS OF CALAMARI IN A CRISPY PANKO CRUST WITH SWEET CHILLI MAYONNAISE — MMM... WHAT DO YOU FANCY, DEAR ?
I fear it's all a bit highfalutin for him —
He's a meat and two veg. man!
UMMM...

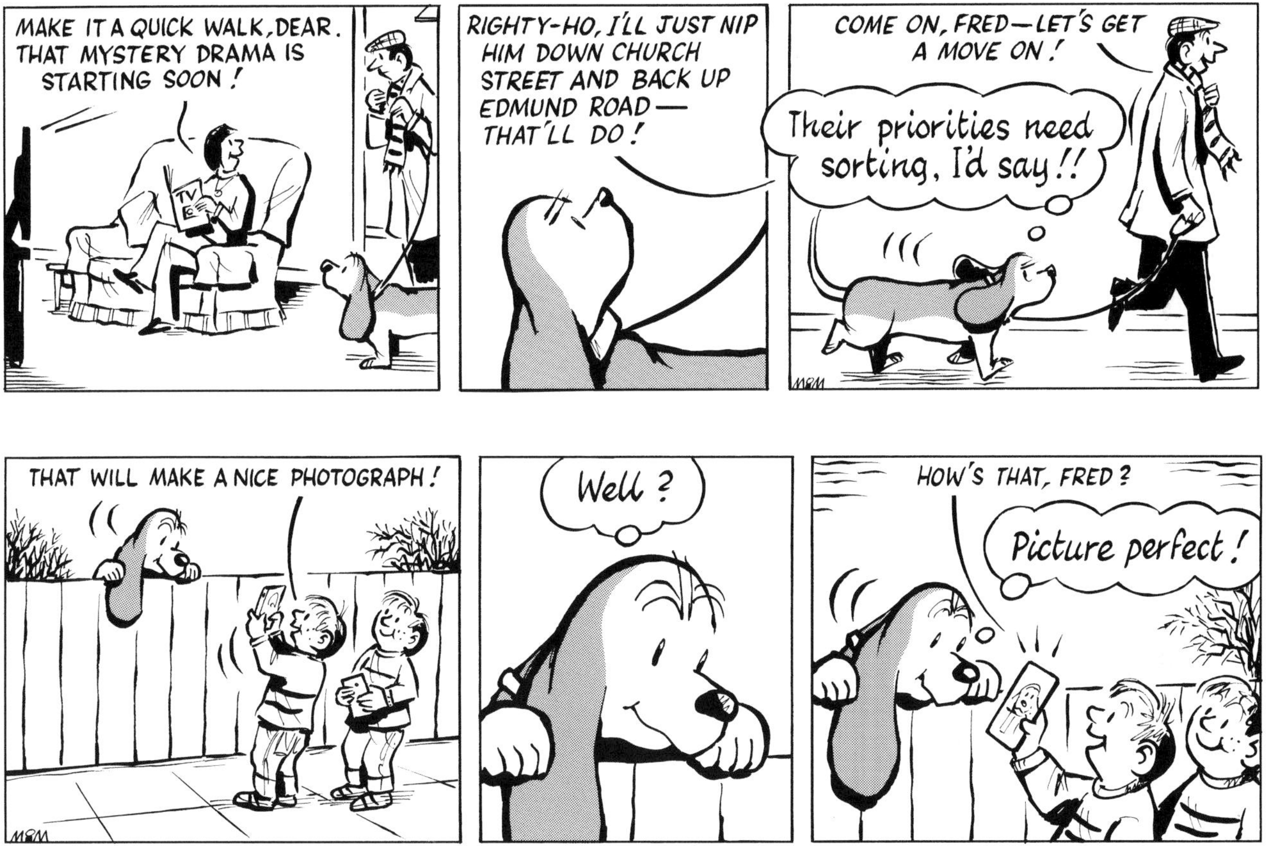
MAKE IT A QUICK WALK, DEAR. THAT MYSTERY DRAMA IS STARTING SOON!
TV
RIGHTY-HO, I'LL JUST NIP HIM DOWN CHURCH STREET AND BACK UP EDMUND ROAD— THAT'LL DO!
COME ON, FRED—LET'S GET A MOVE ON!
Their priorities need sorting, I'd say!!
THAT WILL MAKE A NICE PHOTOGRAPH!
Well?
HOW'S THAT, FRED?
Picture perfect!

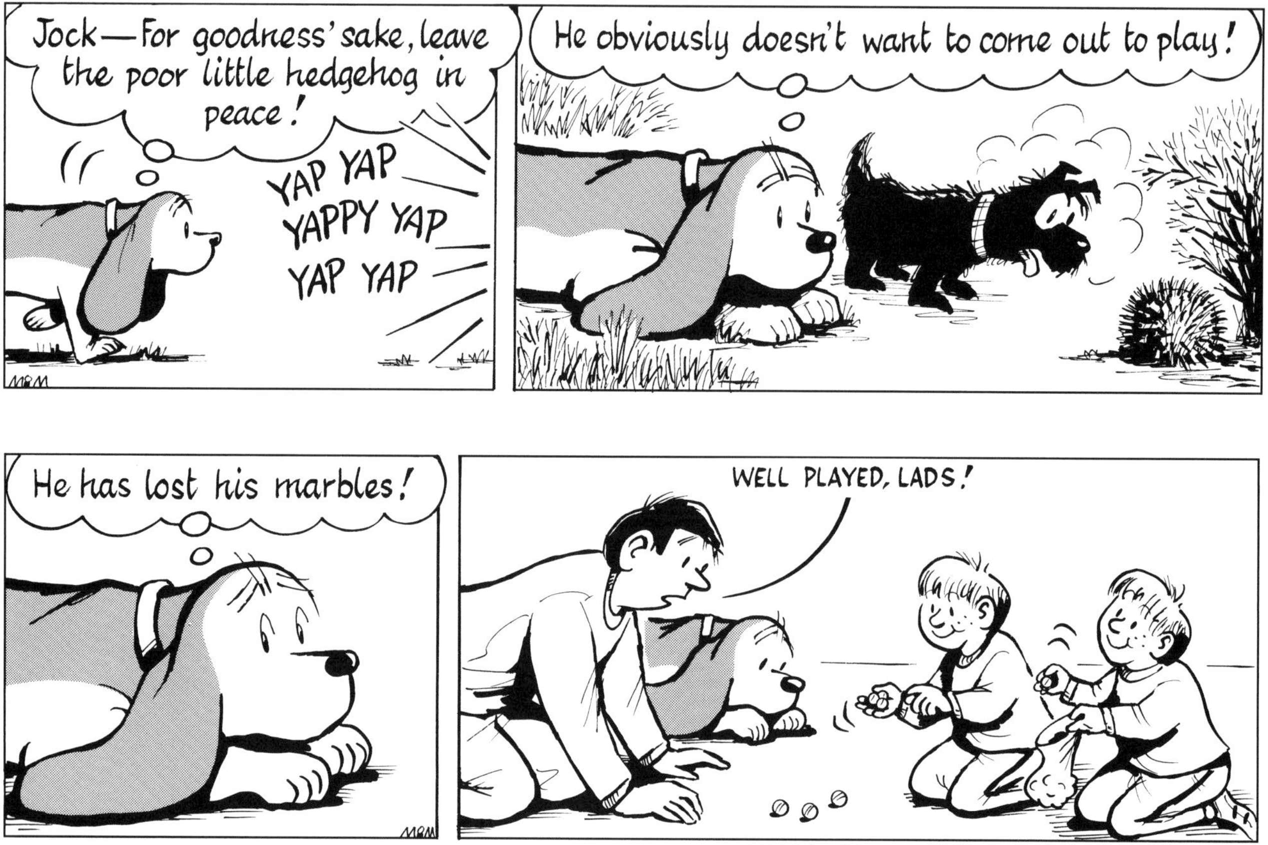
Jock—For goodness' sake, leave the poor little hedgehog in peace!
YAP YAP YAPPY YAP YAP YAP
He obviously doesn't want to come out to play!
He has lost his marbles!
WELL PLAYED, LADS!

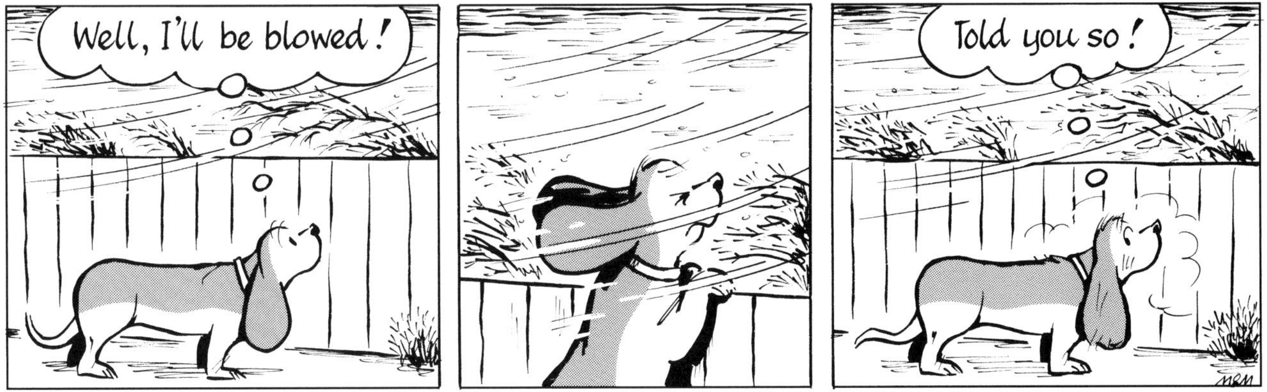
Well, I'll be blowed!
Told you so!

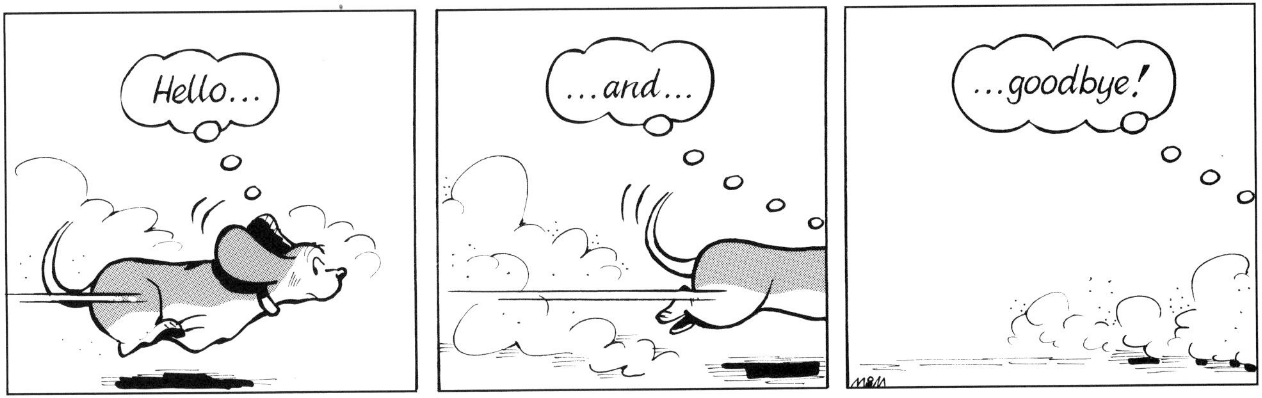
Hello...
...and...
...goodbye!

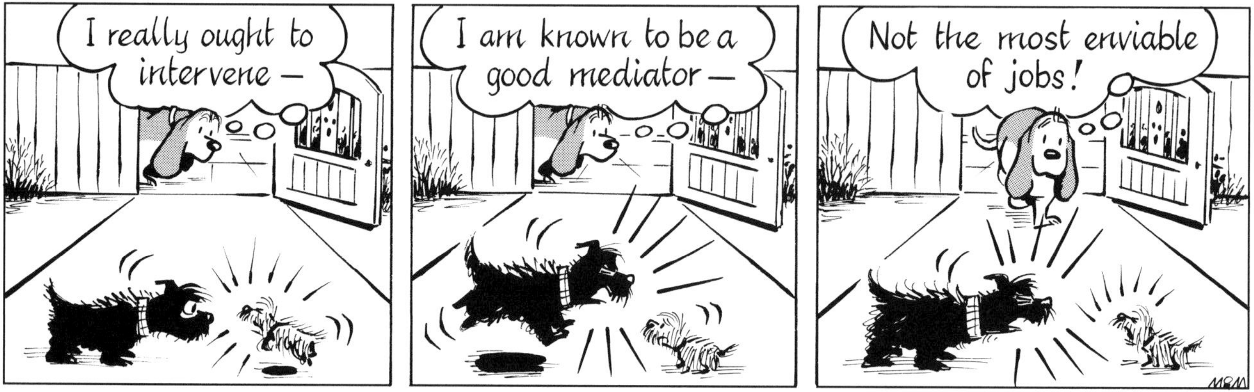
I really ought to intervene –
I am known to be a good mediator –
Not the most enviable of jobs!
MSM

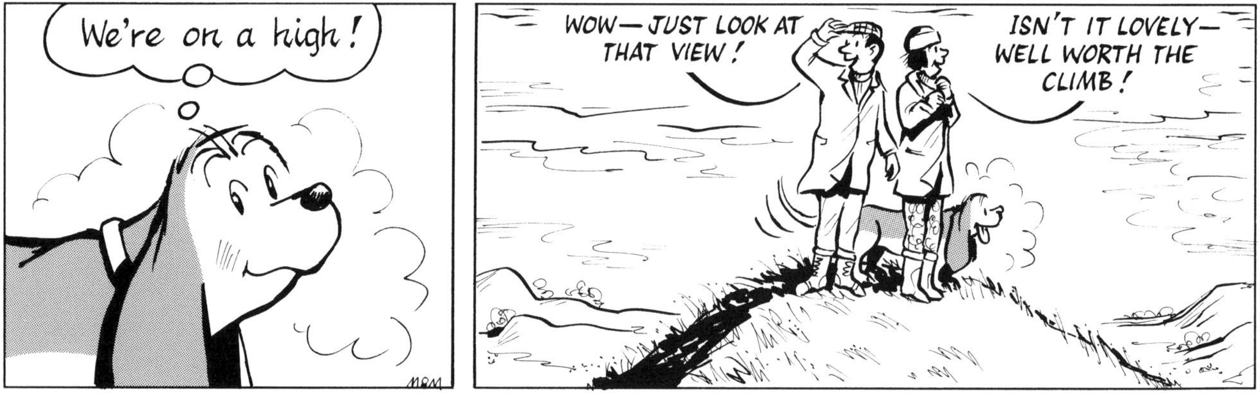
We're on a high!
MSM
WOW — JUST LOOK AT THAT VIEW!
ISN'T IT LOVELY — WELL WORTH THE CLIMB!

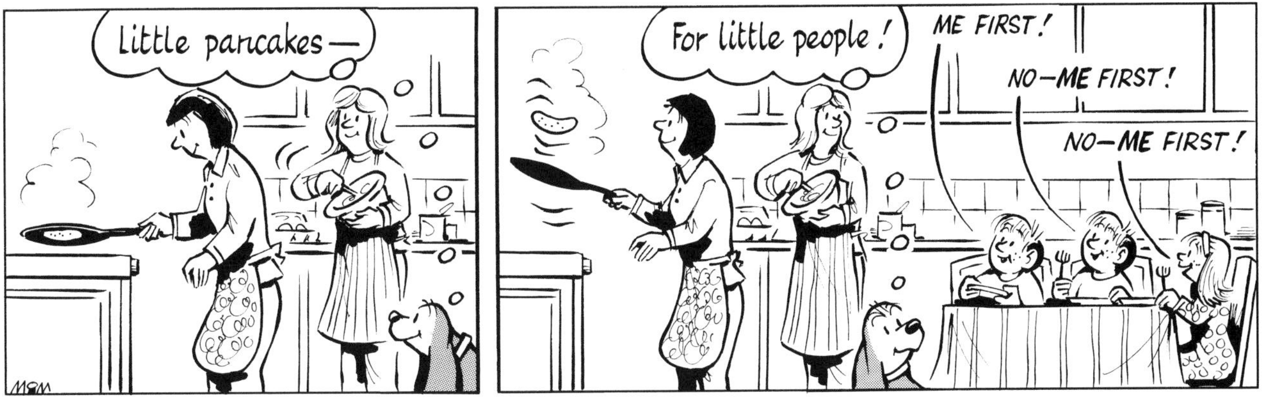
Little pancakes—
For little people!
ME FIRST!
NO—ME FIRST!
NO—ME FIRST!

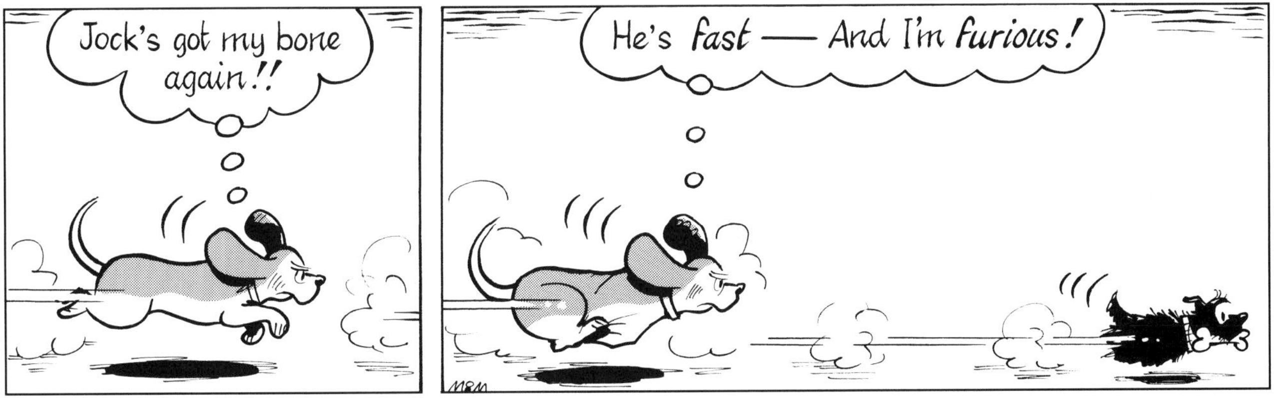
Jock's got my bone again!!
He's fast — And I'm furious!

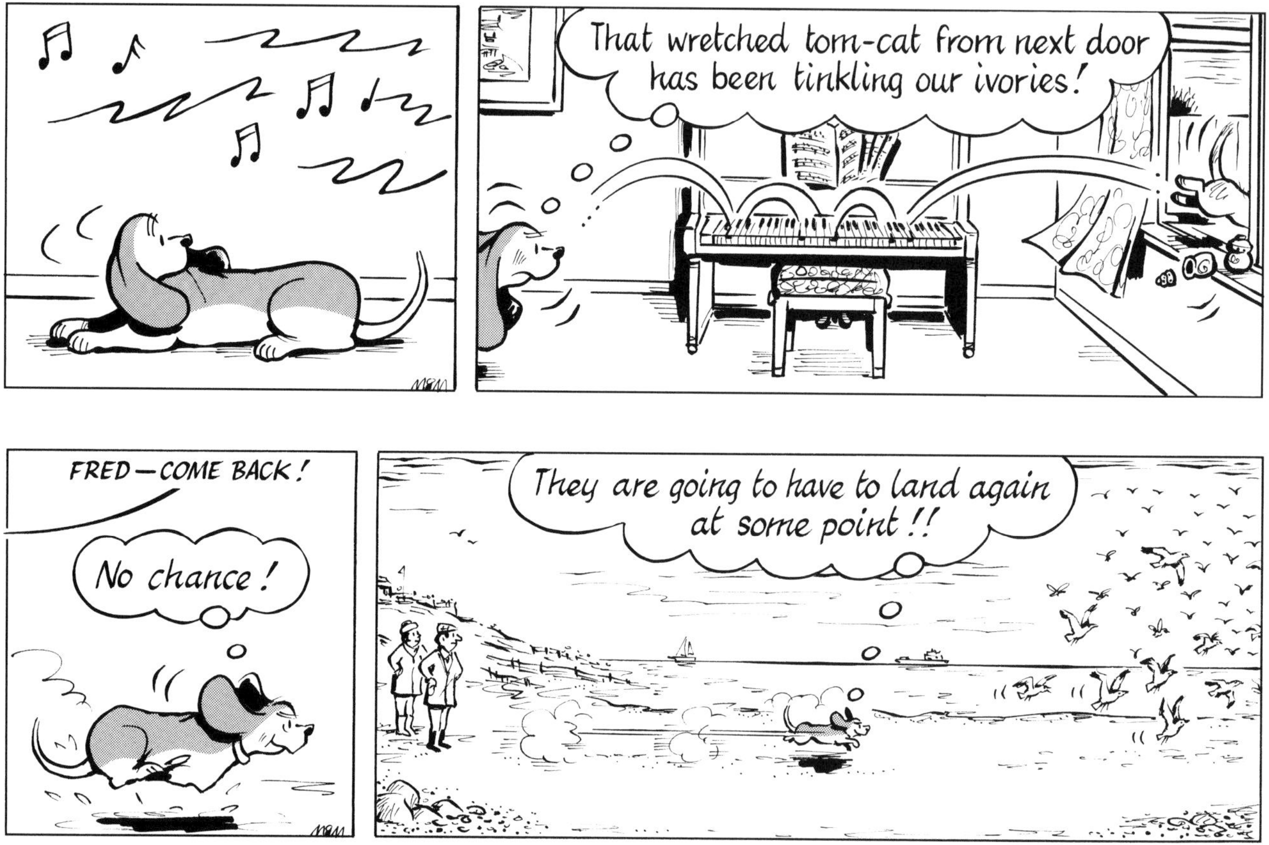
That wretched tom-cat from next door has been tinkling our ivories!
FRED—COME BACK!
No chance!
They are going to have to land again at some point!!

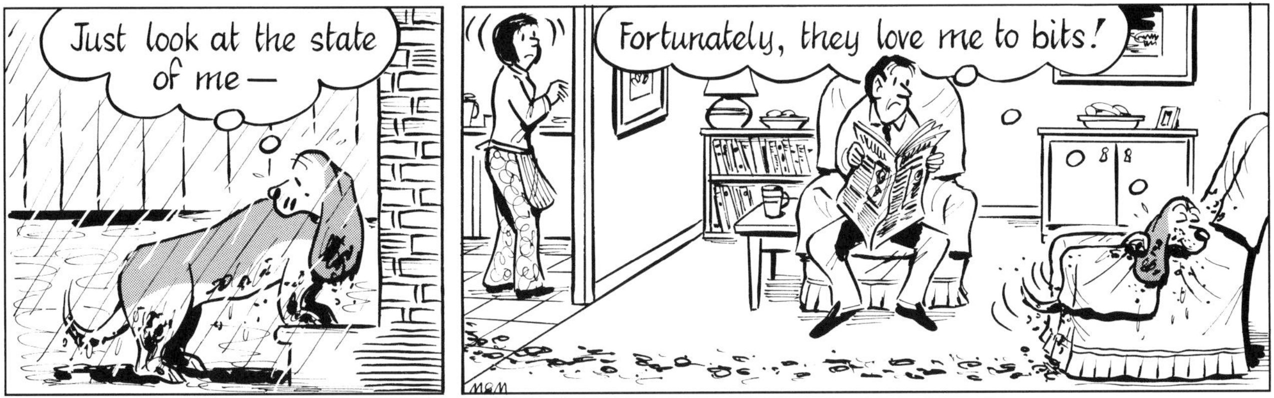
Just look at the state of me —
Fortunately, they love me to bits!

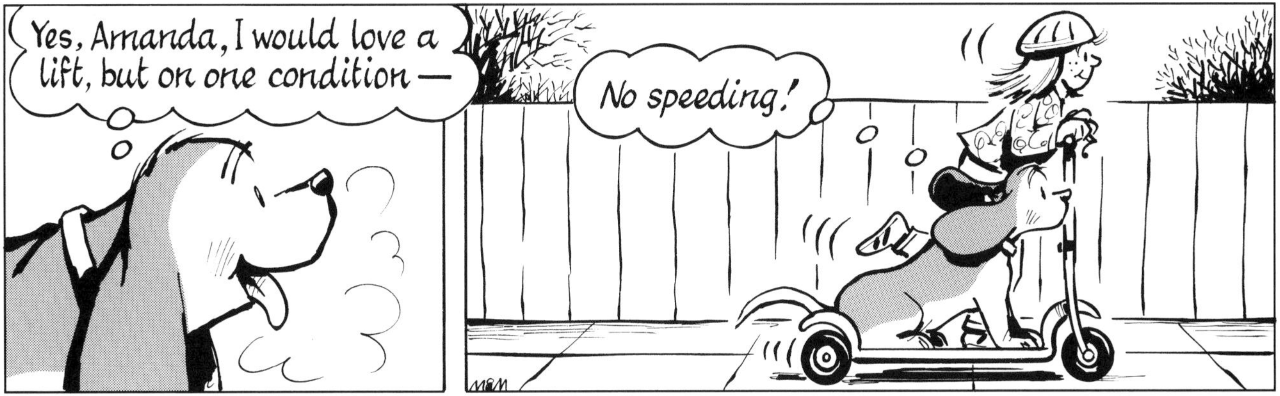
Yes, Amanda, I would love a lift, but on one condition —
No speeding!

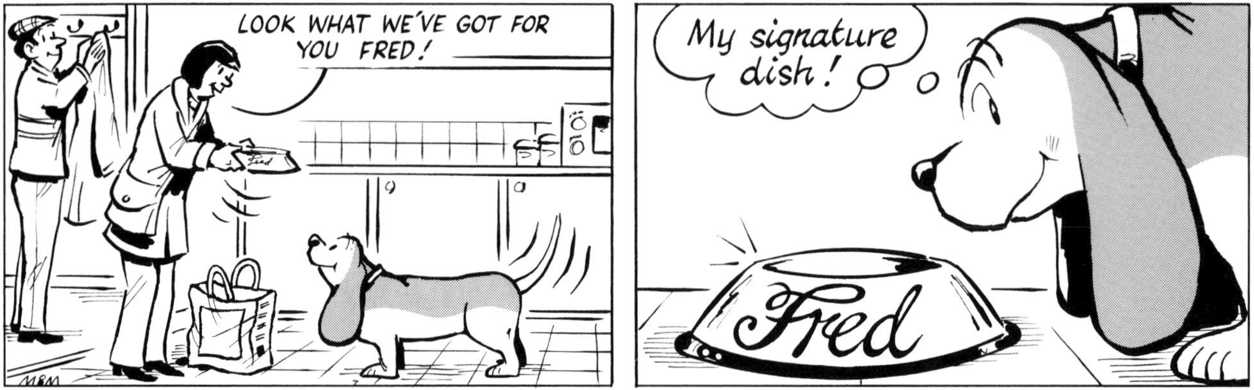
LOOK WHAT WE'VE GOT FOR YOU FRED!
My signature dish!
Fred

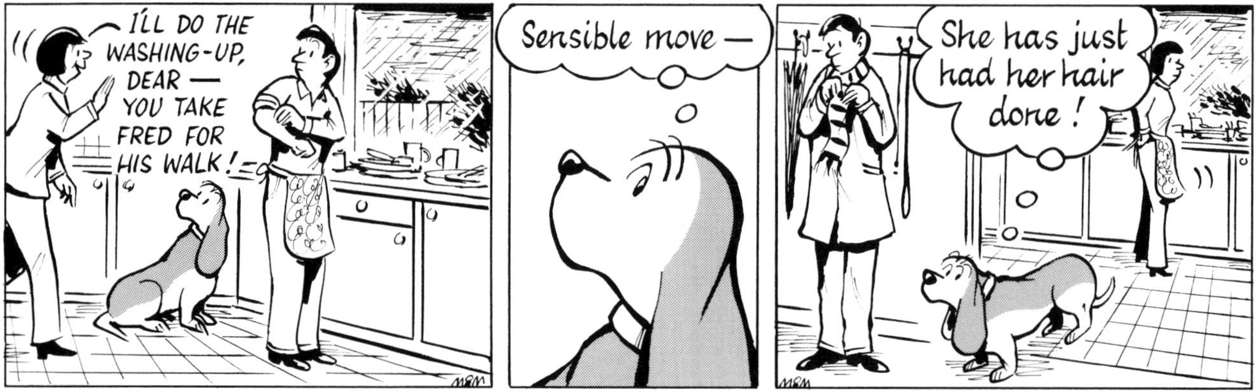
I'LL DO THE WASHING-UP, DEAR — YOU TAKE FRED FOR HIS WALK!
Sensible move —
She has just had her hair done!

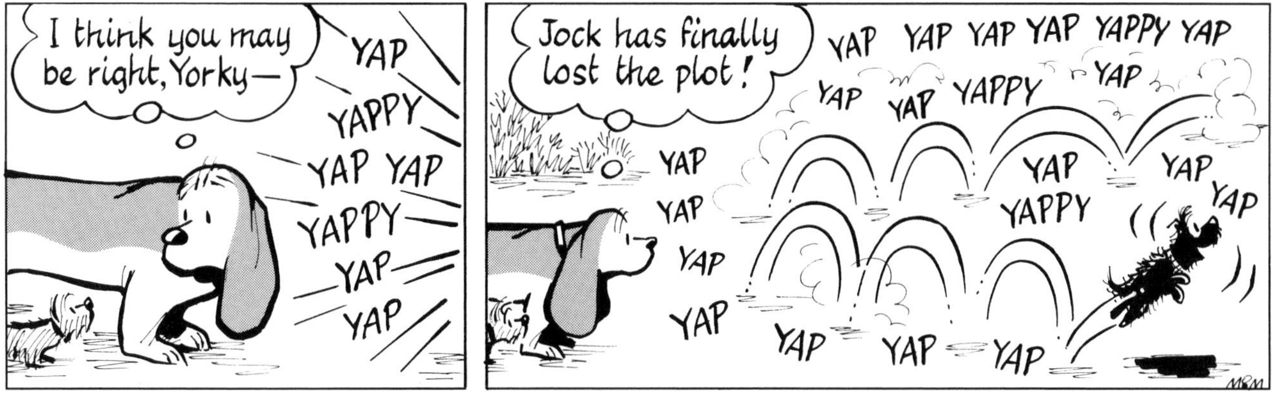
I think you may be right, Yorky—
YAP
YAPPY
YAP YAP
YAPPY
YAP
YAP
Jock has finally lost the plot!
YAP YAP YAP YAP YAPPY YAP
YAP YAP YAPPY YAP
YAP YAP YAP YAP
YAP YAPPY
YAP YAP
YAP YAP YAP YAP

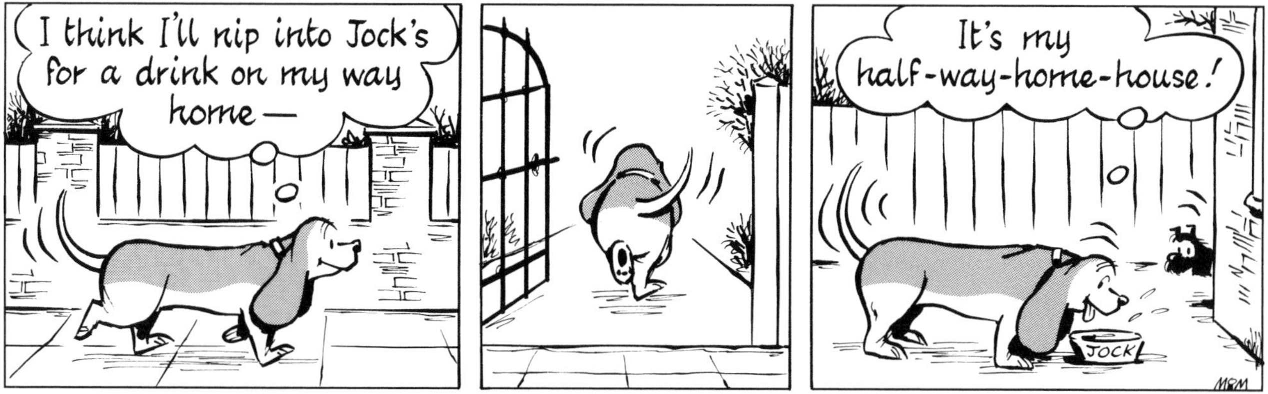
I think I'll nip into Jock's for a drink on my way home—
It's my half-way-home-house!
JOCK

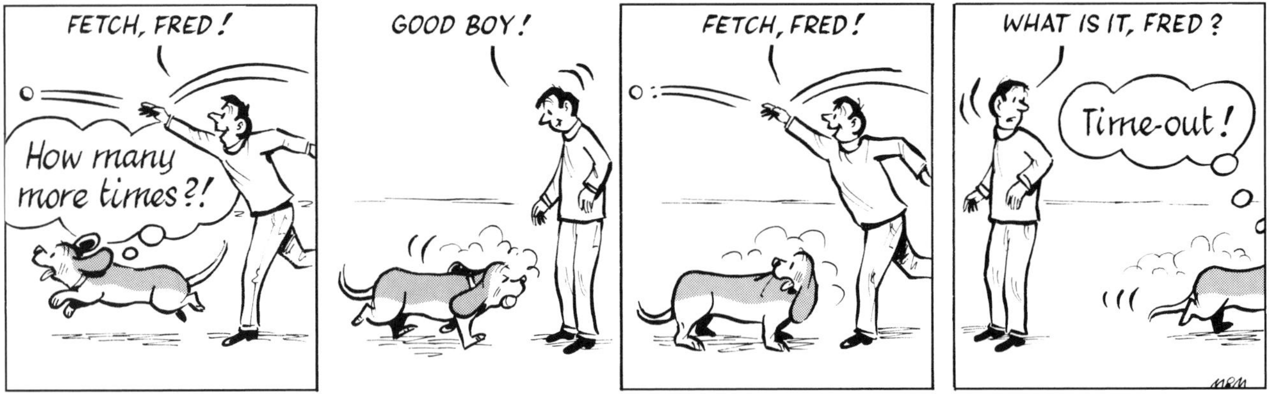
FETCH, FRED!
How many more times?!
GOOD BOY!
FETCH, FRED!
WHAT IS IT, FRED?
Time-out!
MRM

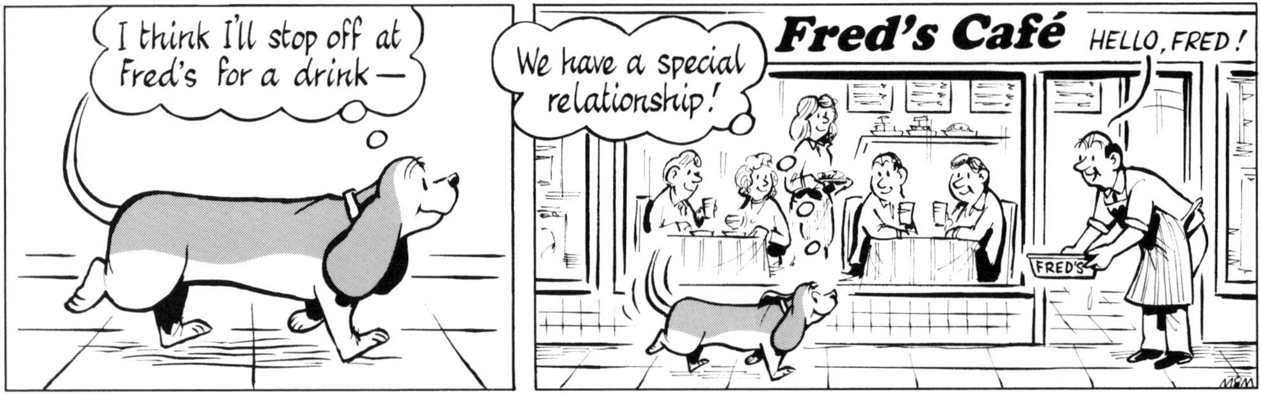
I think I'll stop off at Fred's for a drink —
We have a special relationship!
Fred's Café
HELLO, FRED!
FRED'S
MRM

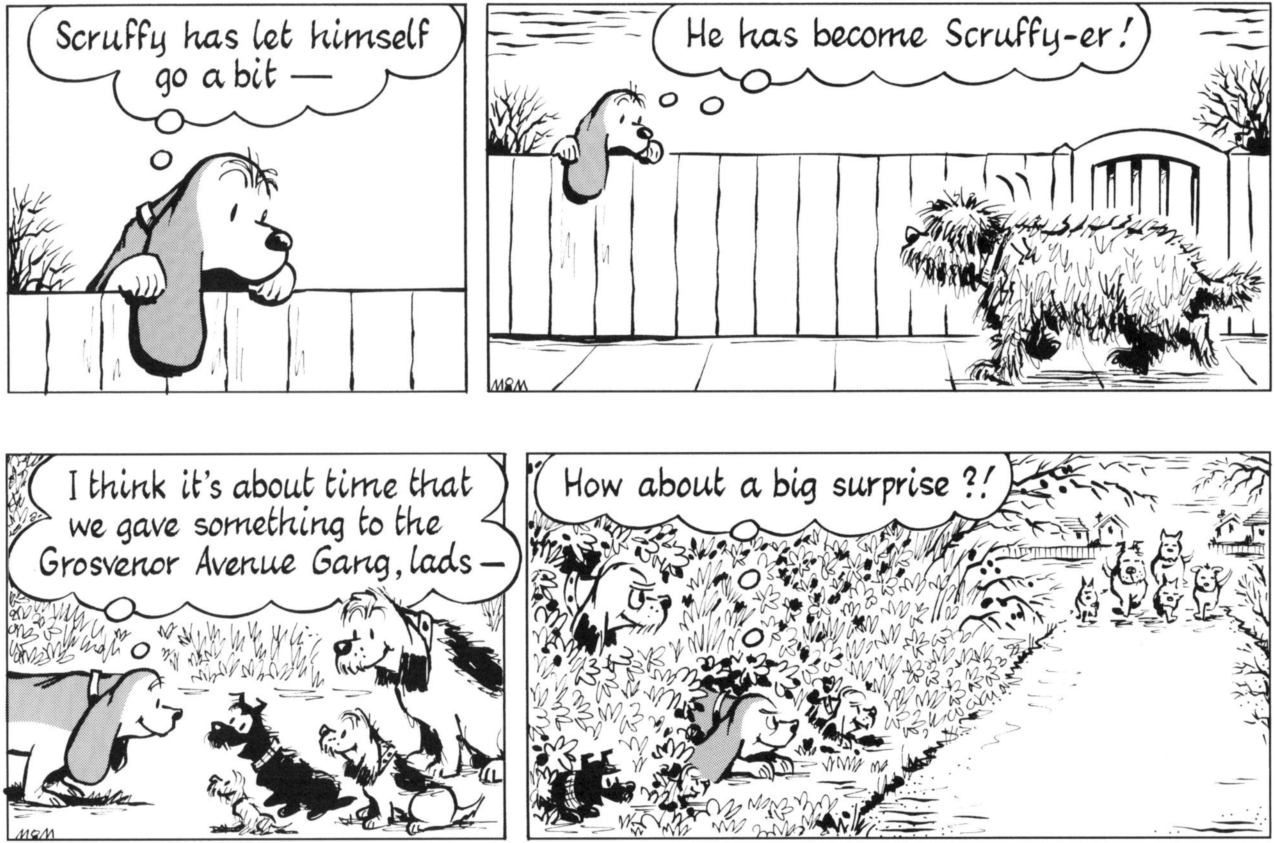
Scruffy has let himself go a bit —
He has become Scruffy-er!
I think it's about time that we gave something to the Grosvenor Avenue Gang, lads —
How about a big surprise ?!

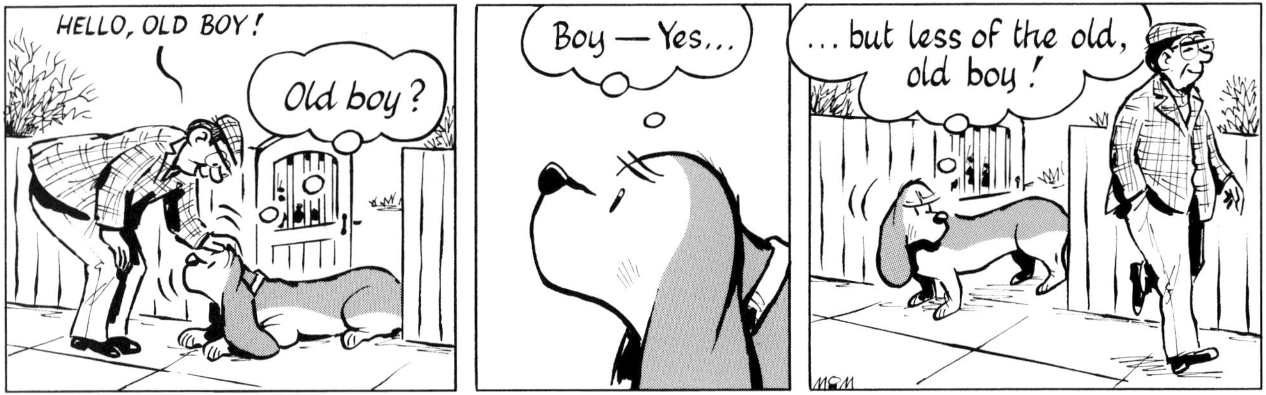
HELLO, OLD BOY!
Old boy?
Boy — Yes...
... but less of the old, old boy!

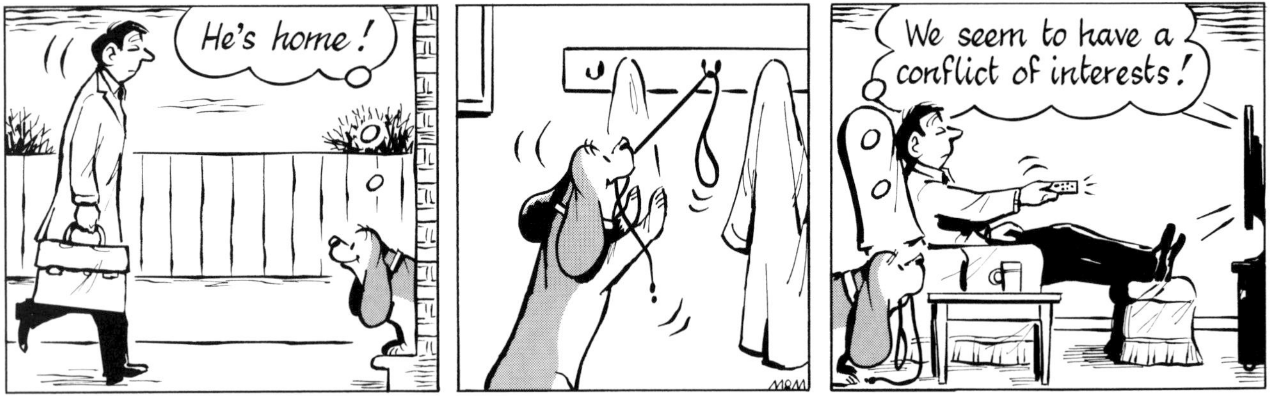
He's home!
We seem to have a conflict of interests!

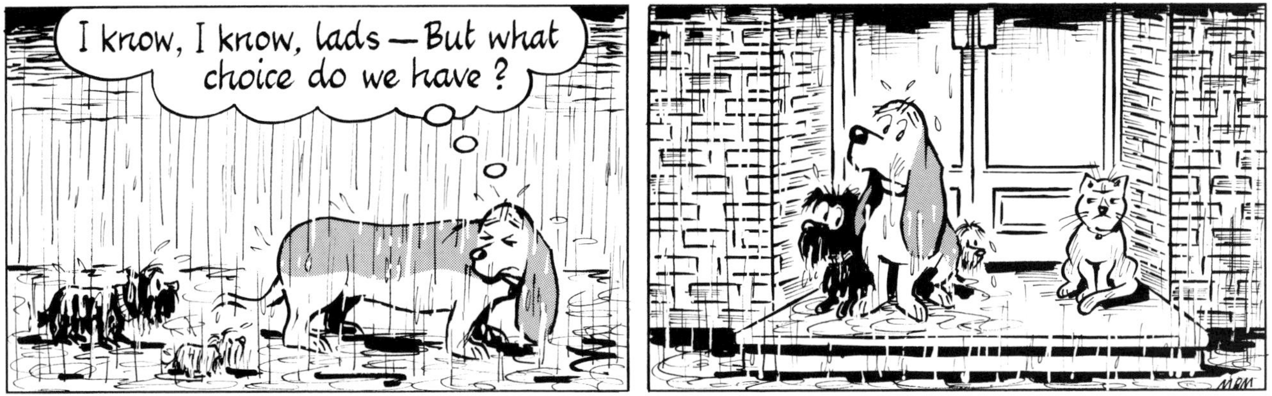
I know, I know, lads — But what choice do we have?

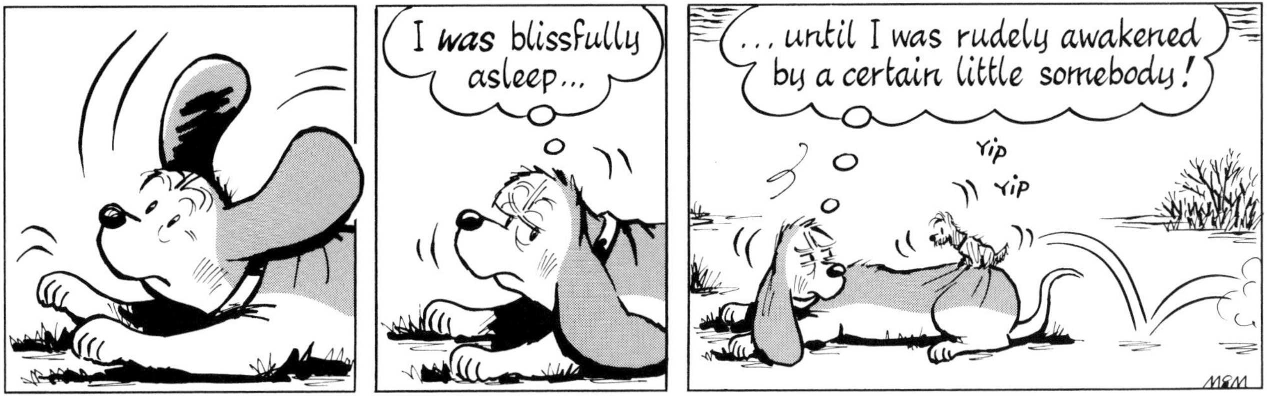
I *was* blissfully asleep...
...until I was rudely awakened by a certain little somebody!
YIP
YIP

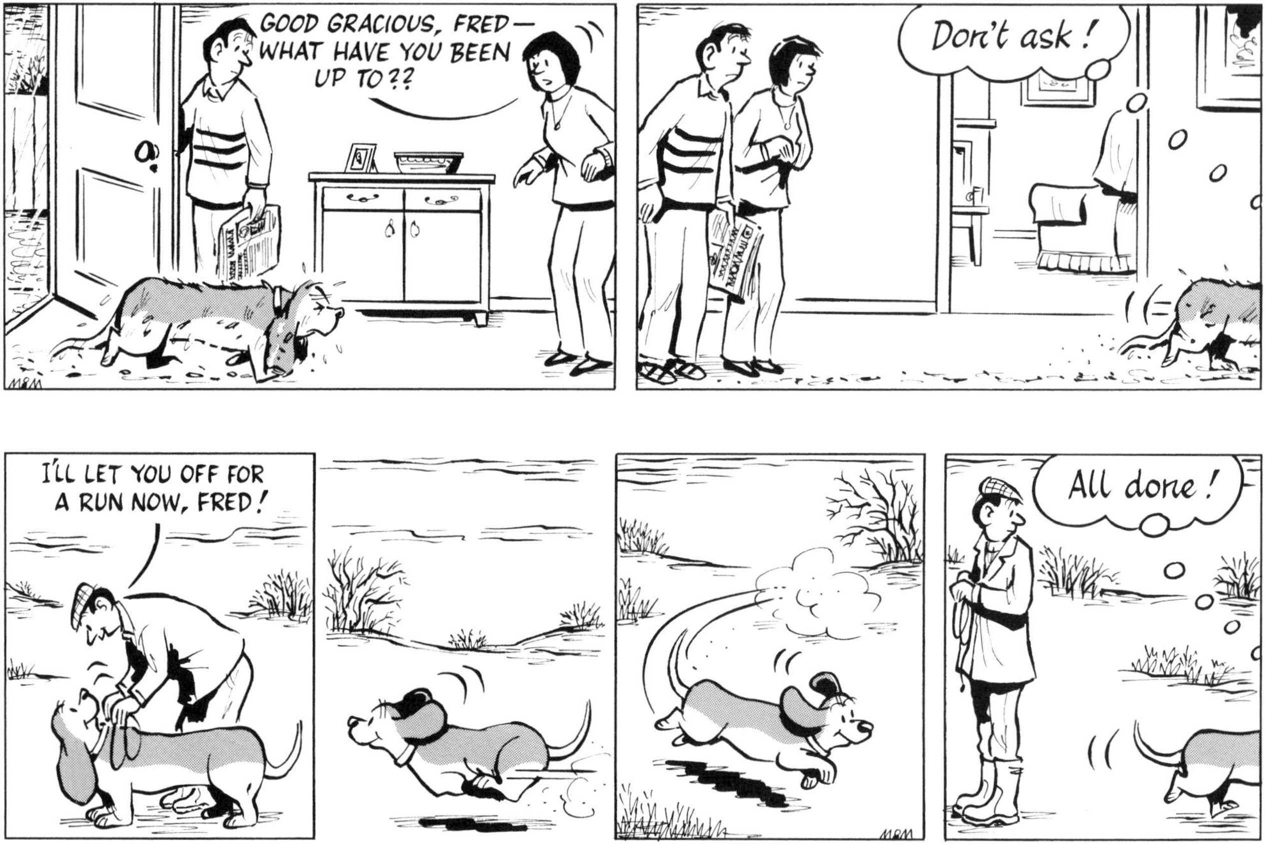
GOOD GRACIOUS, FRED— WHAT HAVE YOU BEEN UP TO??
Don't ask!
I'LL LET YOU OFF FOR A RUN NOW, FRED!
All done!

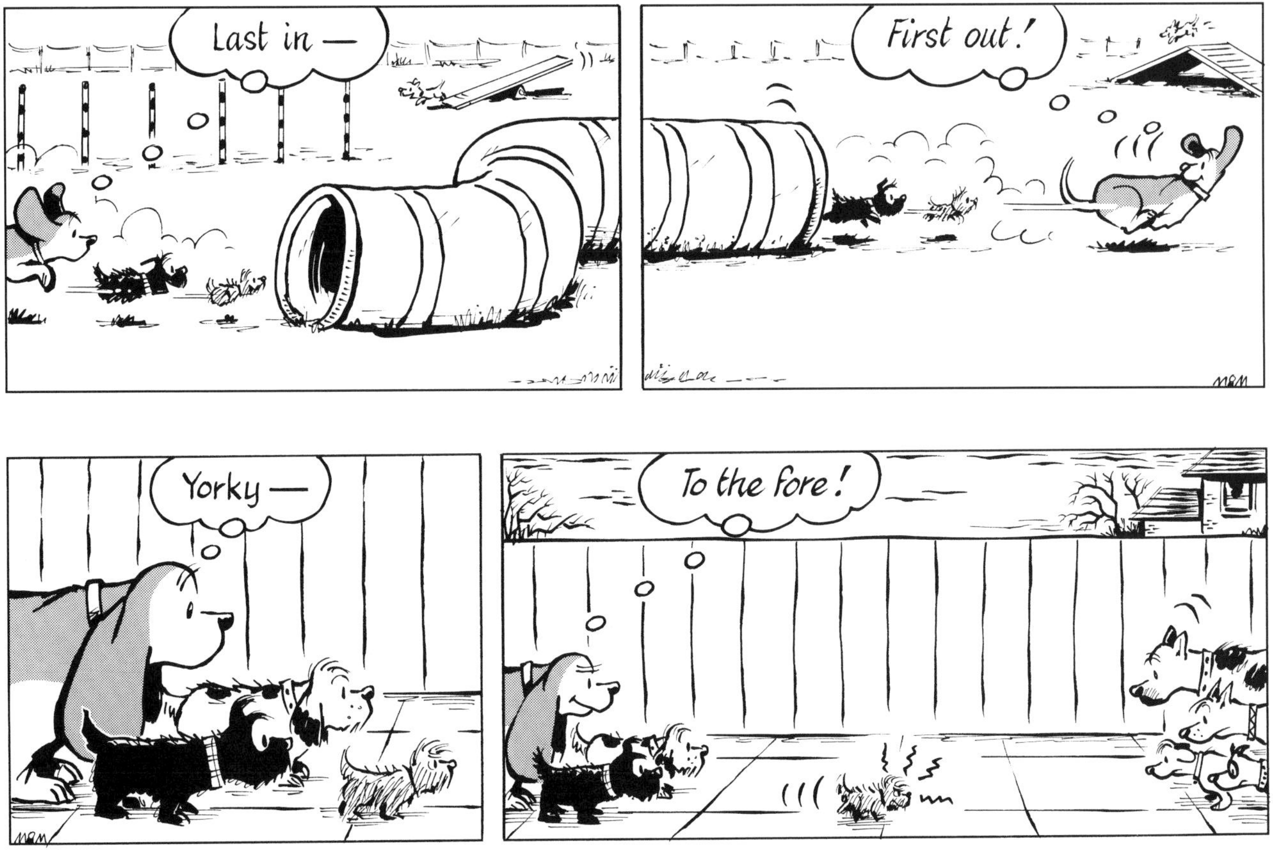
Last in —
First out!
MRM
MRM
Yorky —
To the fore!

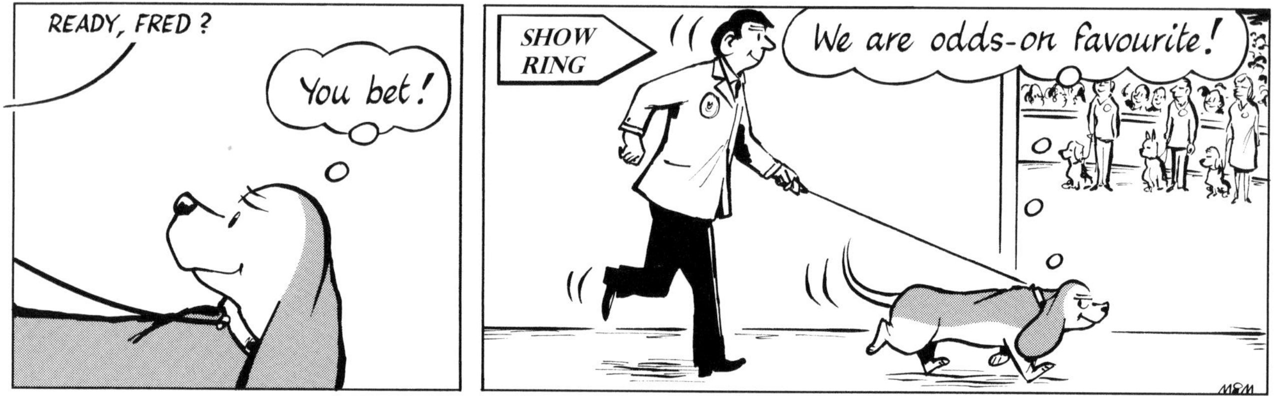
READY, FRED ?
You bet !
SHOW RING
We are odds-on favourite !

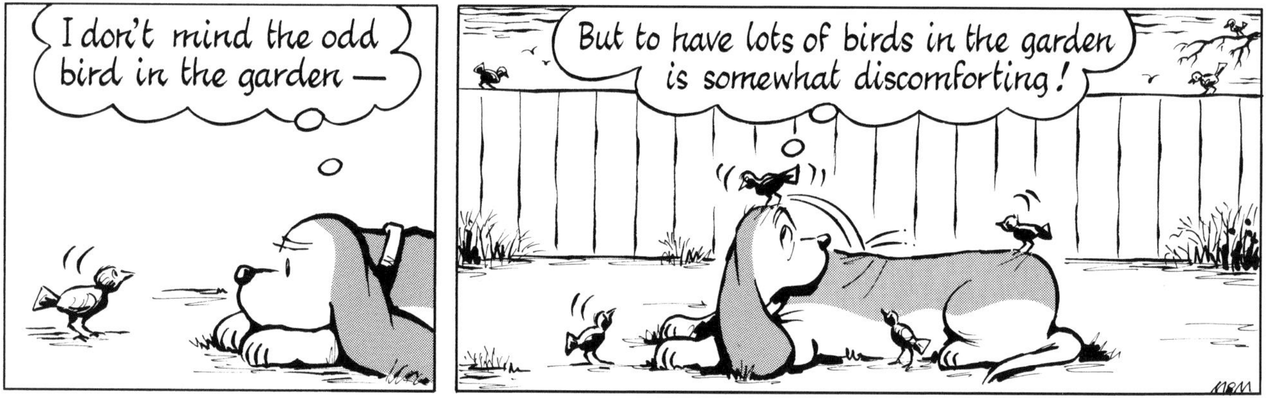
I don't mind the odd bird in the garden —
But to have lots of birds in the garden is somewhat discomforting !

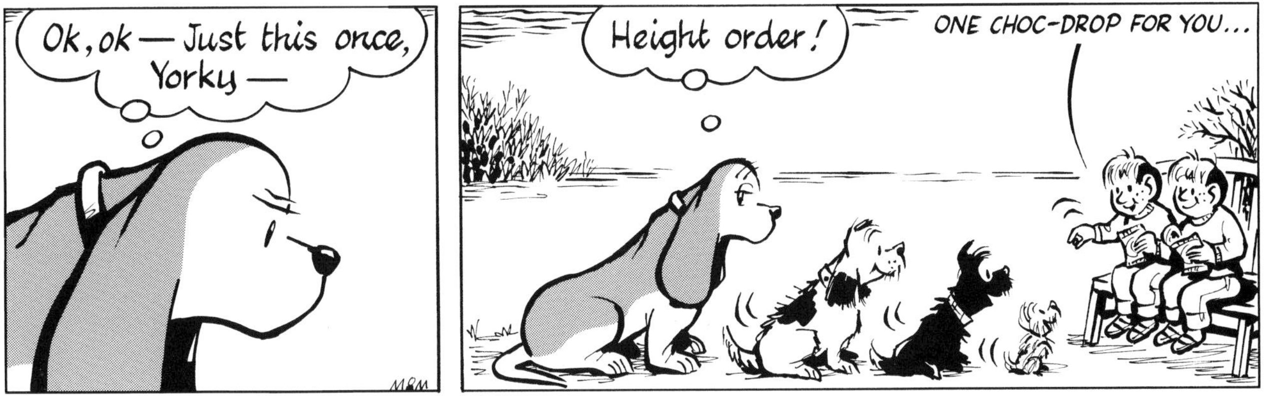
Ok, ok — Just this once, Yorky —
Height order!
ONE CHOC-DROP FOR YOU...

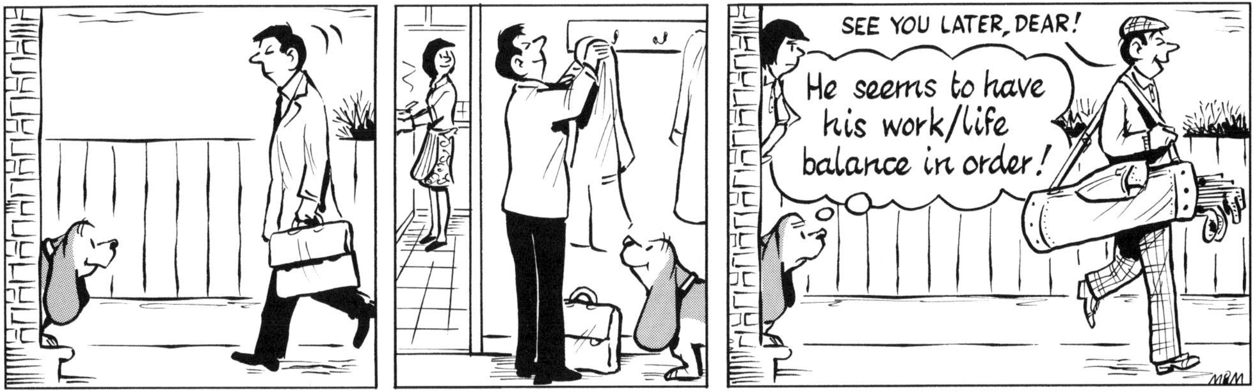
SEE YOU LATER, DEAR!
He seems to have his work/life balance in order!

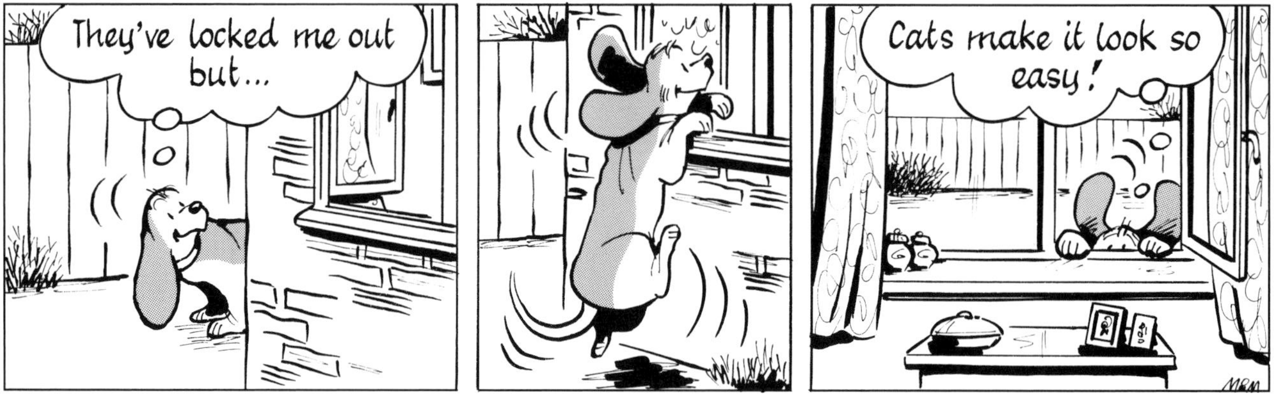
They've locked me out but...
Cats make it look so easy!

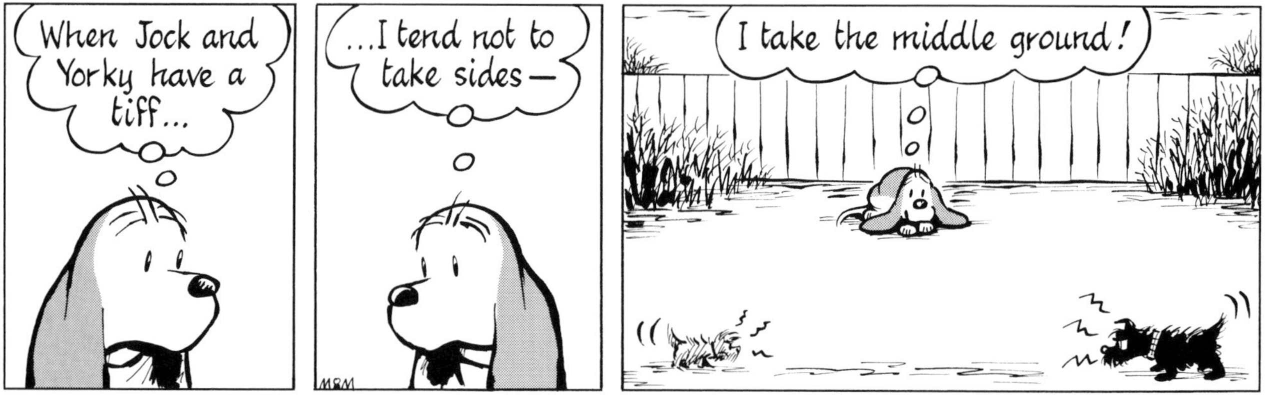
When Jock and Yorky have a tiff...
...I tend not to take sides—
I take the middle ground!

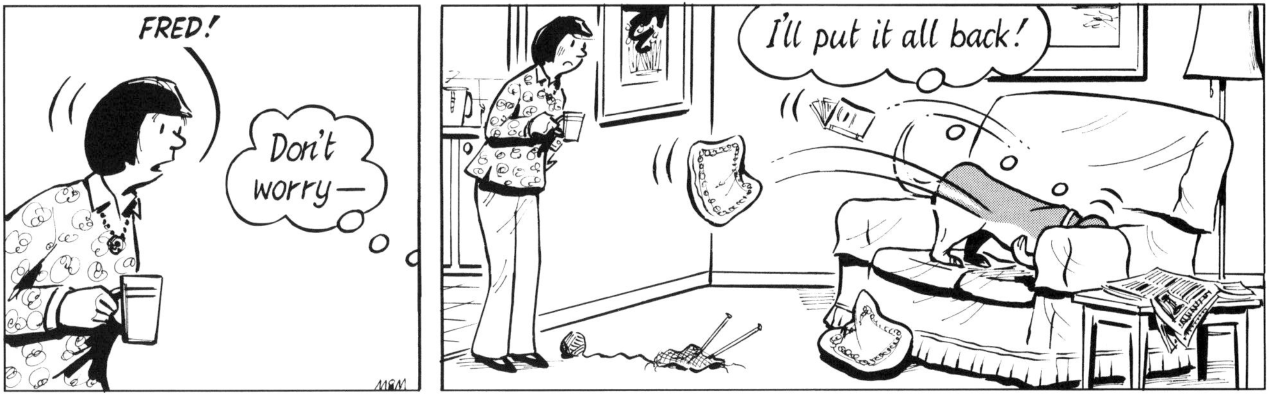
FRED!
Don't worry—
I'll put it all back!

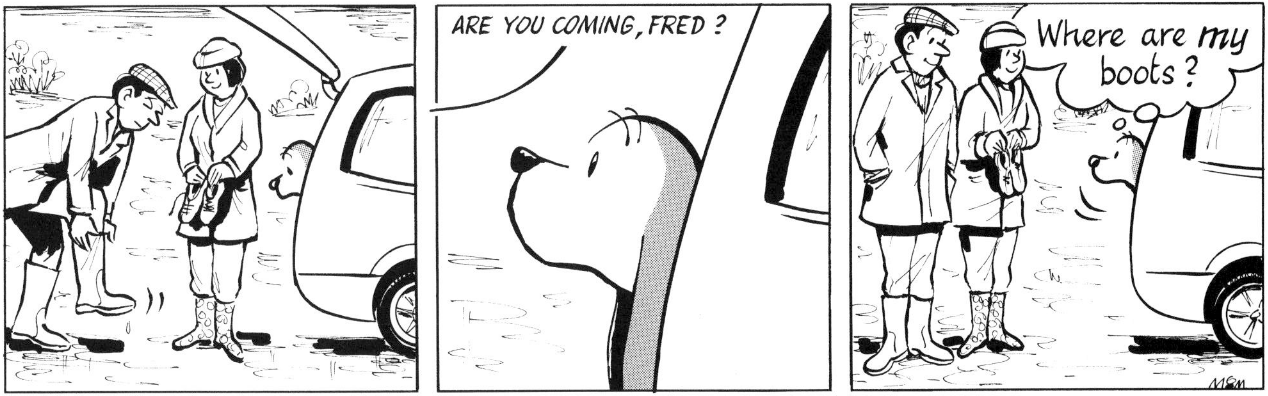
ARE YOU COMING, FRED?
Where are my boots?

I'VE FOUND ONE!
SO HAVE I!
I'VE FOUND TWO!
I'VE FOUND LOADS!
This is all a bit too easy—
I think I will up the ante a little!

OK—COME ON THEN, FRED!
Good manners get you everywhere!

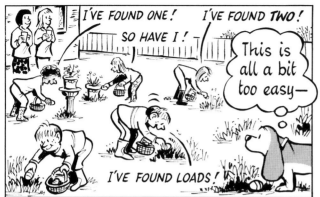

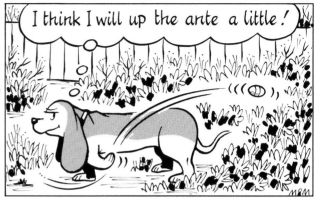

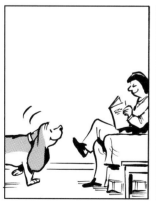

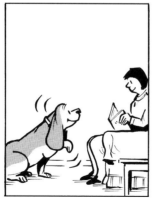

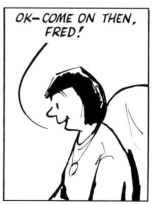

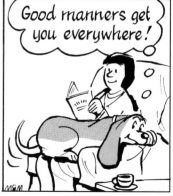

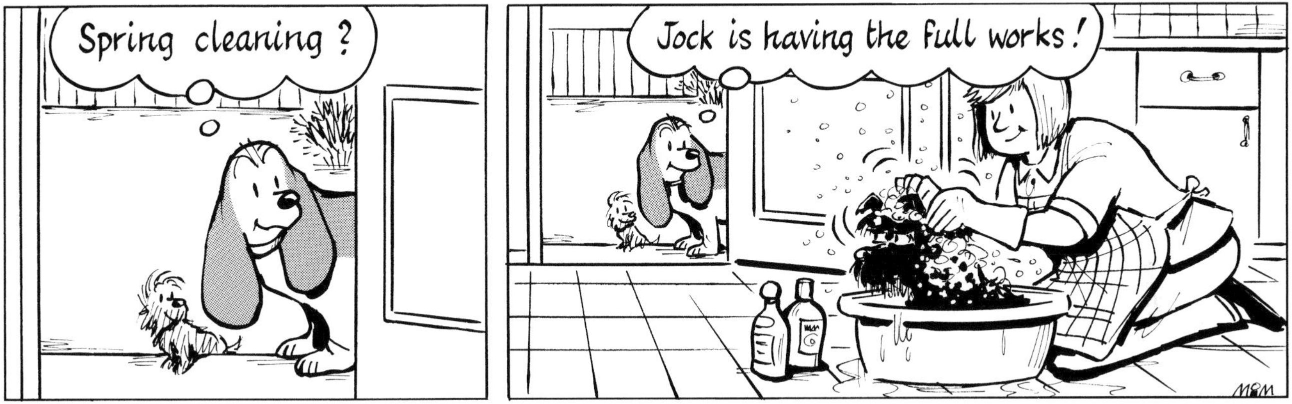
Spring cleaning ?
Jock is having the full works !

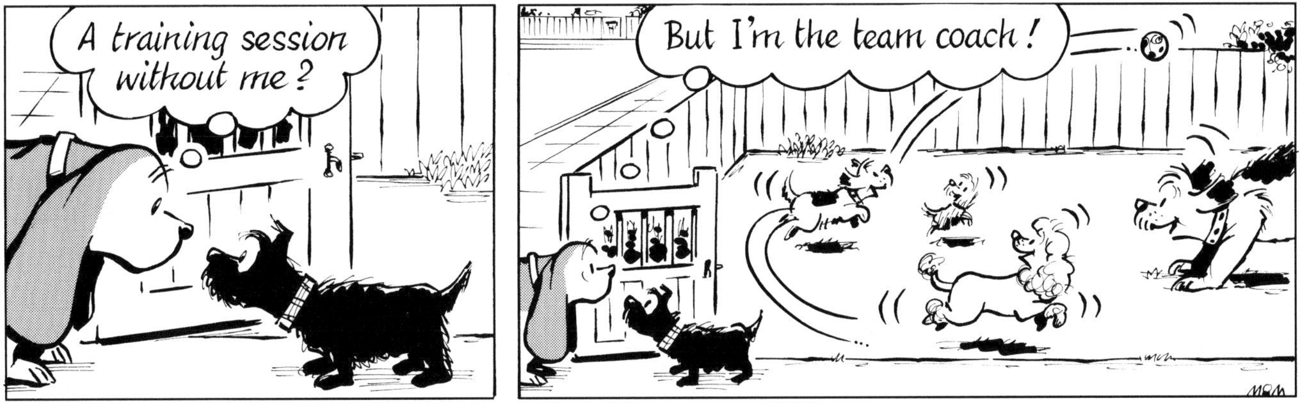
A training session without me ?
But I'm the team coach !

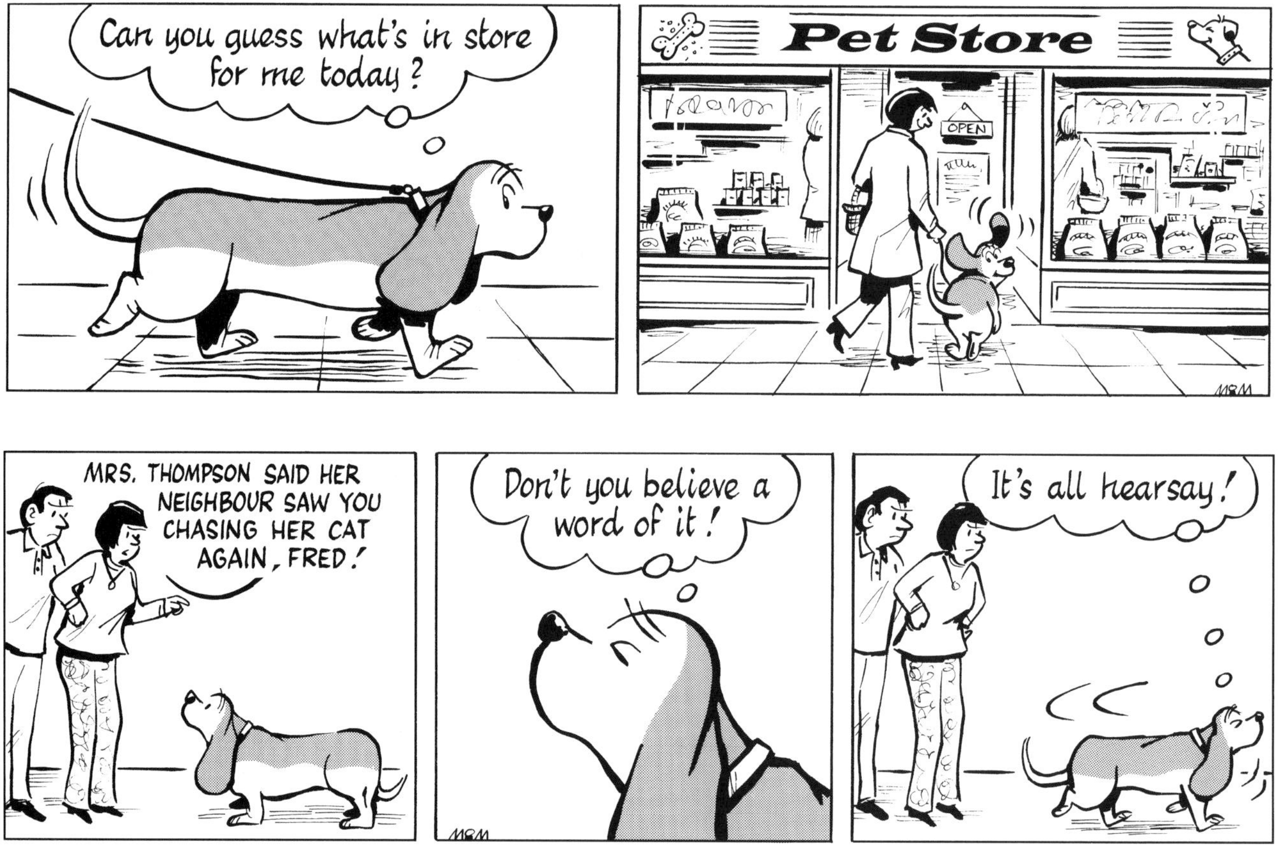
Can you guess what's in store for me today?
Pet Store
OPEN
MRS. THOMPSON SAID HER NEIGHBOUR SAW YOU CHASING HER CAT AGAIN, FRED!
Don't you believe a word of it!
It's all hearsay!

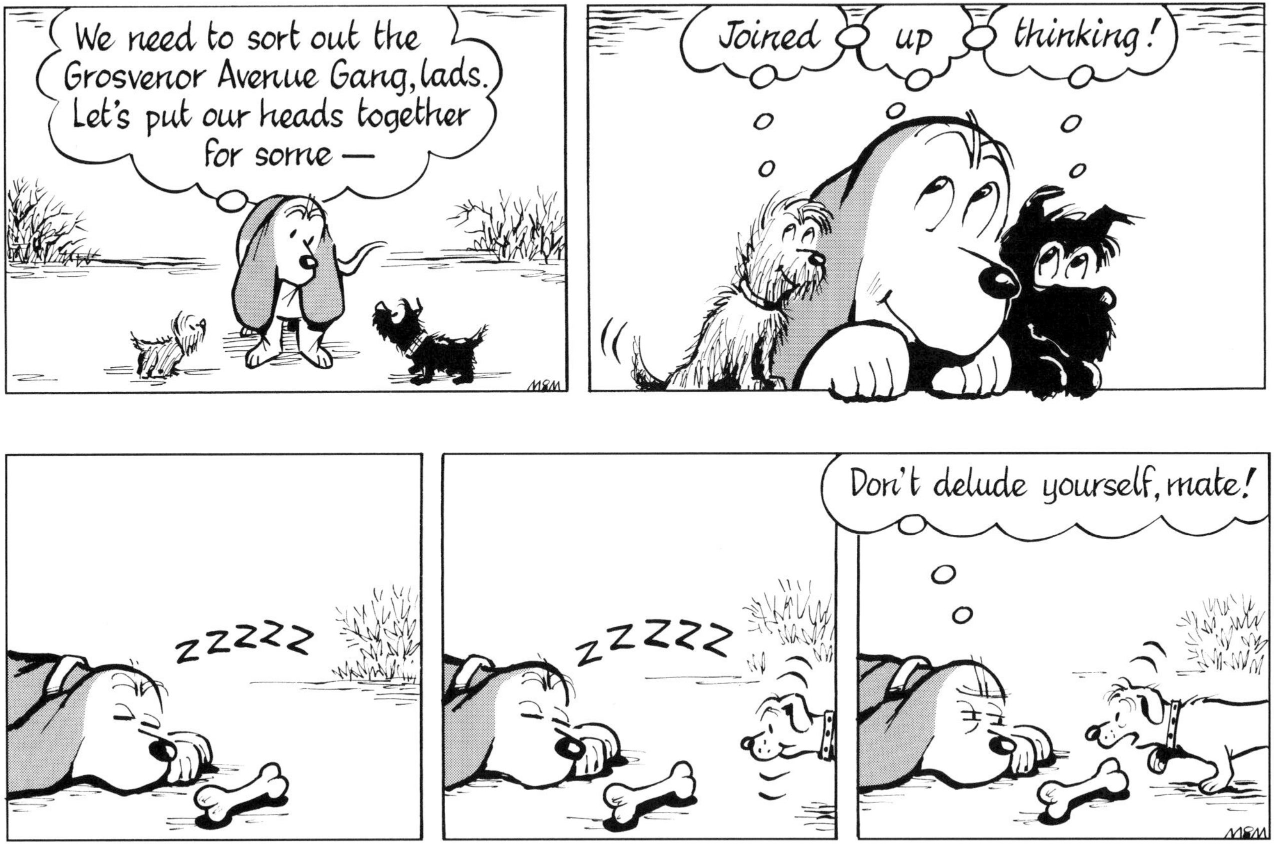
We need to sort out the Grosvenor Avenue Gang, lads. Let's put our heads together for some —
Joined
up
thinking!
ZZZZZ
ZZZZZ
Don't delude yourself, mate!
M&M

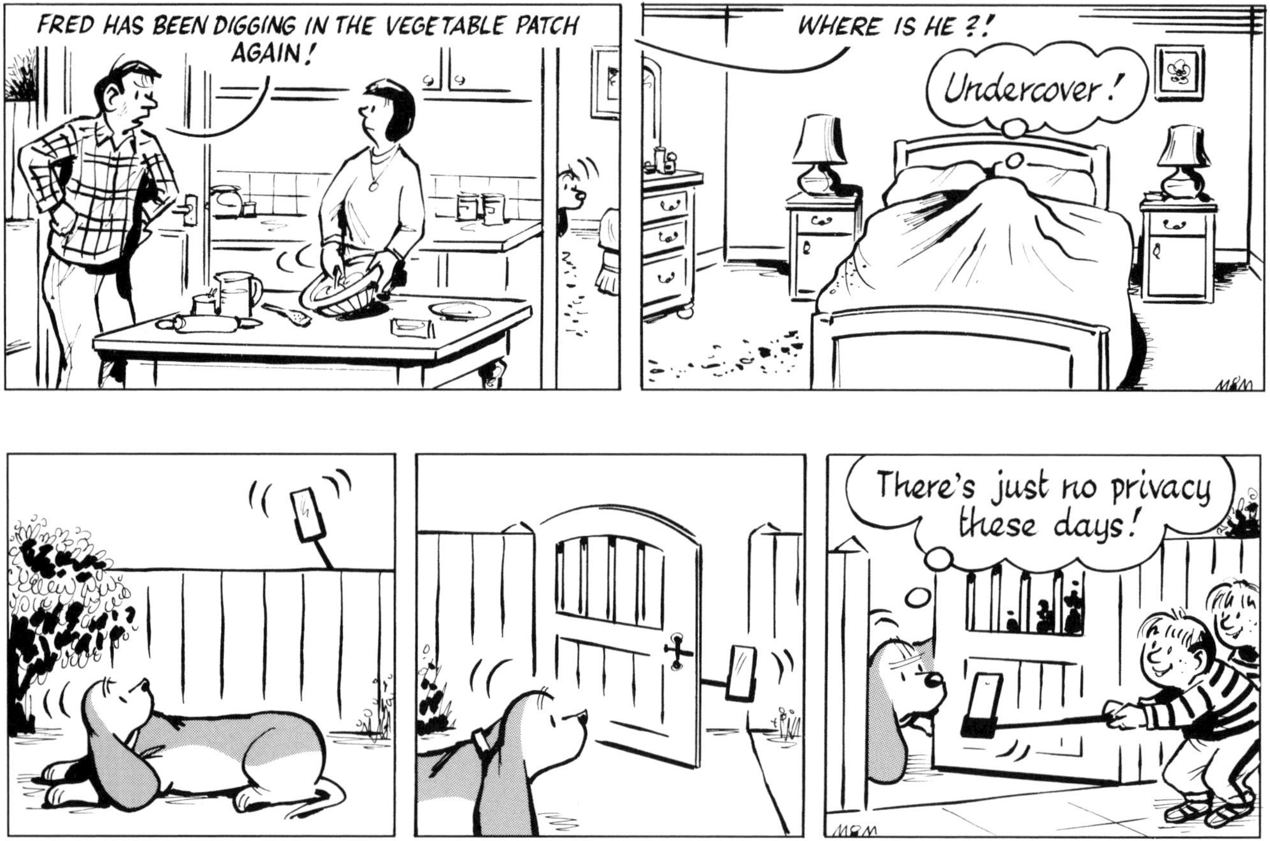
FRED HAS BEEN DIGGING IN THE VEGETABLE PATCH AGAIN!
WHERE IS HE ?!
Undercover!
There's just no privacy these days!

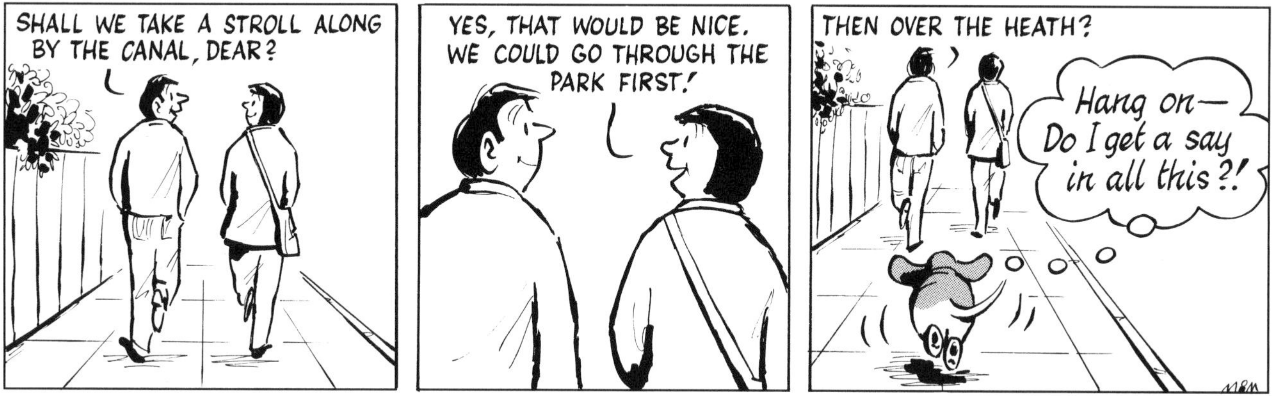
SHALL WE TAKE A STROLL ALONG BY THE CANAL, DEAR?
YES, THAT WOULD BE NICE. WE COULD GO THROUGH THE PARK FIRST!
THEN OVER THE HEATH?
Hang on— Do I get a say in all this?!
MBM

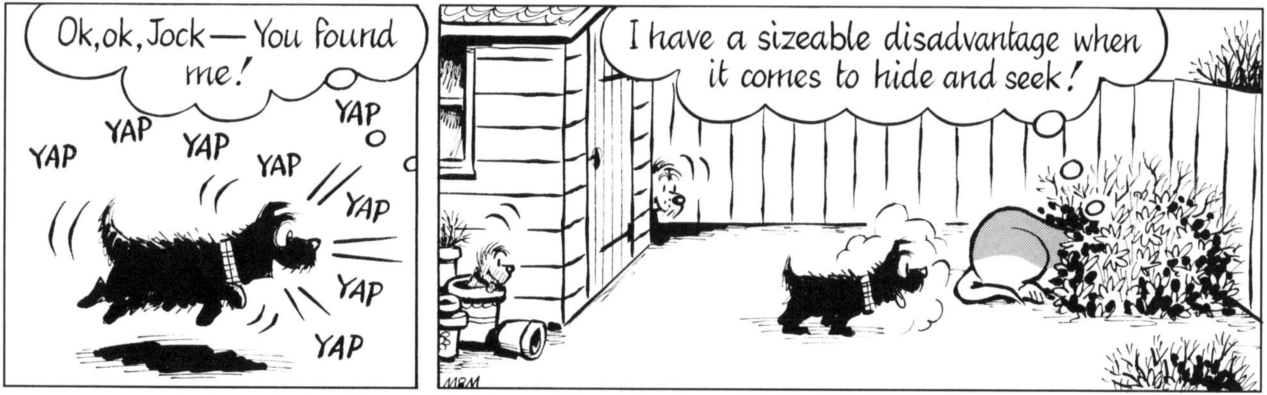
Ok, ok, Jock — You found me!
YAP YAP YAP YAP YAP YAP YAP YAP
I have a sizeable disadvantage when it comes to hide and seek!
MBM

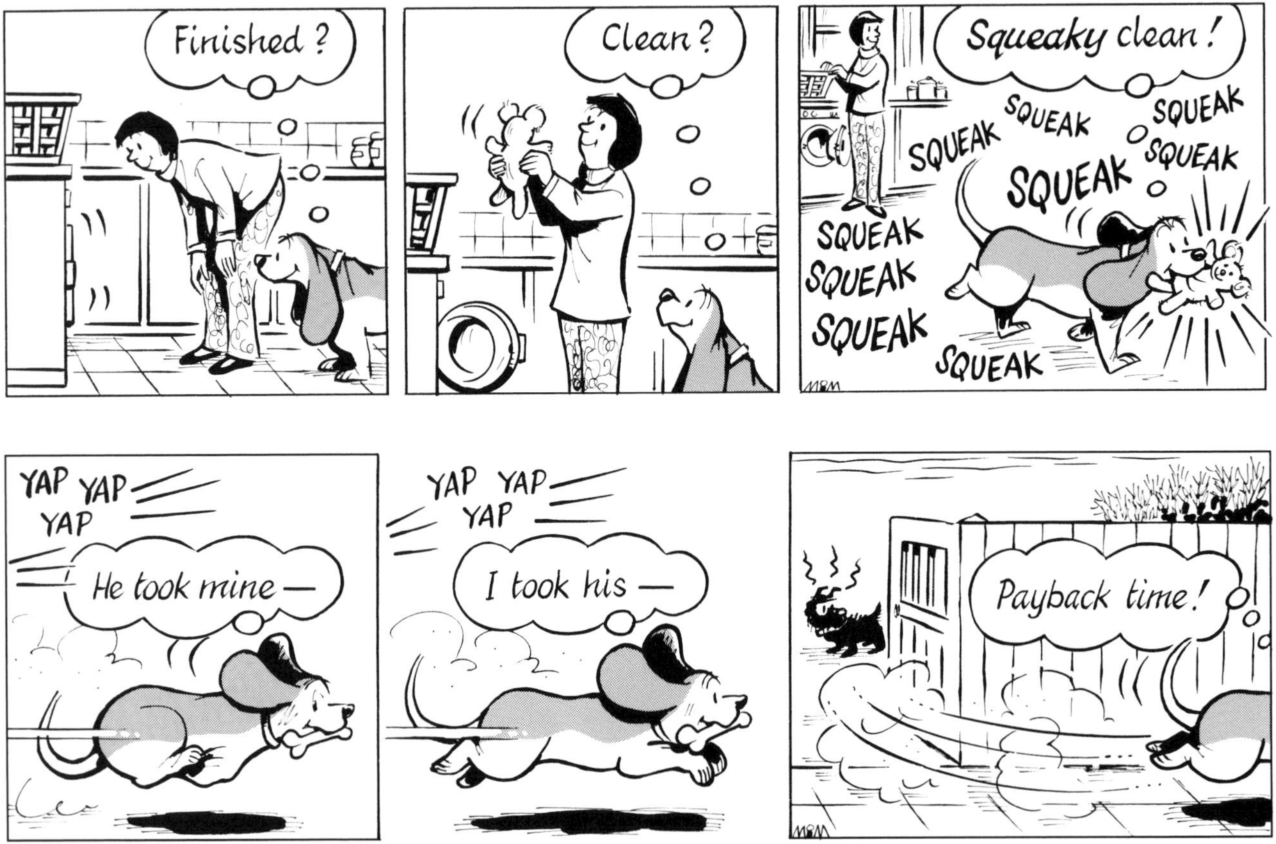
Finished?
Clean?
Squeaky clean!
SQUEAK SQUEAK SQUEAK SQUEAK SQUEAK SQUEAK SQUEAK SQUEAK SQUEAK SQUEAK
M&M
YAP YAP YAP
He took mine —
YAP YAP YAP
I took his —
Payback time!
M&M

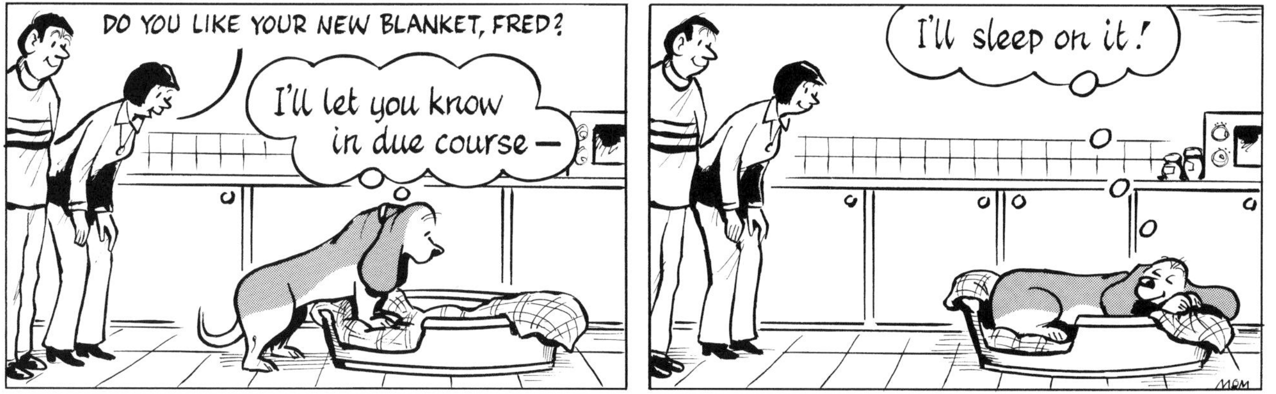
DO YOU LIKE YOUR NEW BLANKET, FRED?
I'll let you know in due course —
I'll sleep on it!

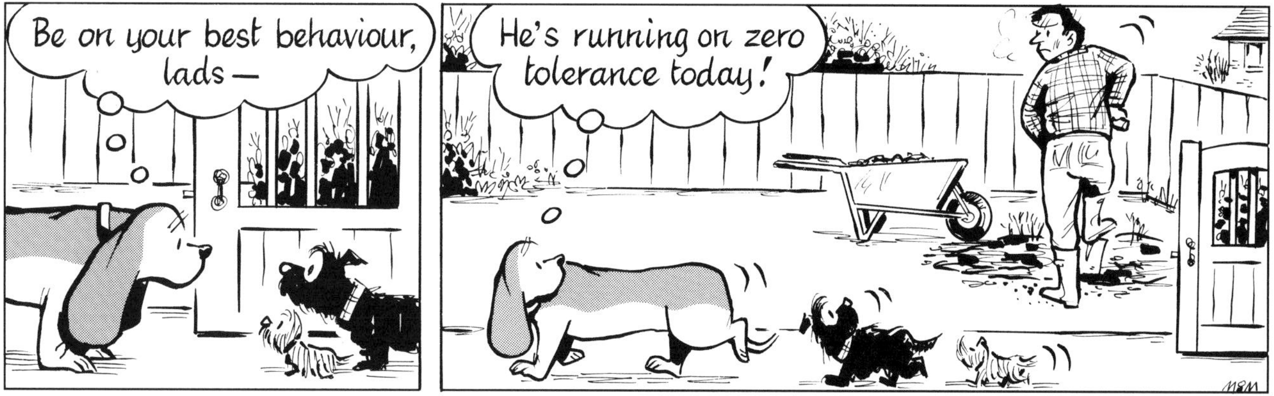
Be on your best behaviour, lads —
He's running on zero tolerance today!

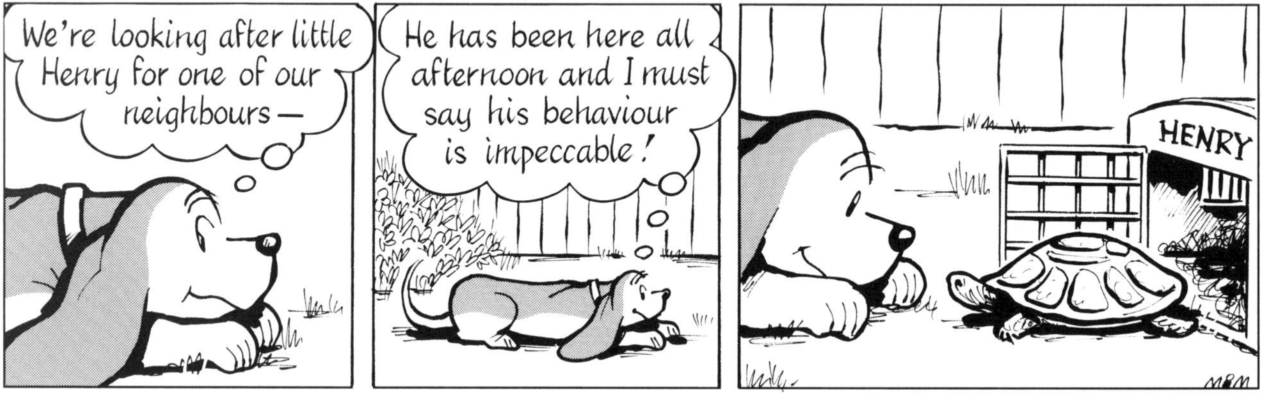
We're looking after little Henry for one of our neighbours—
He has been here all afternoon and I must say his behaviour is impeccable!
HENRY

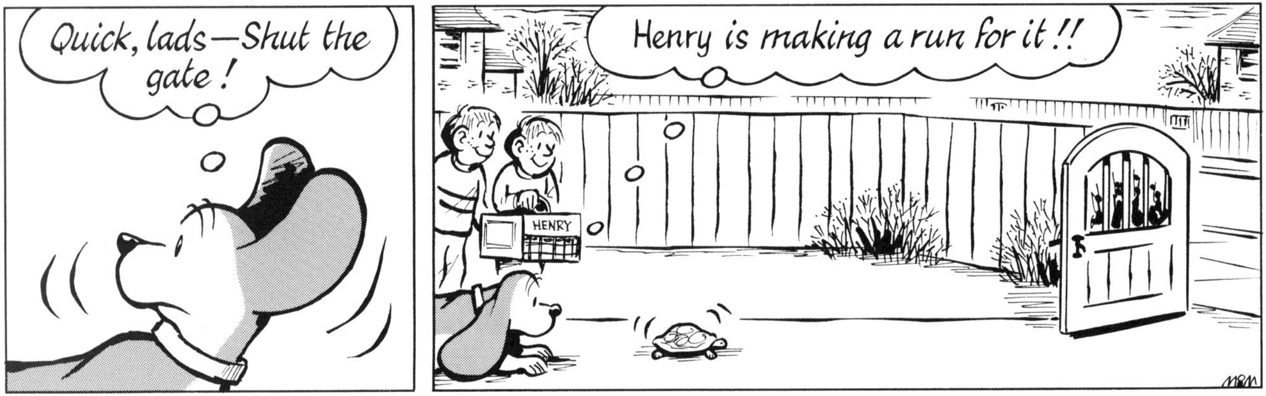
Quick, lads—Shut the gate!
Henry is making a run for it!!
HENRY

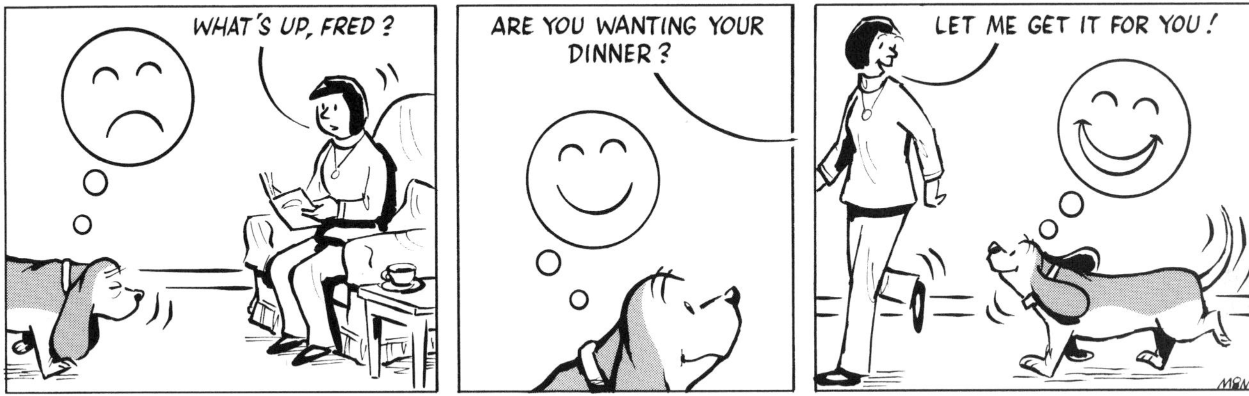
WHAT'S UP, FRED?
ARE YOU WANTING YOUR DINNER?
LET ME GET IT FOR YOU!

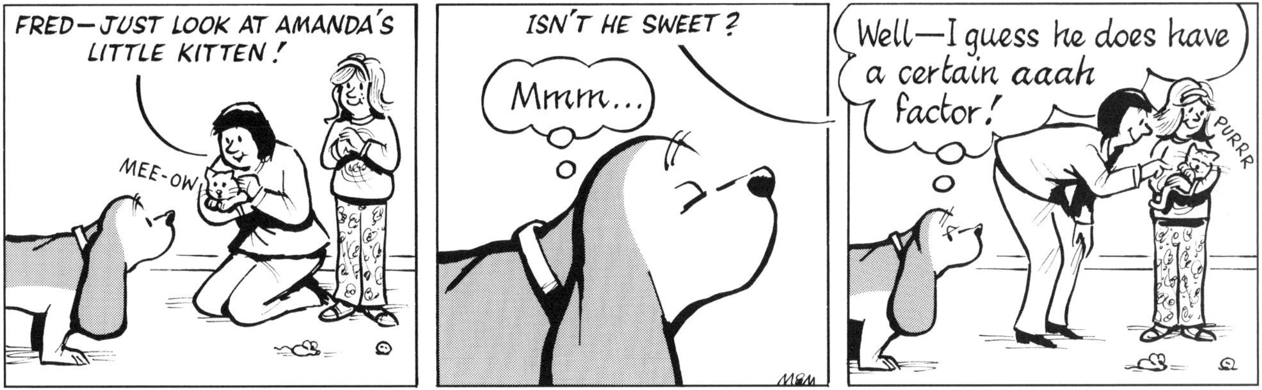
FRED—JUST LOOK AT AMANDA'S LITTLE KITTEN!
MEE-OW
ISN'T HE SWEET?
Mmm...
Well—I guess he does have a certain aaah factor!
PURRR

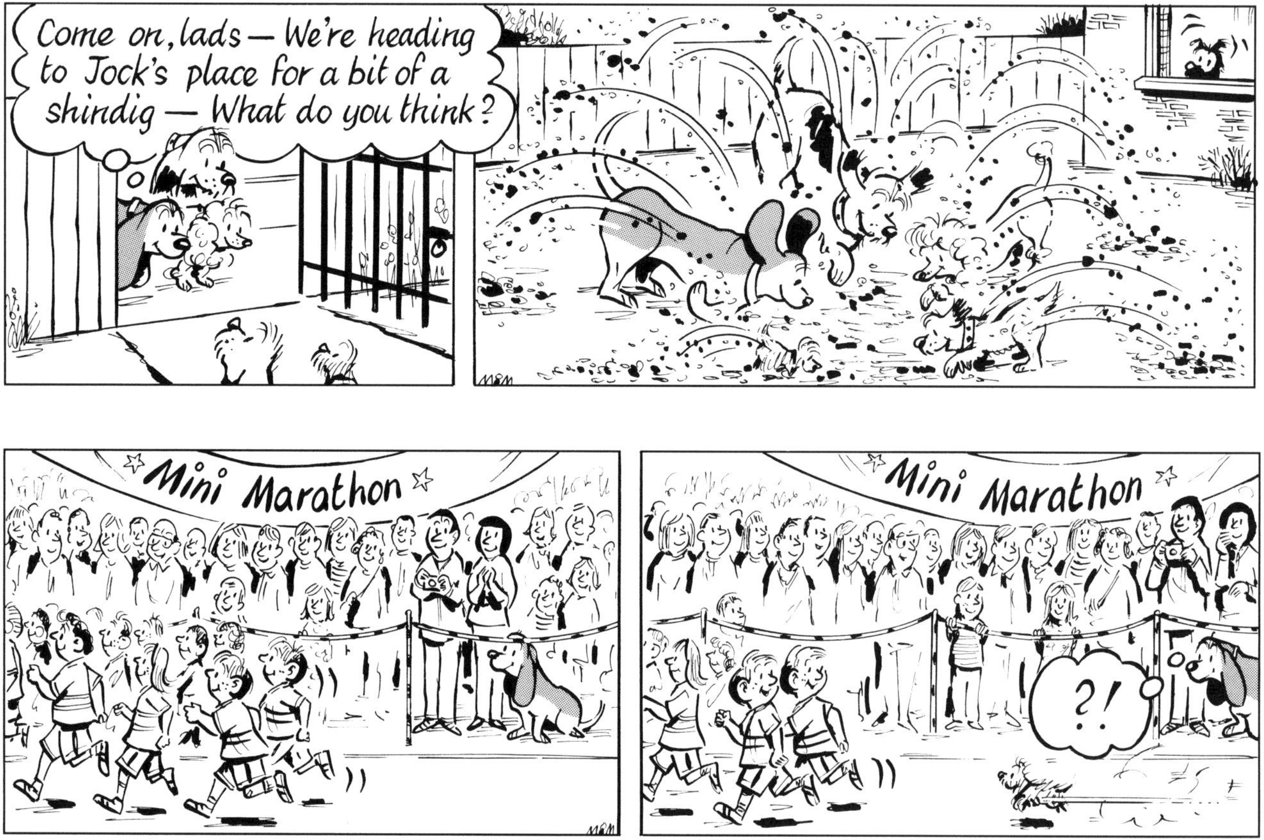
Come on, lads — We're heading to Jock's place for a bit of a shindig — What do you think?
Mini Marathon
Mini Marathon
?!

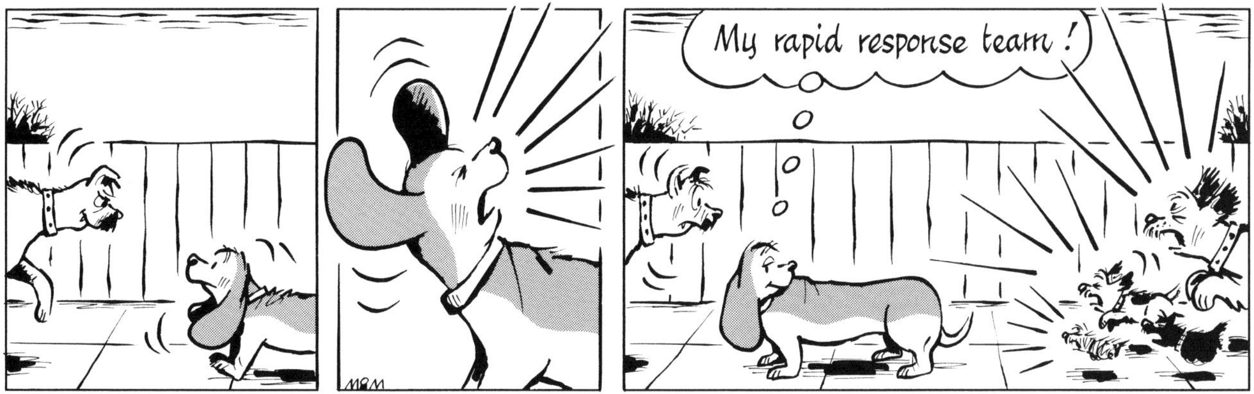
My rapid response team!
MGM

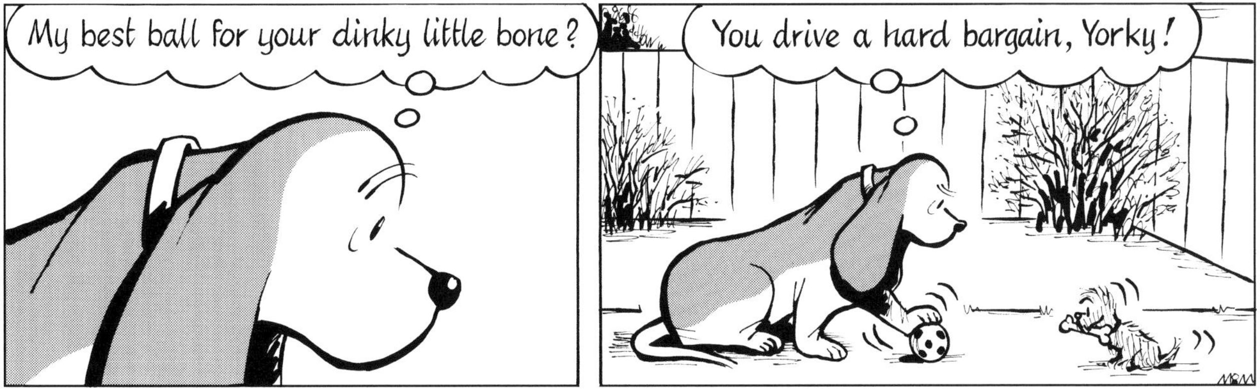
My best ball for your dinky little bone?
You drive a hard bargain, Yorky!
MGM

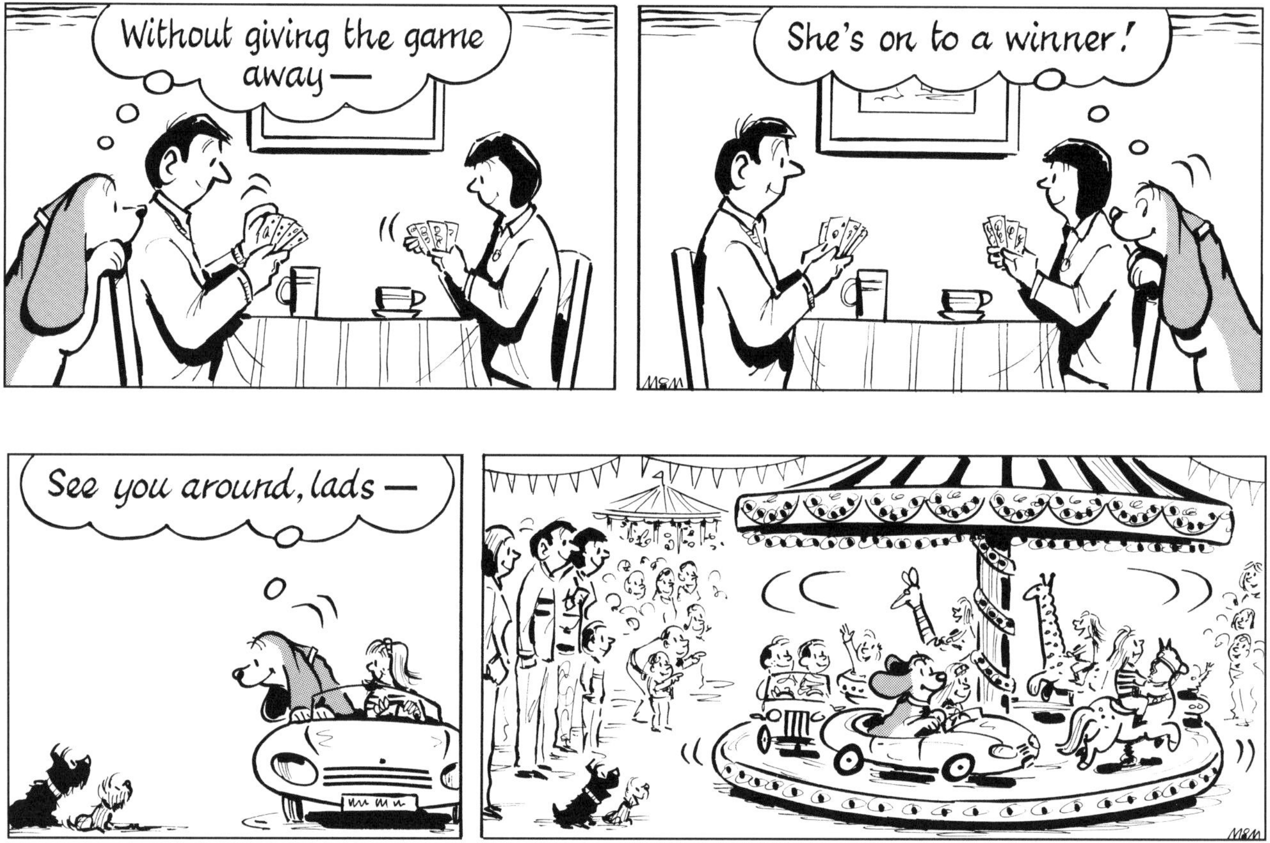
Without giving the game away—
She's on to a winner!
See you around, lads—

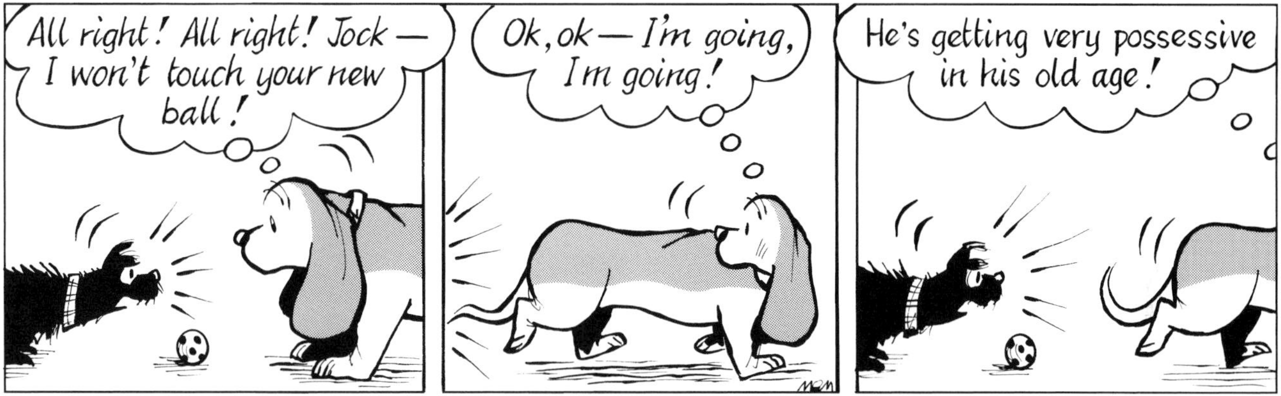
All right! All right! Jock — I won't touch your new ball!
Ok, ok — I'm going, I'm going!
He's getting very possessive in his old age!

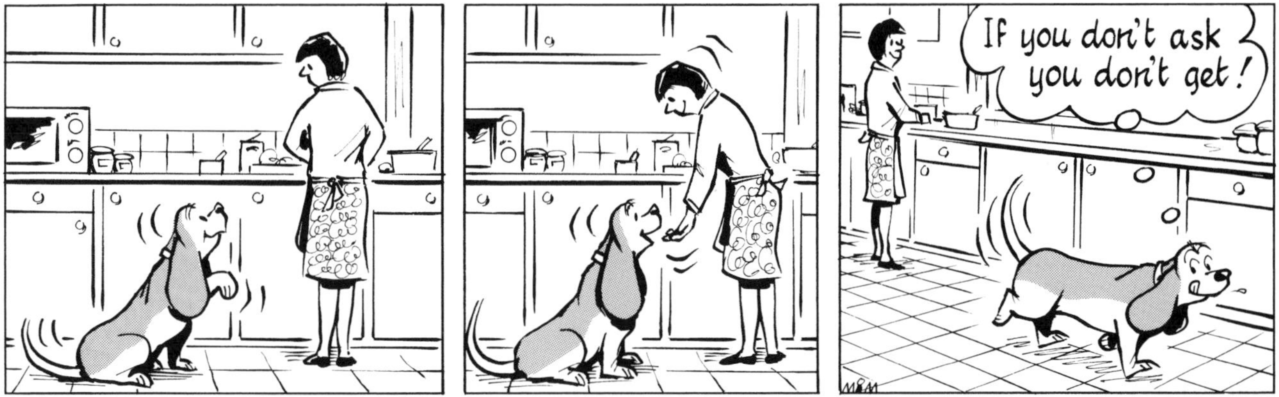
If you don't ask you don't get!

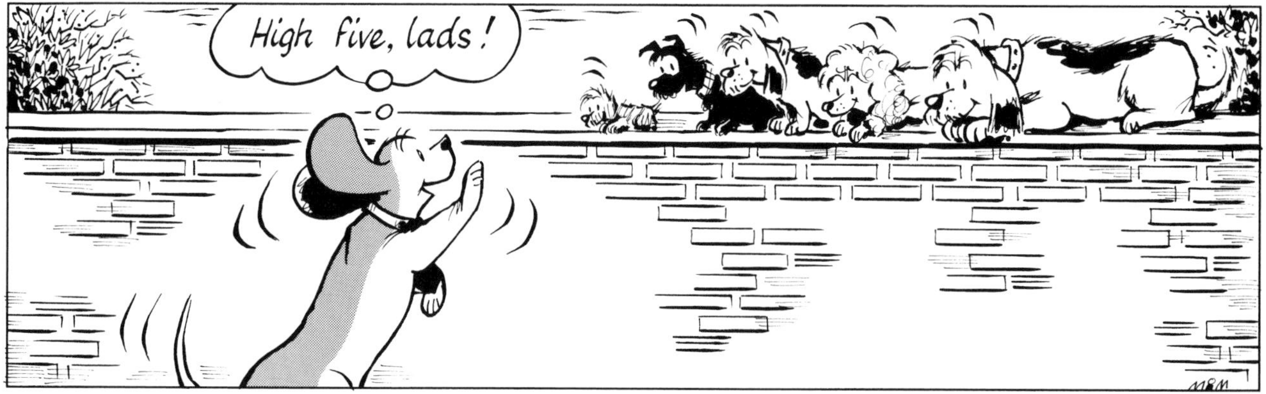
High five, lads!

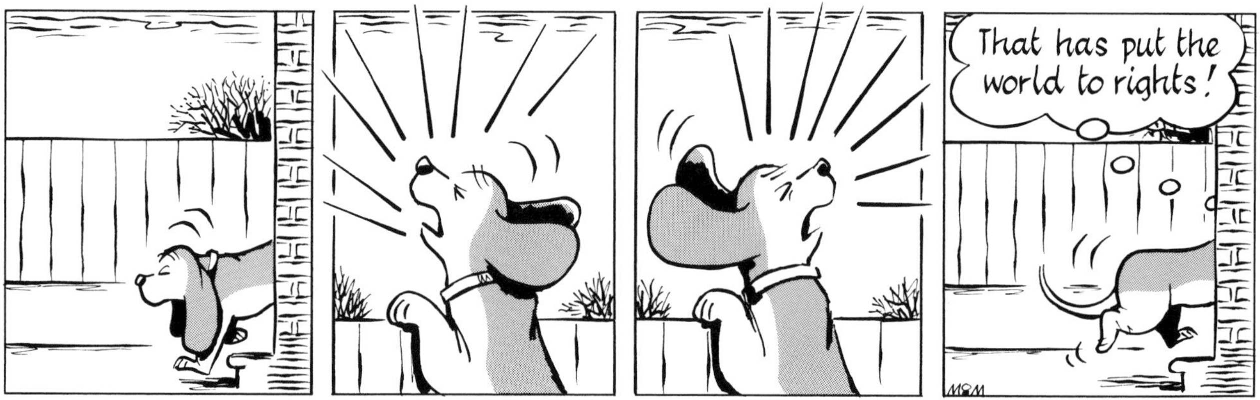
That has put the world to rights!

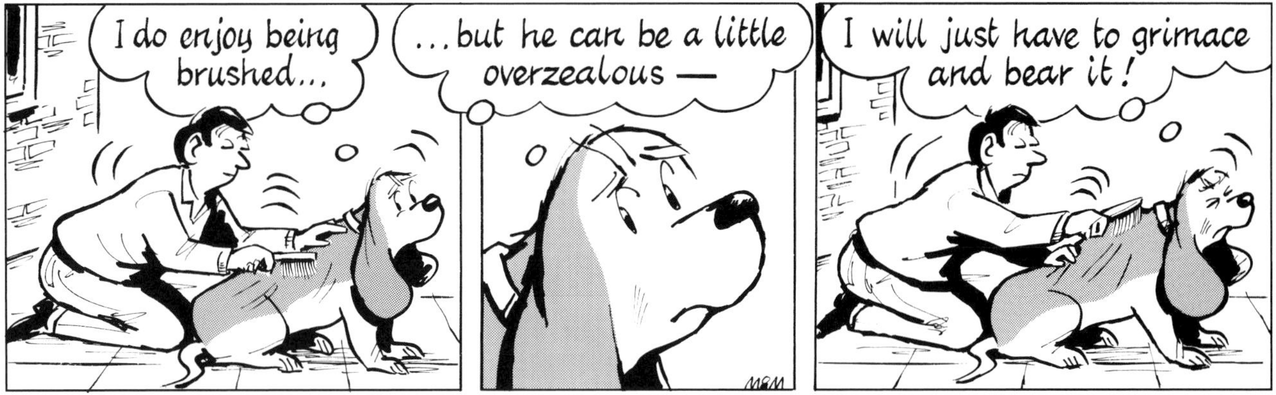
I do enjoy being brushed...
...but he can be a little overzealous —
I will just have to grimace and bear it!

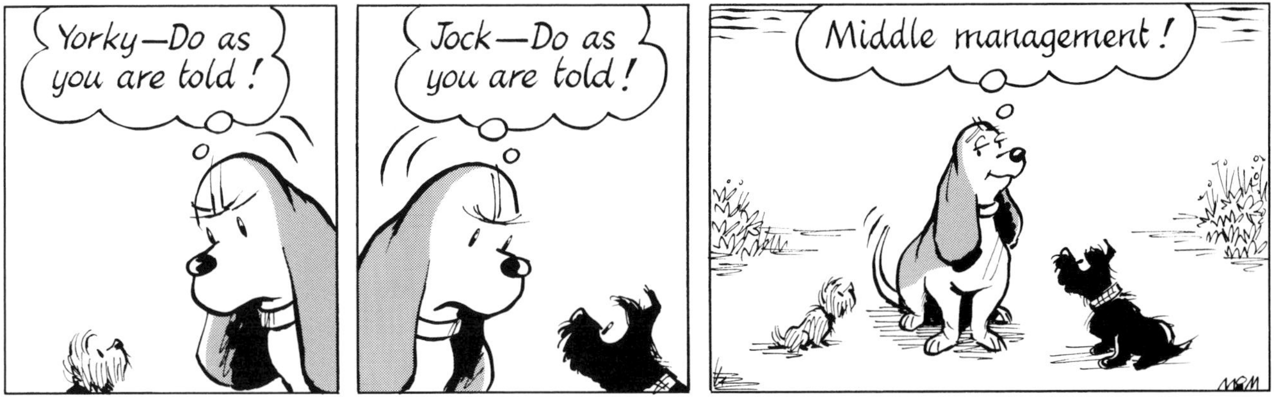
Yorky—Do as you are told!
Jock—Do as you are told!
Middle management!

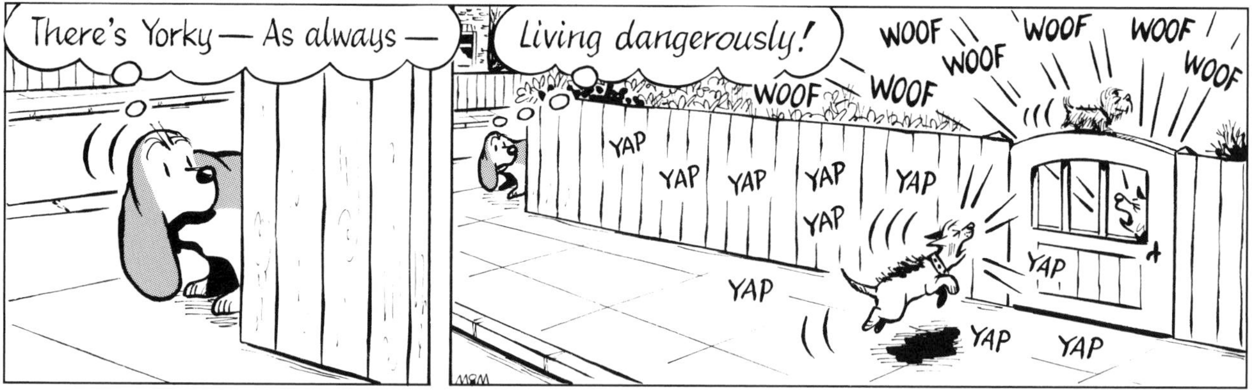
There's Yorky — As always —
Living dangerously!
WOOF WOOF WOOF WOOF WOOF WOOF WOOF
YAP YAP YAP YAP YAP YAP YAP YAP YAP YAP

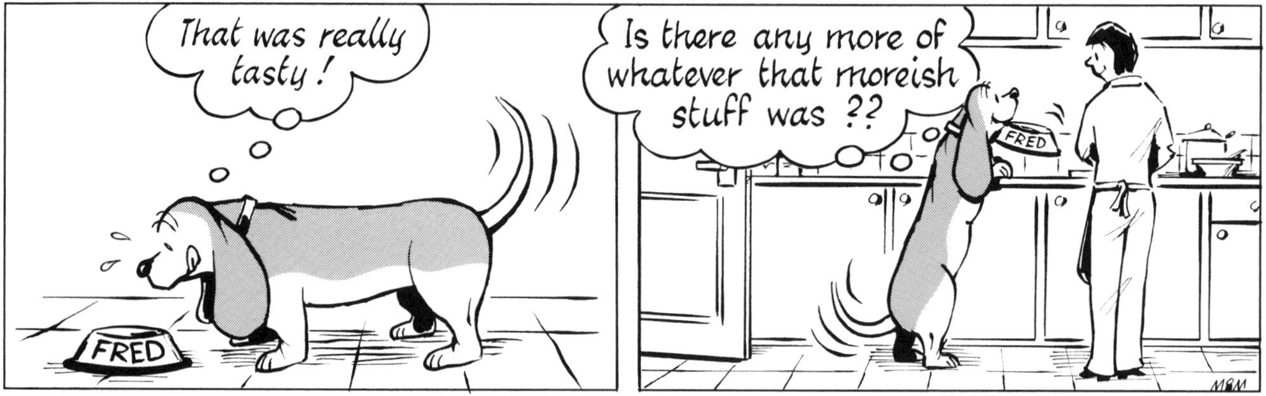
That was really tasty!
FRED
Is there any more of whatever that moreish stuff was ??
FRED

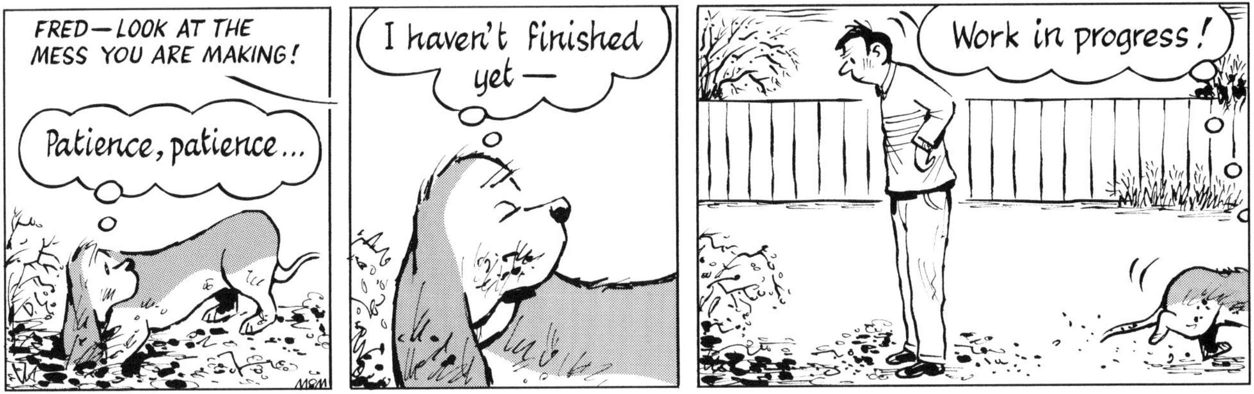
FRED—LOOK AT THE MESS YOU ARE MAKING!
Patience, patience...
I haven't finished yet—
Work in progress!
MSM

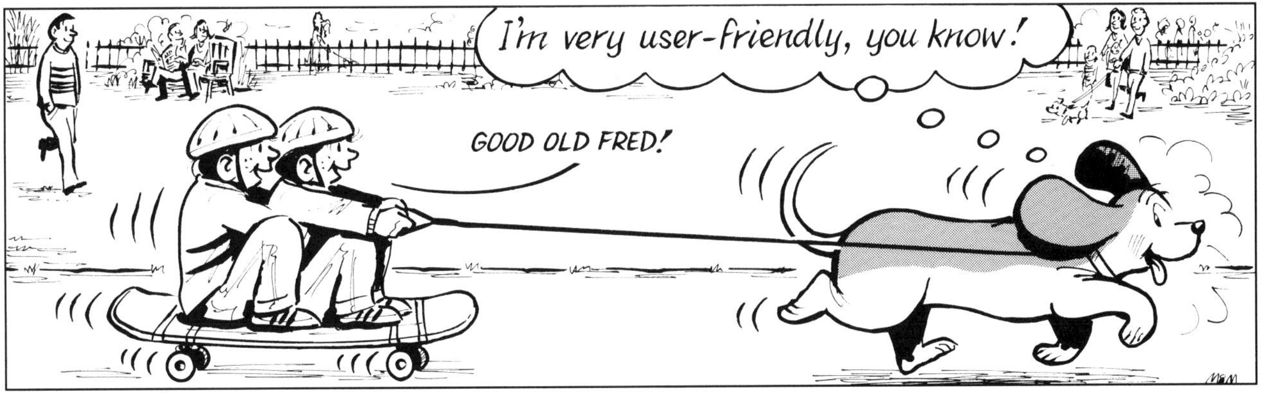
I'm very user-friendly, you know!
GOOD OLD FRED!
MSM

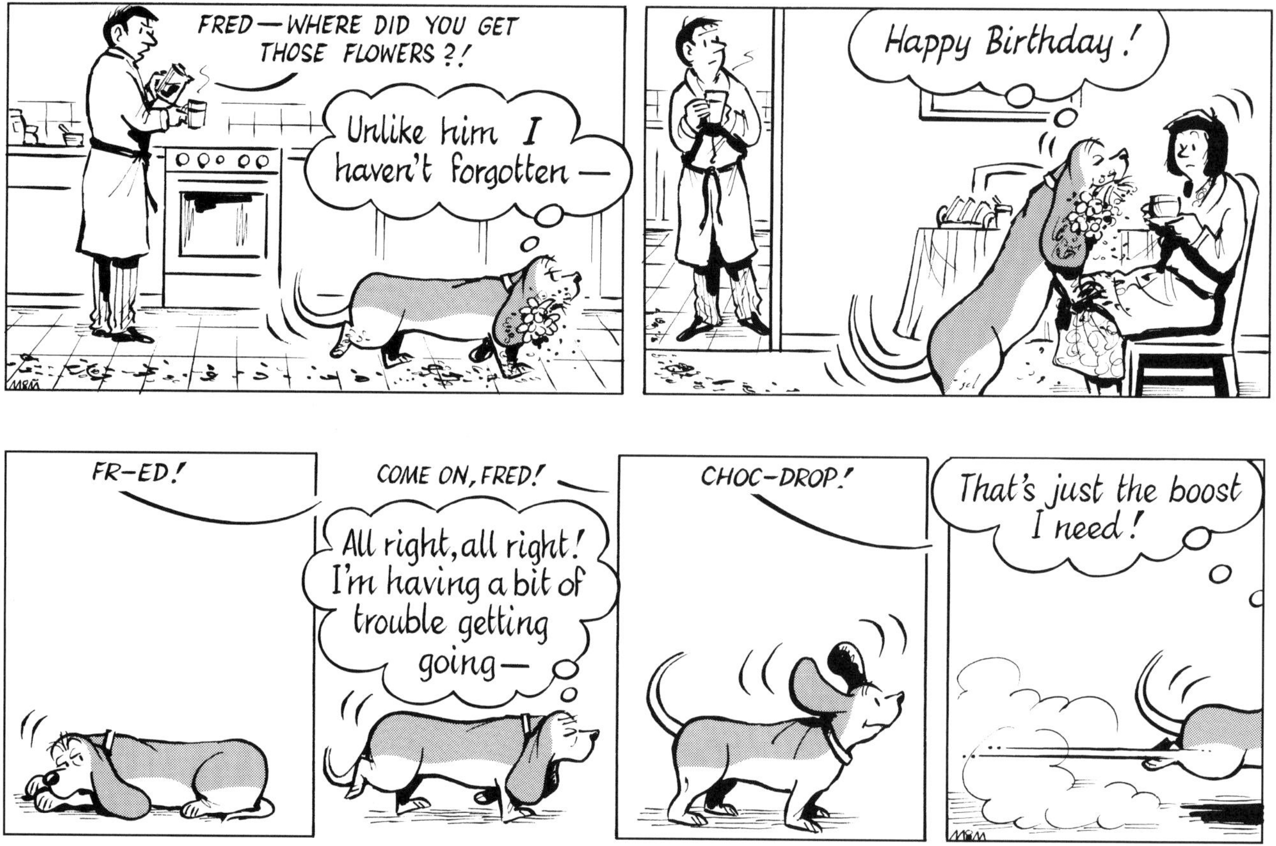
FRED — WHERE DID YOU GET THOSE FLOWERS ?!
Unlike him I haven't forgotten —
Happy Birthday!
FR-ED!
COME ON, FRED!
All right, all right! I'm having a bit of trouble getting going—
CHOC-DROP!
That's just the boost I need!

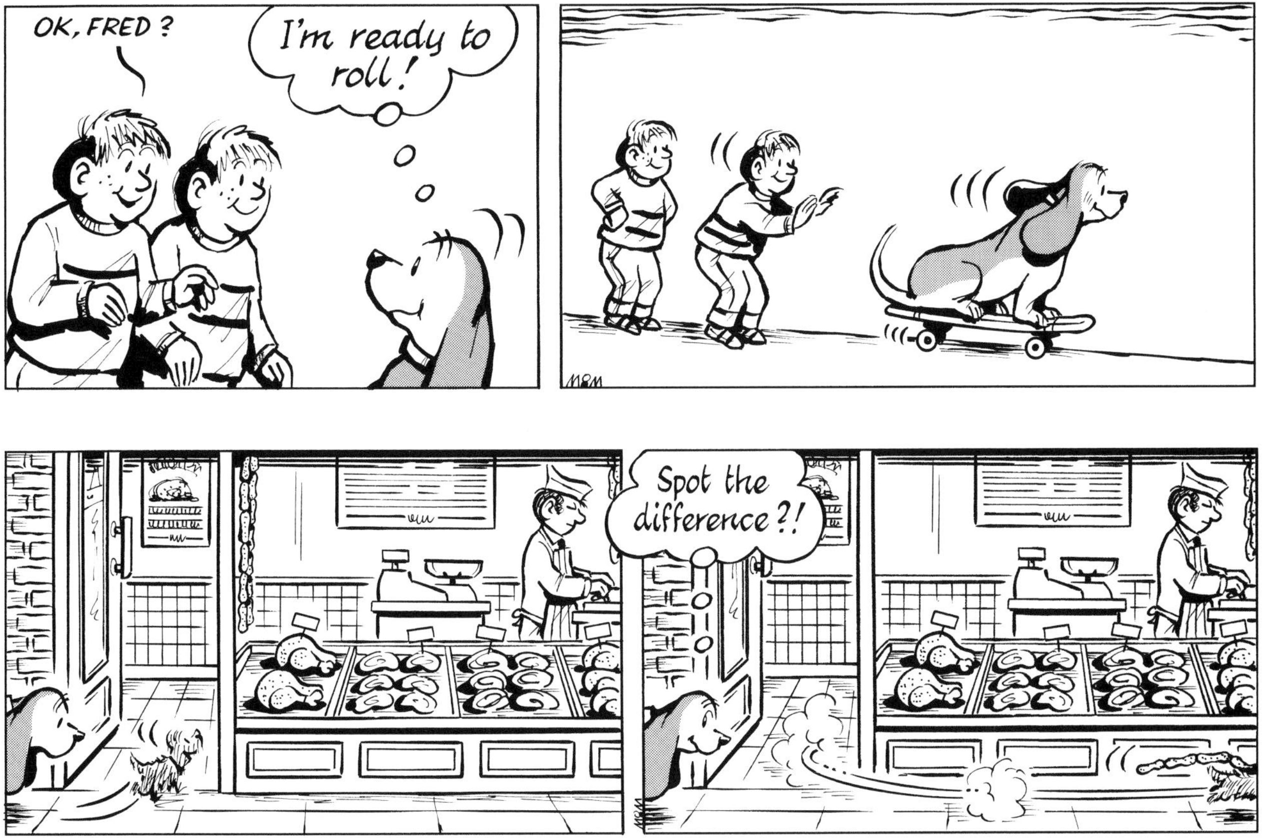
OK, FRED ?
I'm ready to roll!
Spot the difference ?!

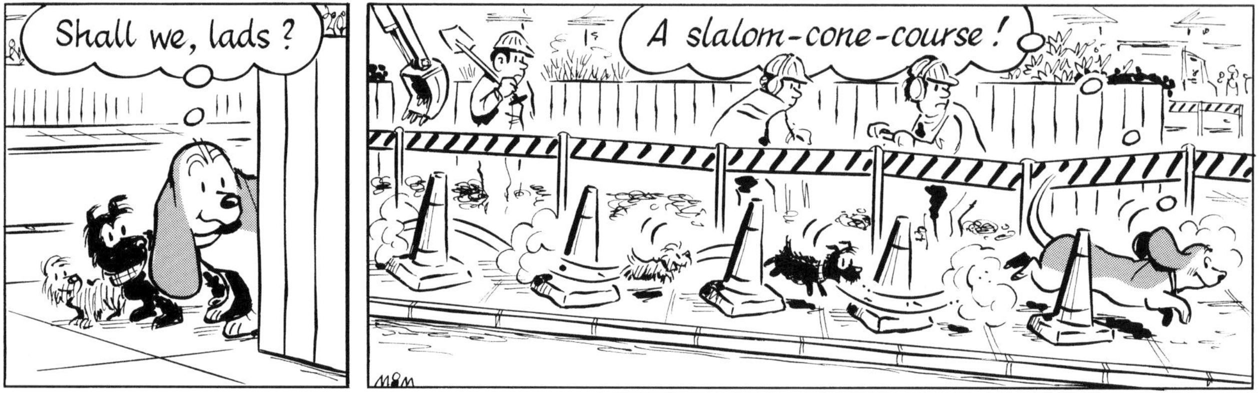
Shall we, lads?
A slalom-cone-course!

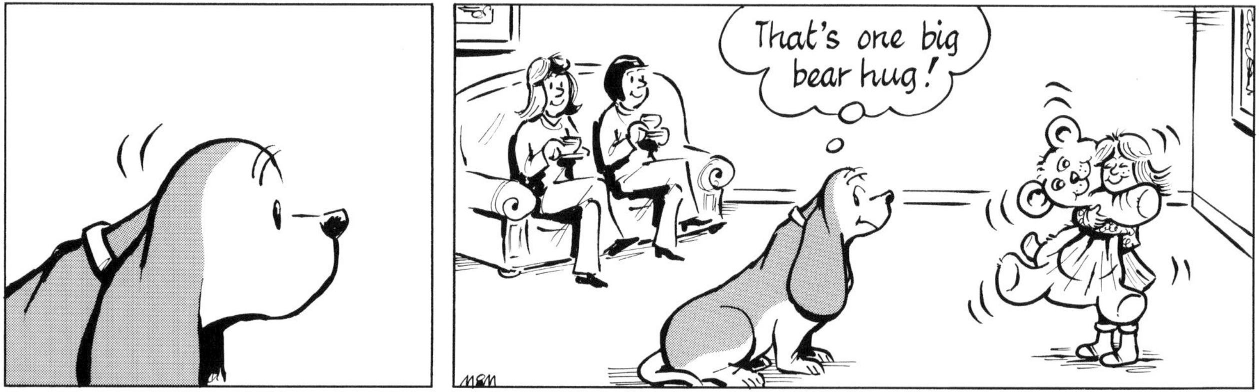
That's one big bear hug!

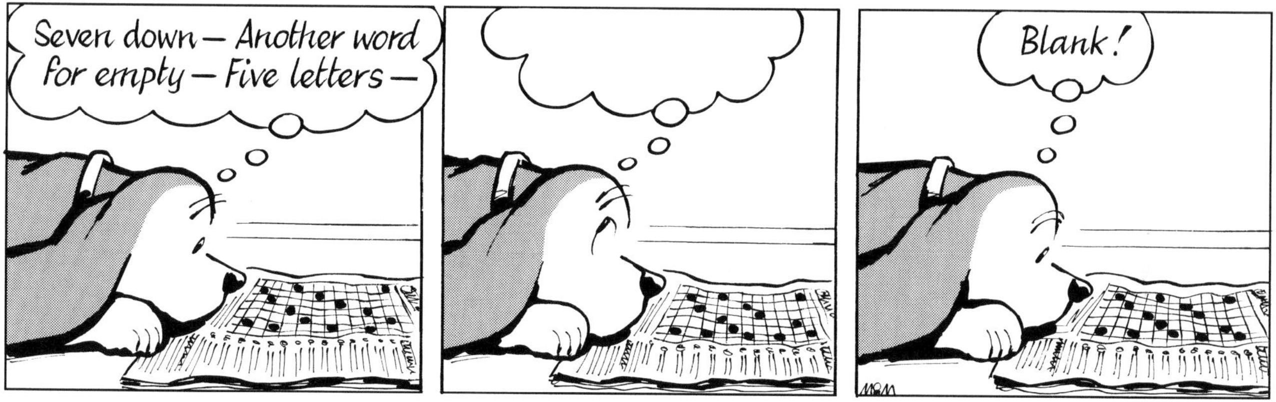
Seven down — Another word for empty — Five letters —
Blank!

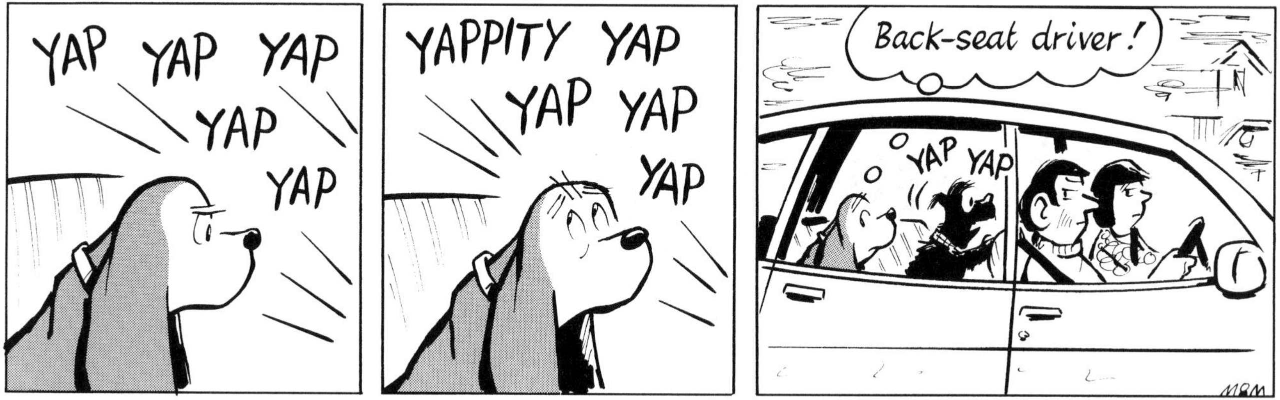
YAP YAP YAP
YAP
YAP
YAPPITY YAP
YAP YAP
YAP
Back-seat driver!
YAP YAP

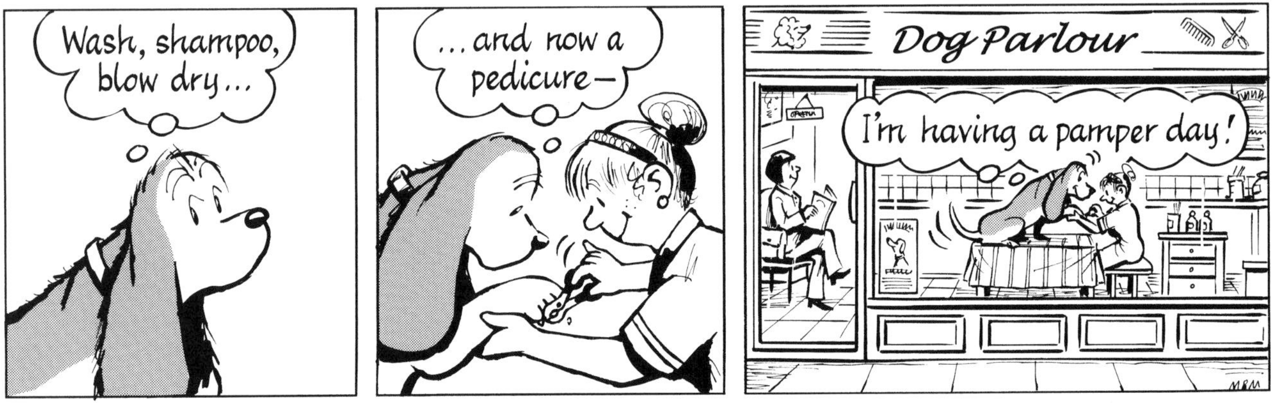
Wash, shampoo, blow dry...
...and now a pedicure–
Dog Parlour
I'm having a pamper day!

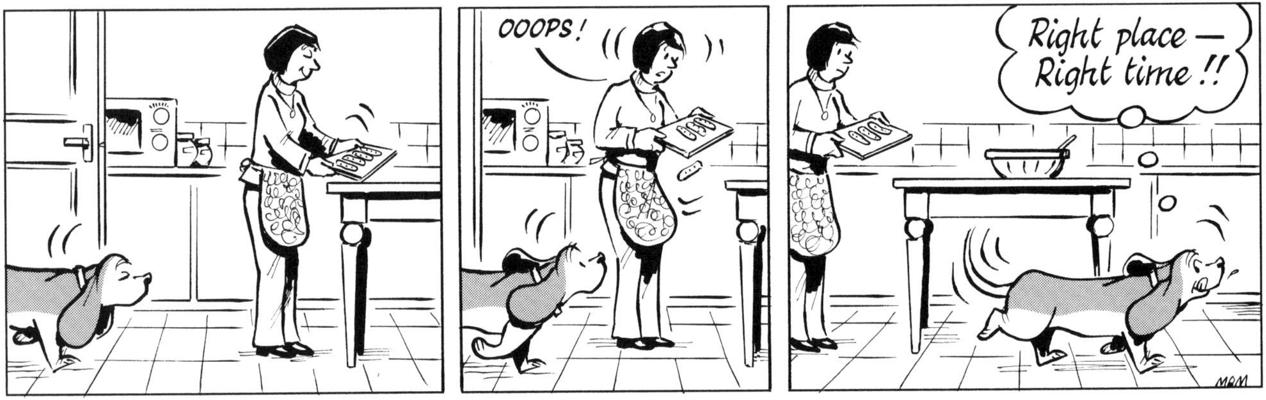
OOOPS!
Right place – Right time!!

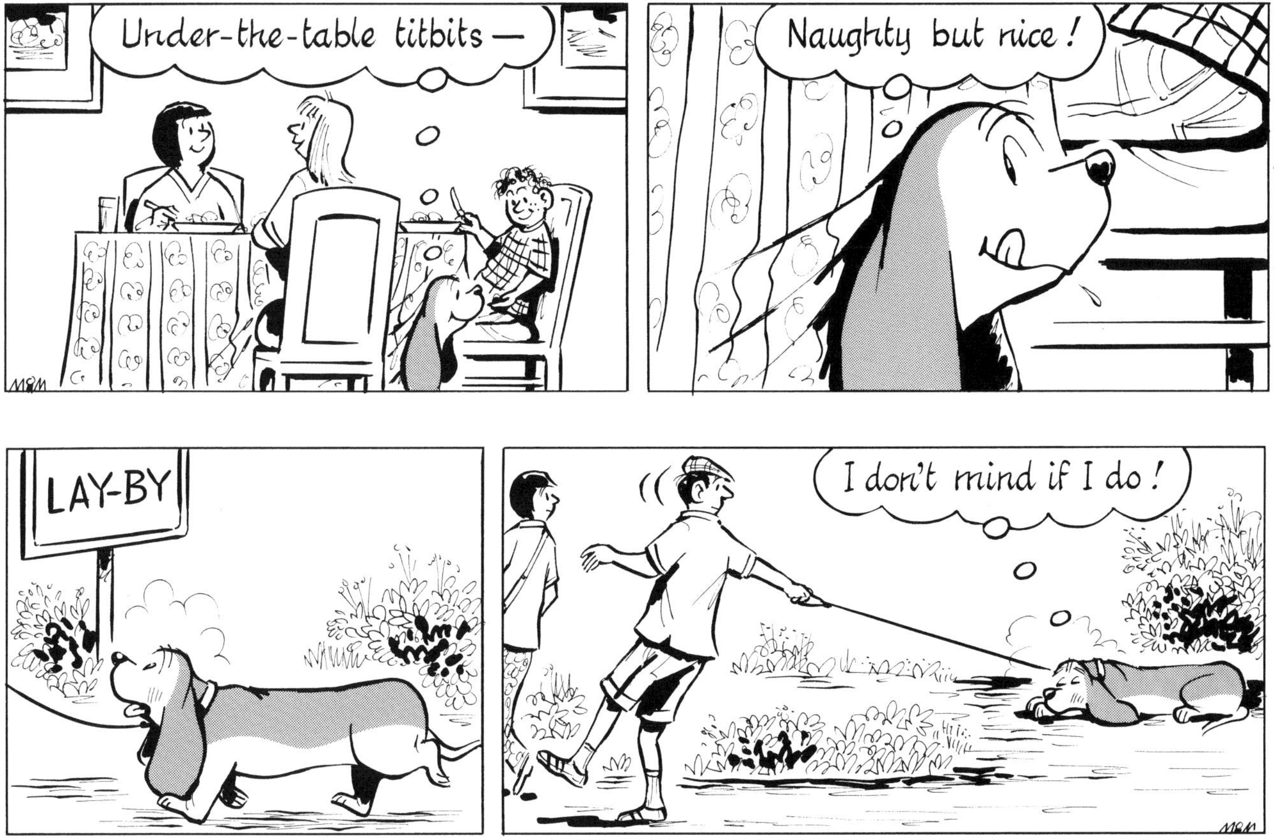
Under-the-table titbits —
MSM
Naughty but nice!
LAY-BY
I don't mind if I do!
MSM

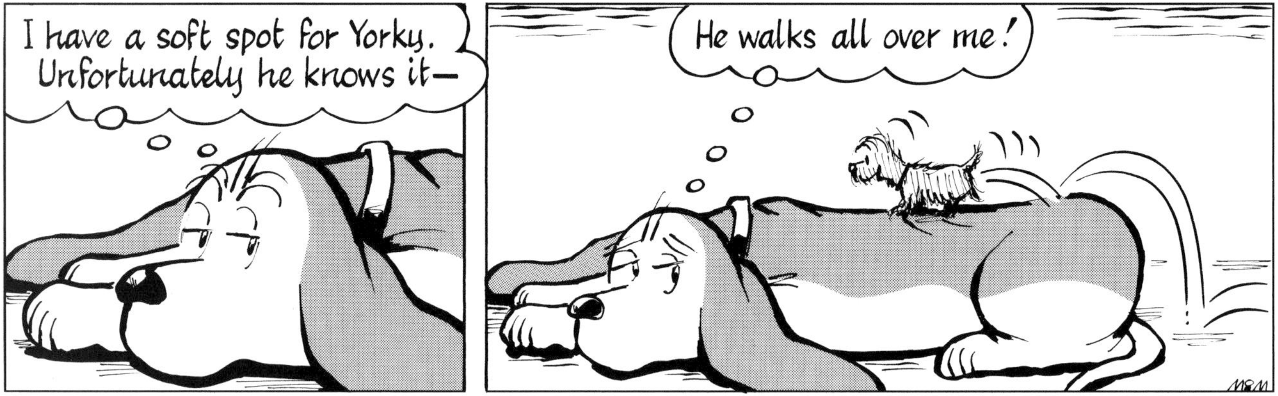
I have a soft spot for Yorky. Unfortunately he knows it—
He walks all over me!

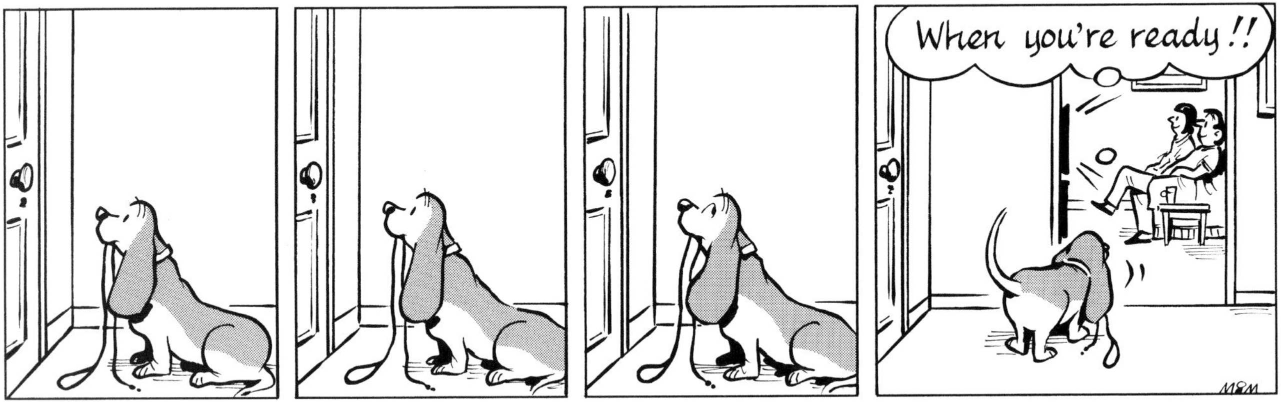
When you're ready!!

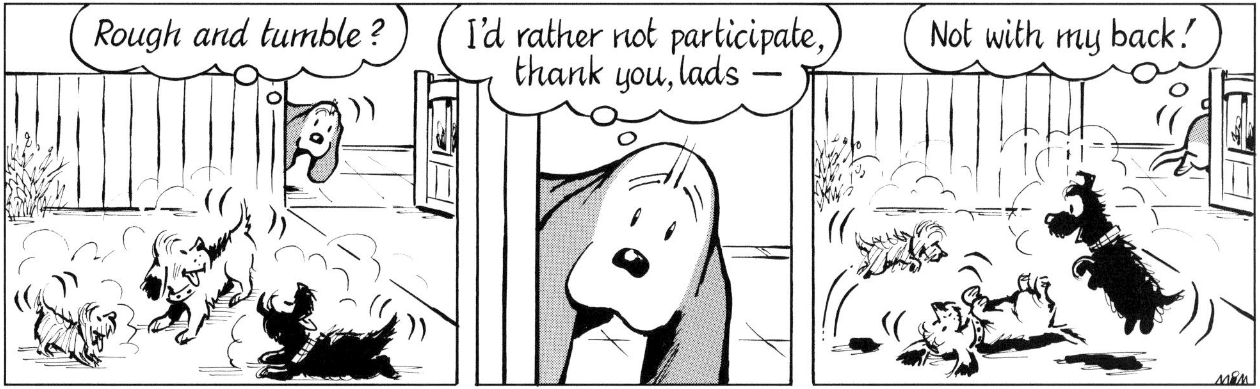
Rough and tumble?
I'd rather not participate, thank you, lads —
Not with my back!

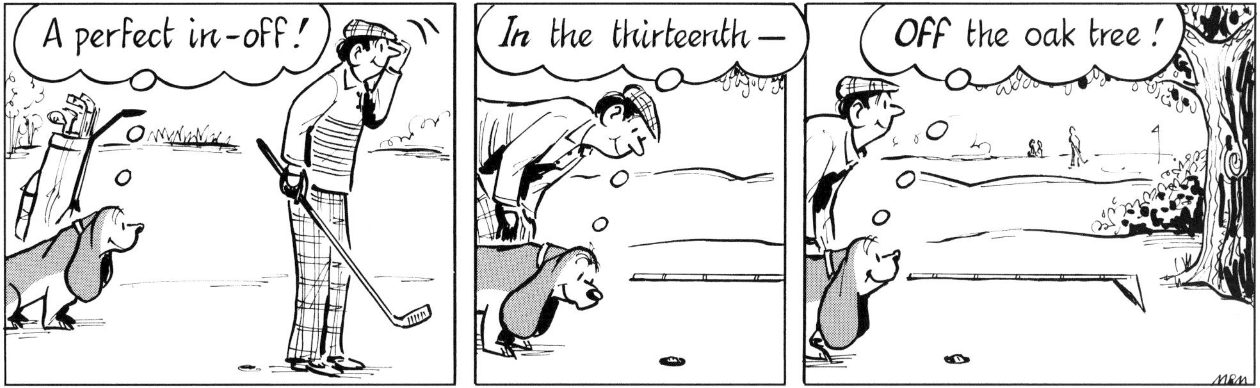
A perfect in-off!
In the thirteenth —
OFF the oak tree!

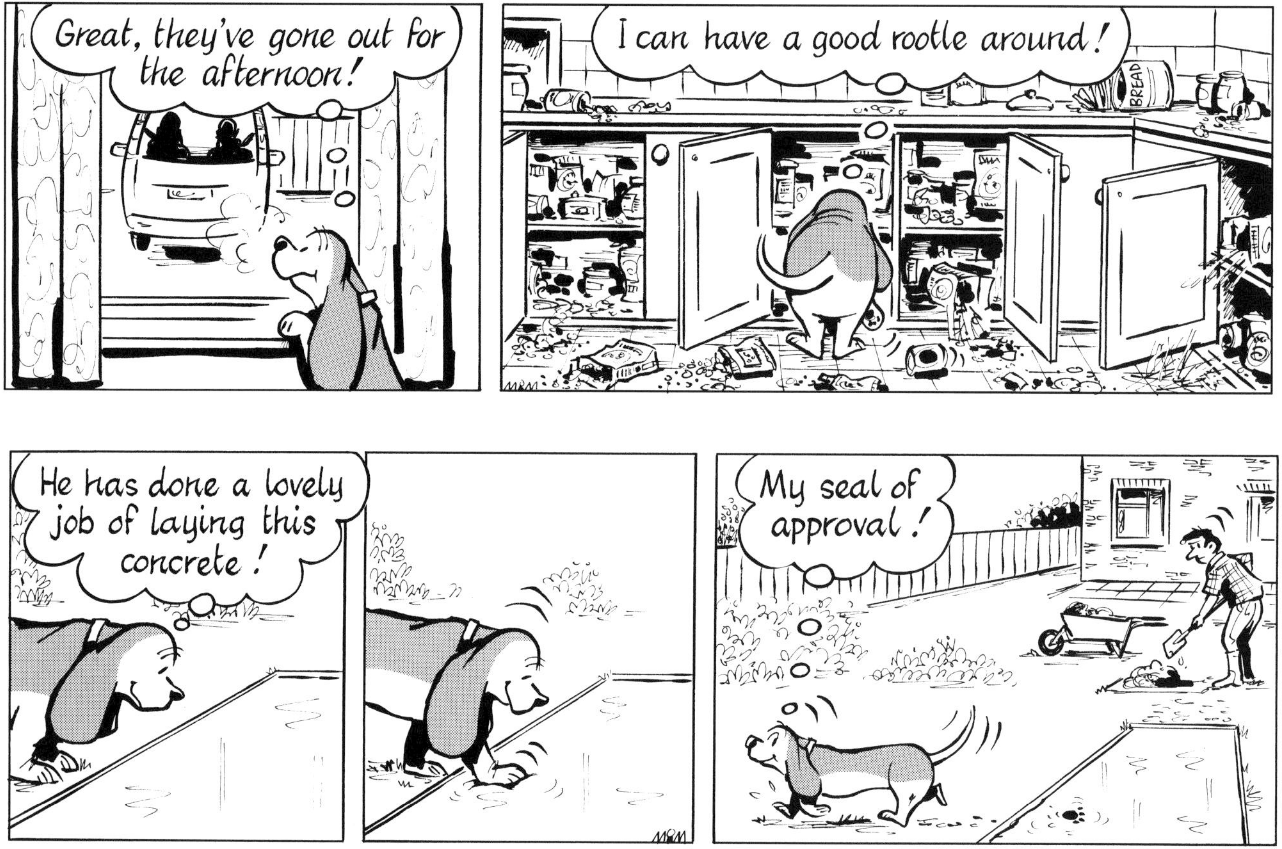
Great, they've gone out for the afternoon!
I can have a good rootle around!
BREAD
He has done a lovely job of laying this concrete!
My seal of approval!

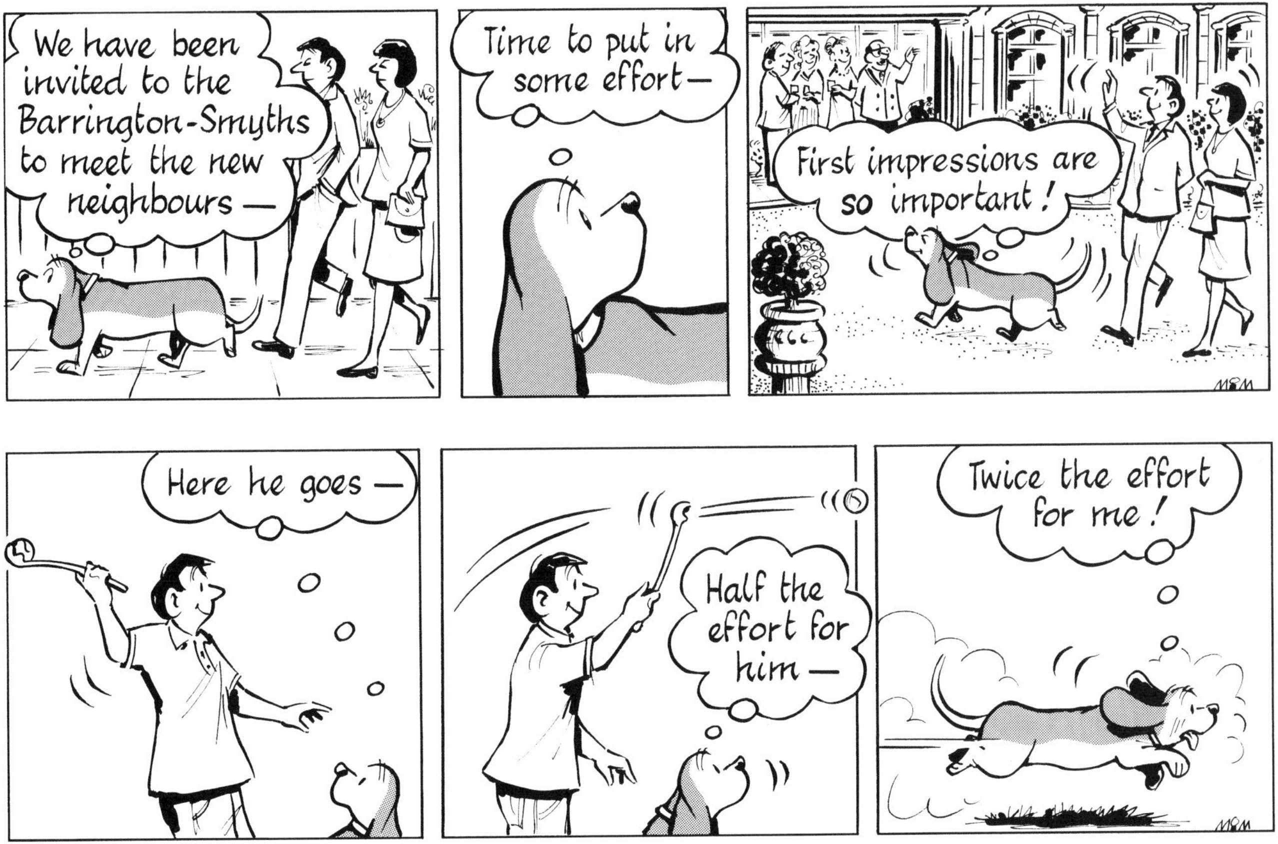
We have been invited to the Barrington-Smyths to meet the new neighbours —
Time to put in some effort —
First impressions are so important!
M&M
Here he goes —
Half the effort for him —
Twice the effort for me!
M&M

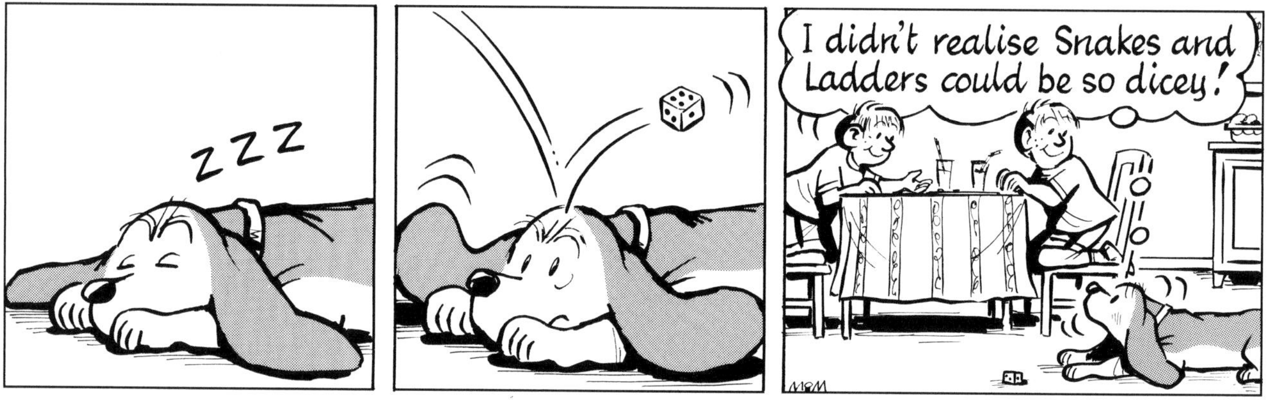
Z Z Z
I didn't realise Snakes and Ladders could be so dicey!

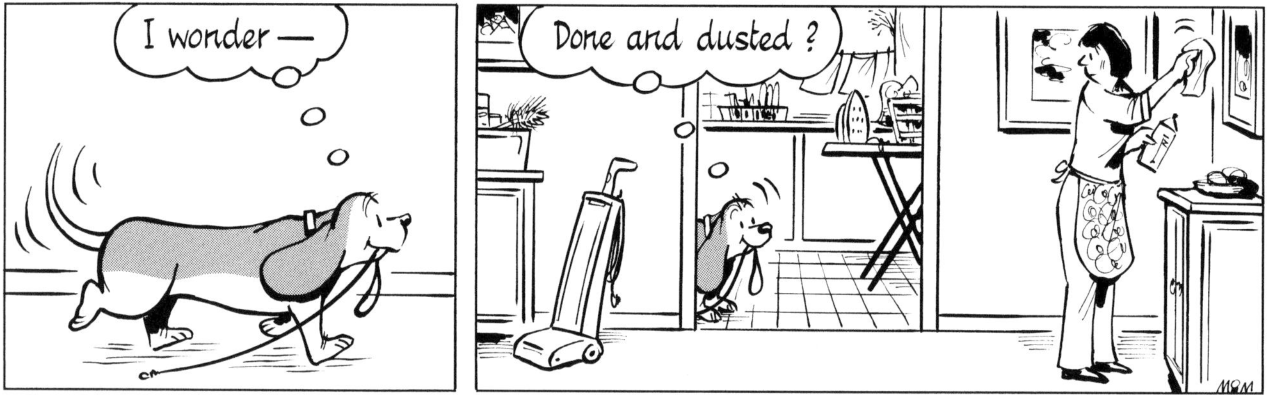
I wonder —
Done and dusted ?

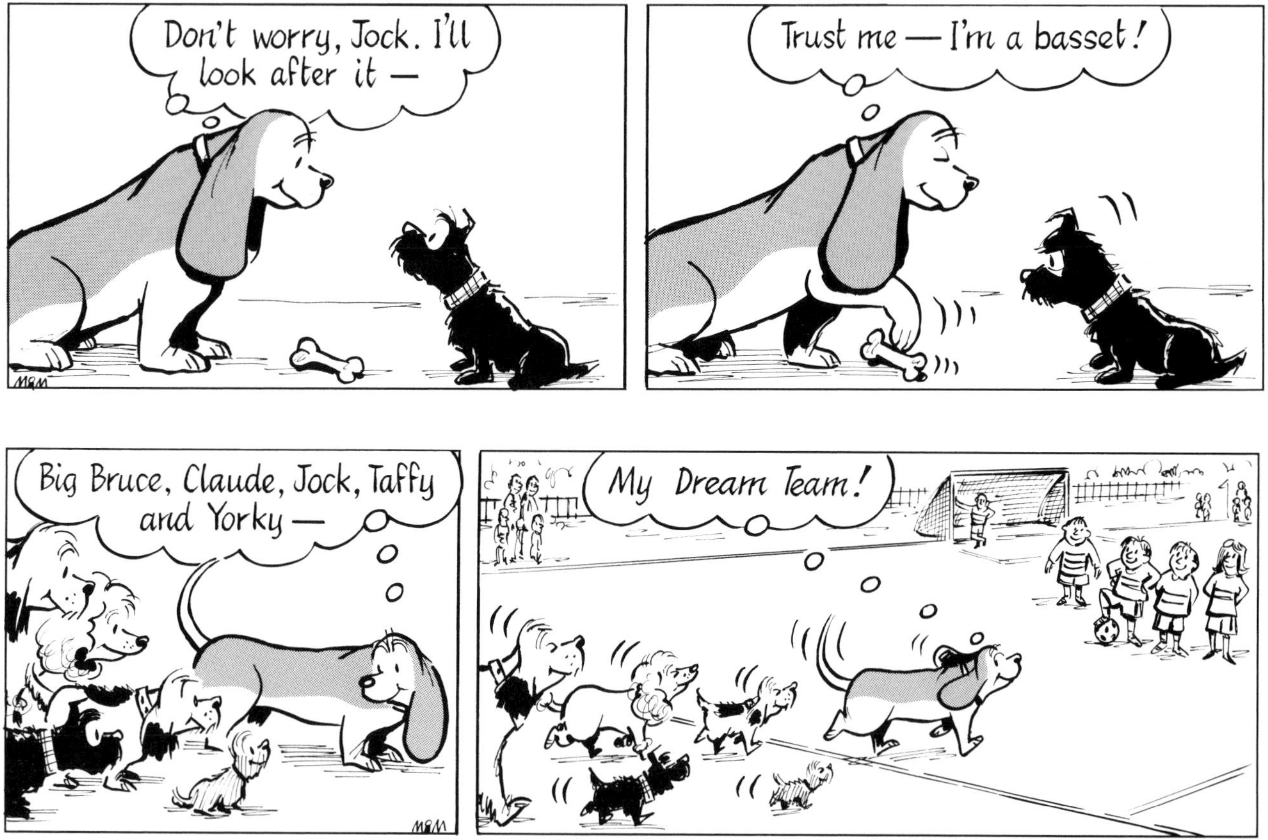
Don't worry, Jock. I'll look after it —
Trust me — I'm a basset!
Big Bruce, Claude, Jock, Taffy and Yorky —
My Dream Team!

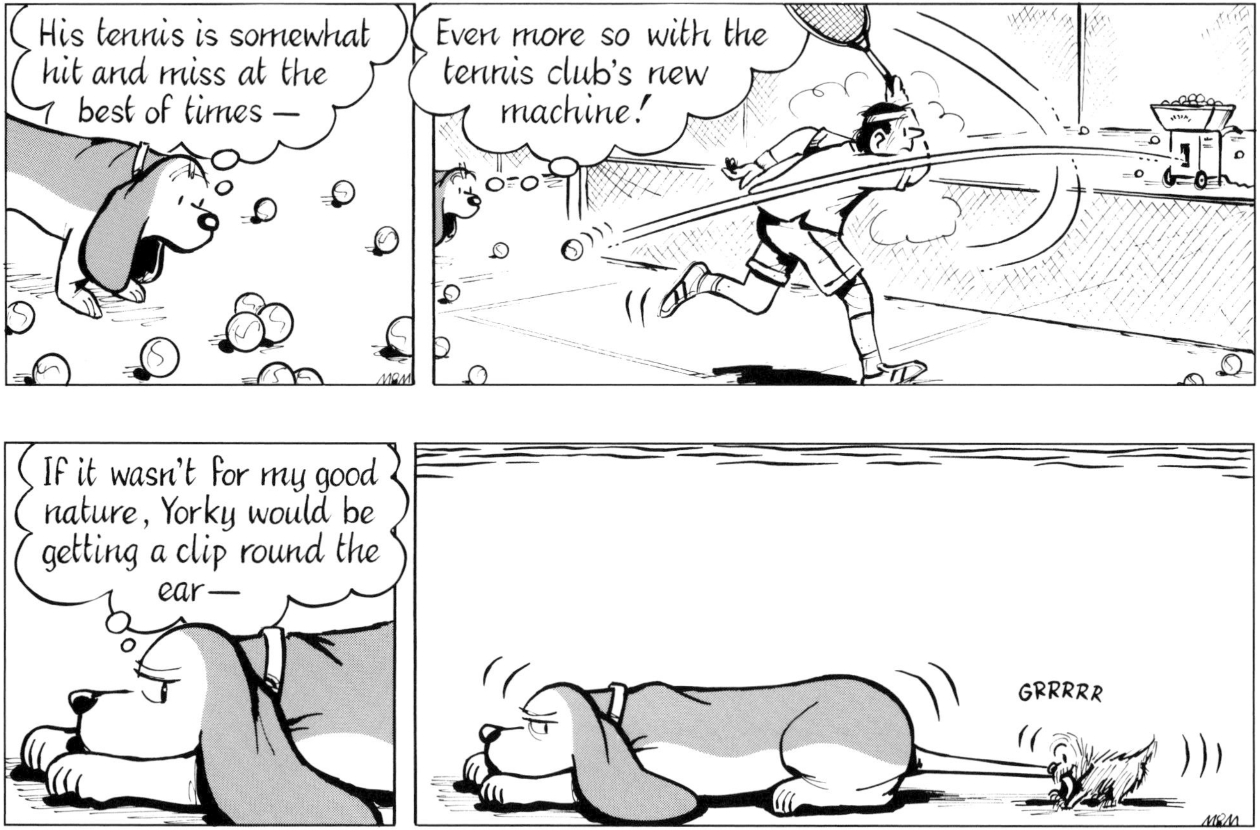
His tennis is somewhat hit and miss at the best of times —
Even more so with the tennis club's new machine!
If it wasn't for my good nature, Yorky would be getting a clip round the ear—
GRRRRR

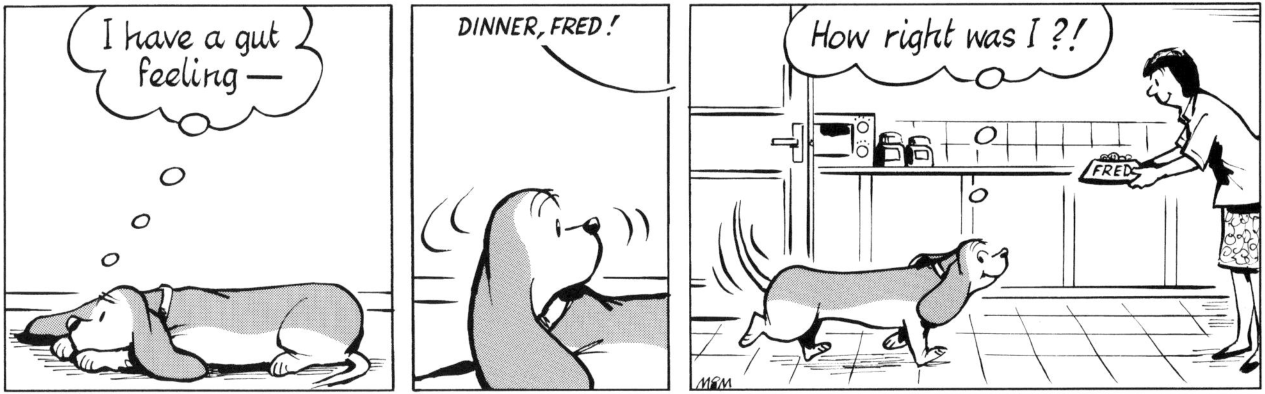
I have a gut feeling —
DINNER, FRED!
How right was I ?!
FRED

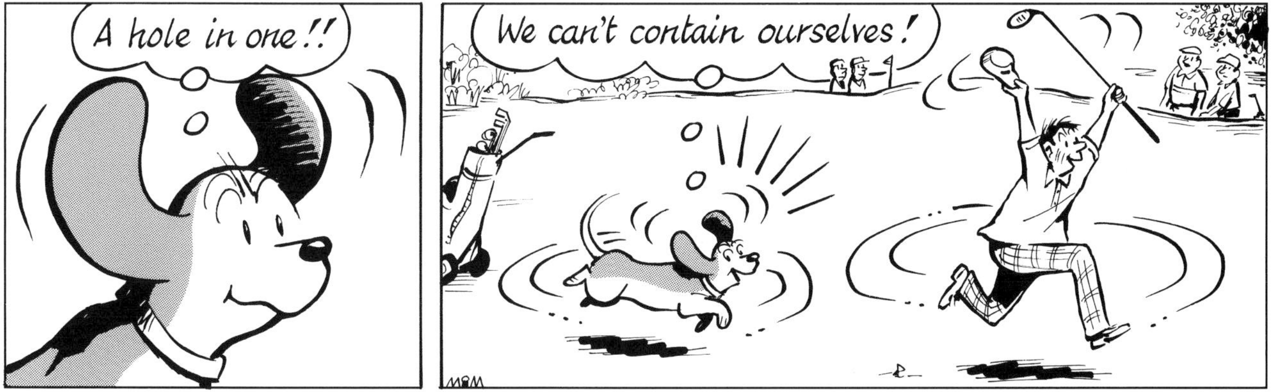
A hole in one!!
We can't contain ourselves!

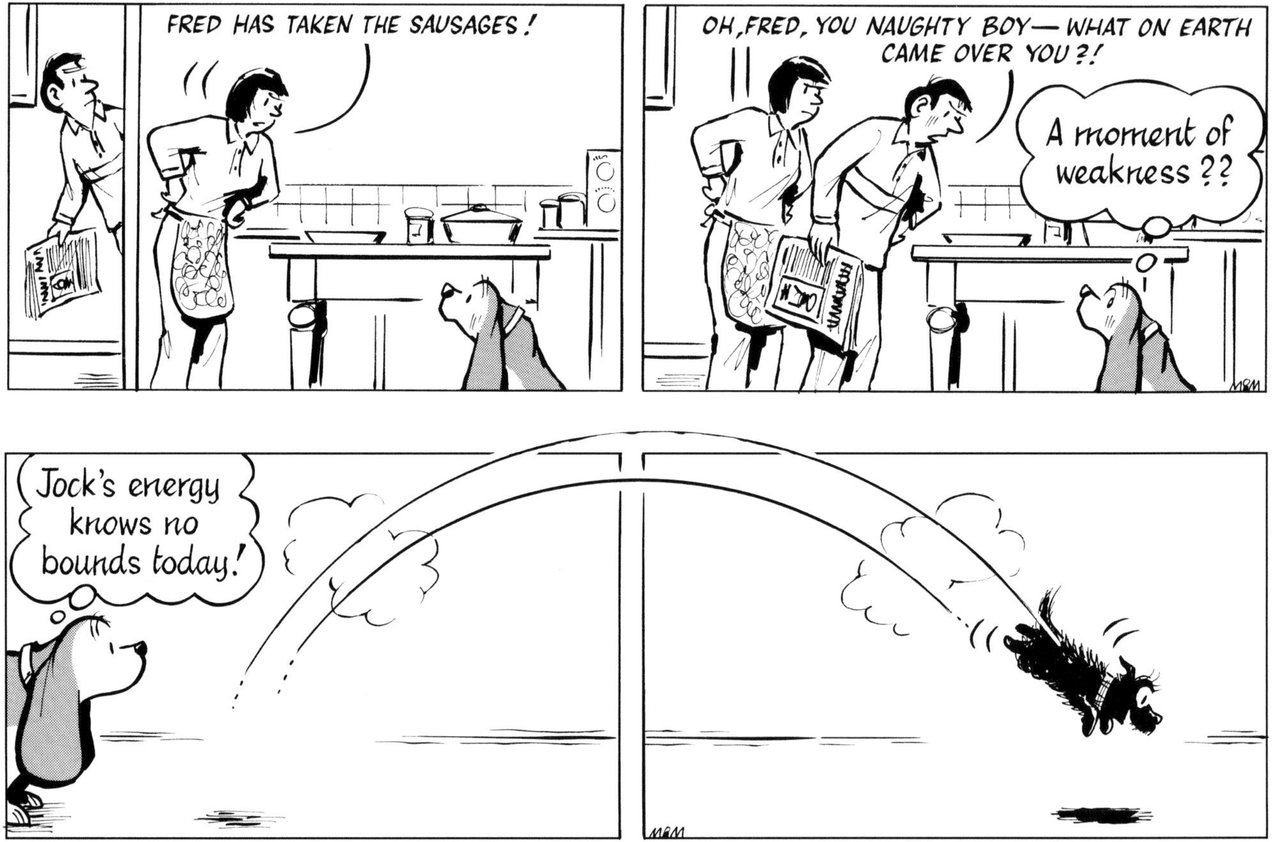
FRED HAS TAKEN THE SAUSAGES!
OH, FRED, YOU NAUGHTY BOY— WHAT ON EARTH CAME OVER YOU?!
A moment of weakness??
Jock's energy knows no bounds today!
MBM

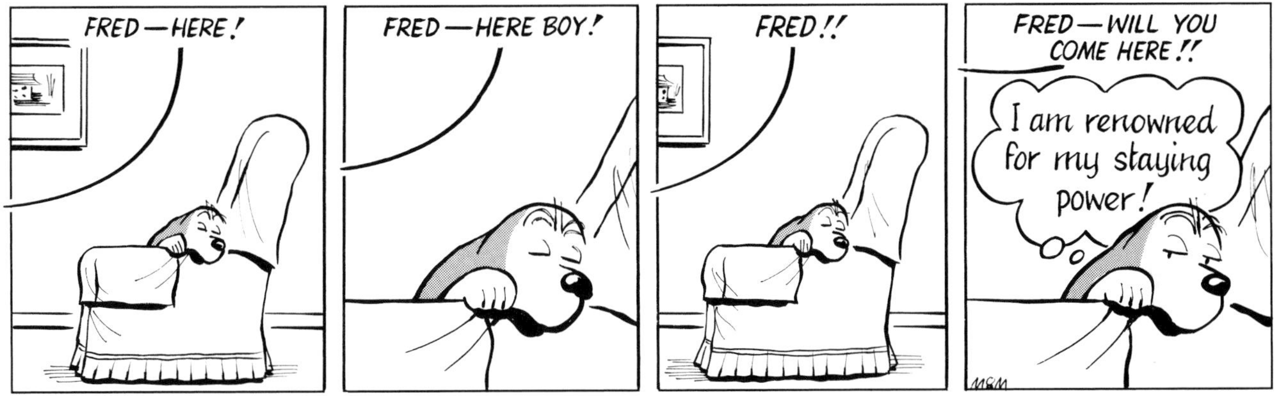
FRED—HERE!
FRED—HERE BOY!
FRED!!
FRED—WILL YOU COME HERE!!
I am renowned for my staying power!
M&M

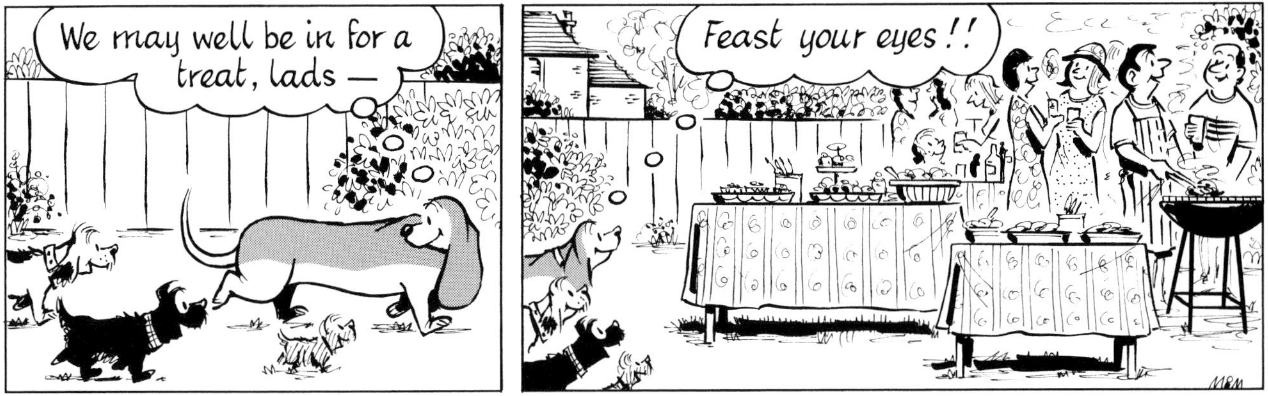
We may well be in for a treat, lads —
Feast your eyes!!
M&M

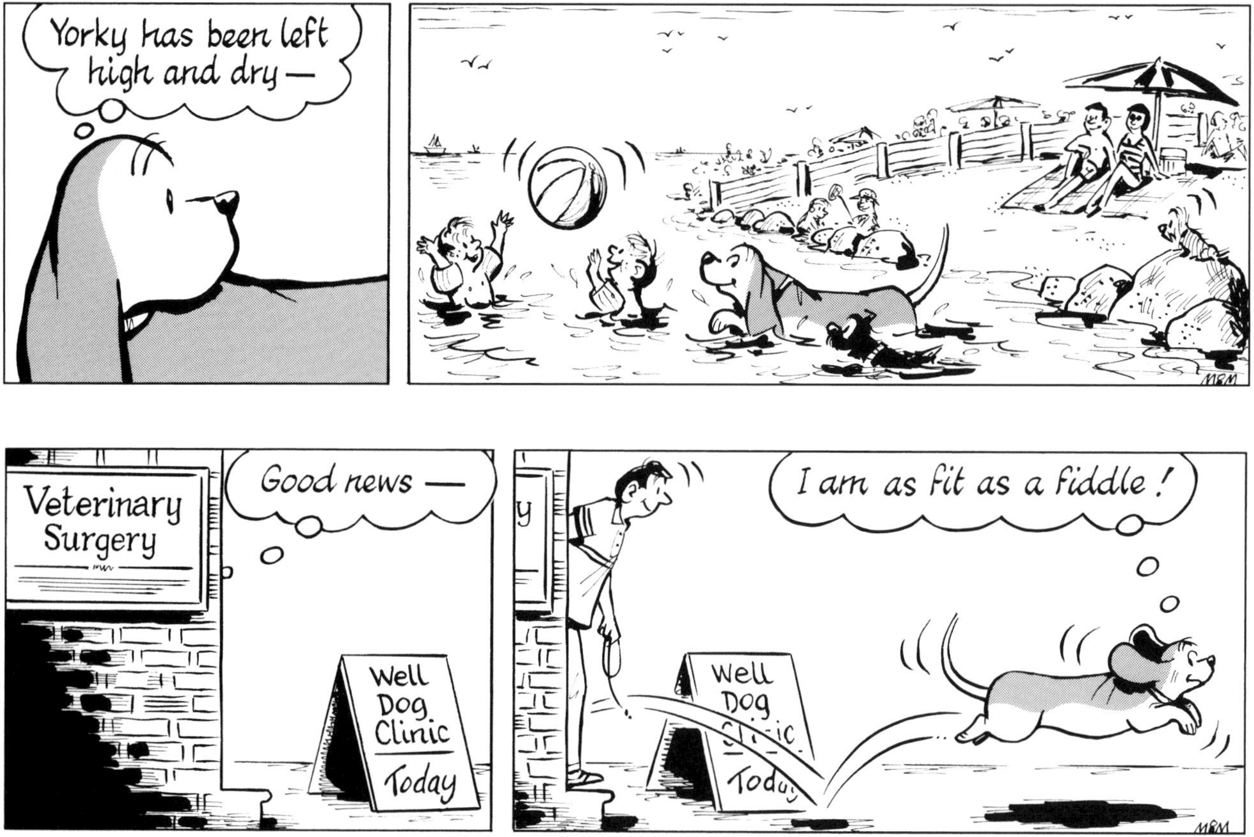
Yorky has been left high and dry —
Veterinary Surgery
Good news —
Well Dog Clinic
Today
I am as fit as a fiddle !

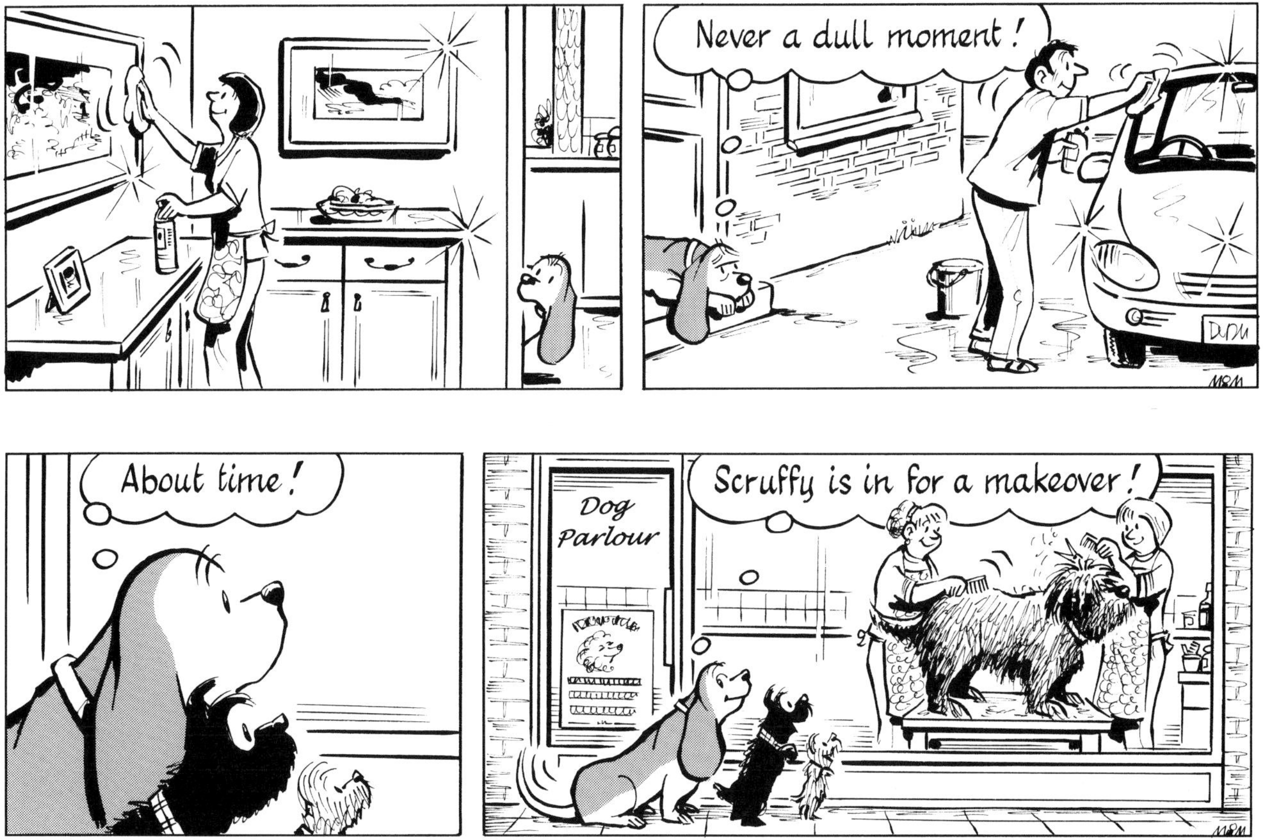
Never a dull moment!
About time!
Dog Parlour
Scruffy is in for a makeover!

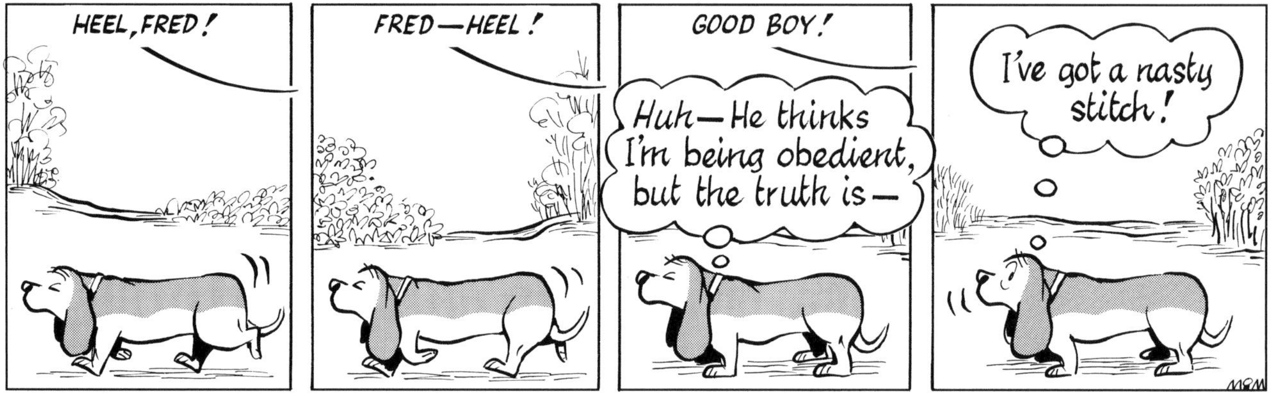
HEEL, FRED!
FRED—HEEL!
GOOD BOY!
Huh—He thinks I'm being obedient, but the truth is—
I've got a nasty stitch!

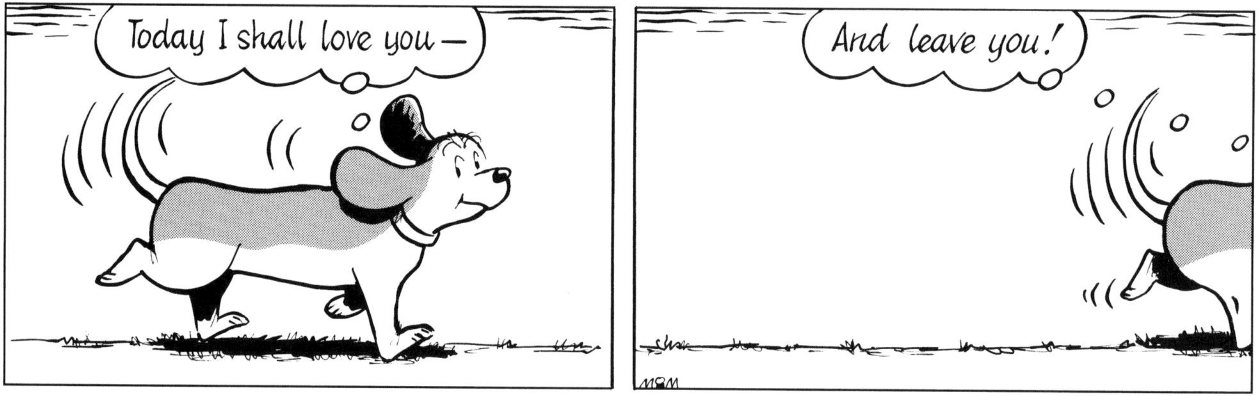
Today I shall love you—
And leave you!

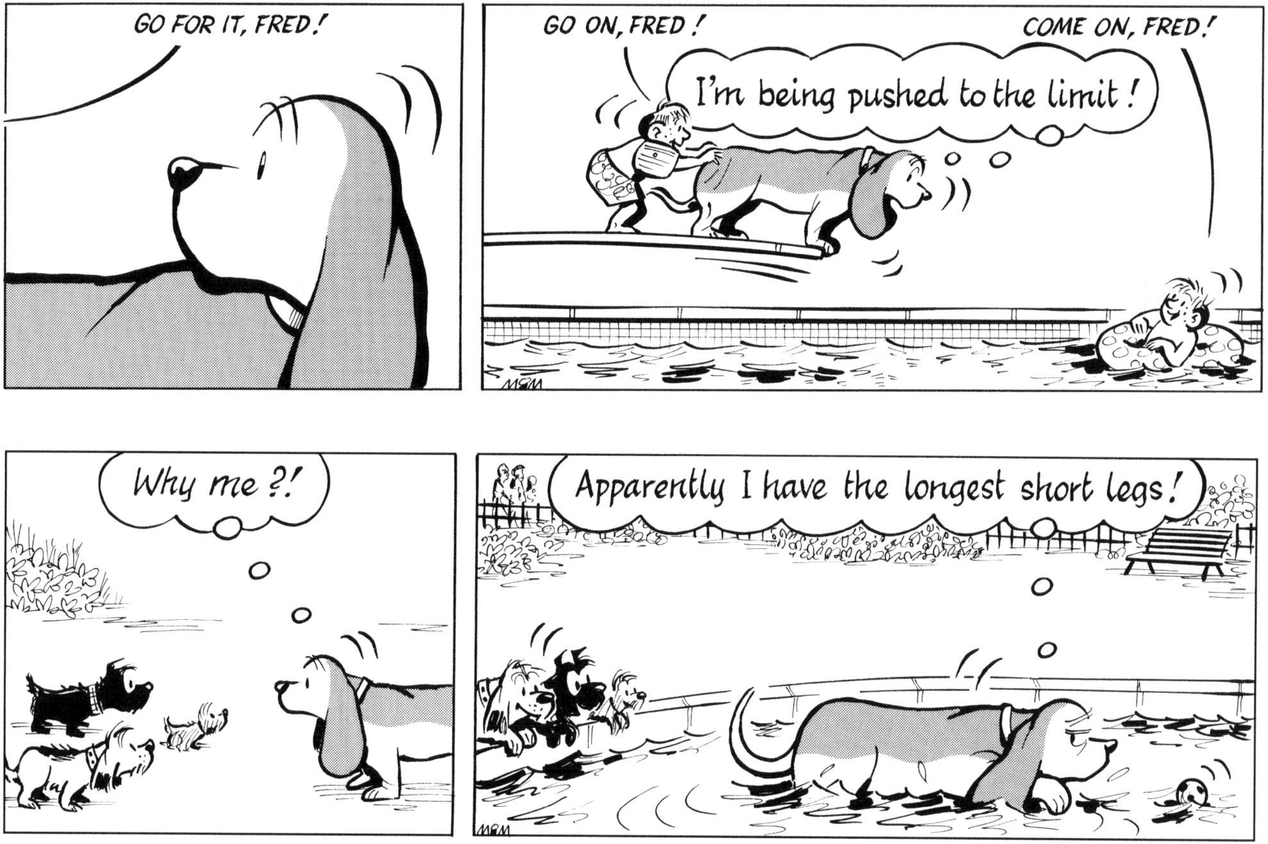
GO FOR IT, FRED!
GO ON, FRED!
COME ON, FRED!
I'm being pushed to the limit!
Why me?!
Apparently I have the longest short legs!

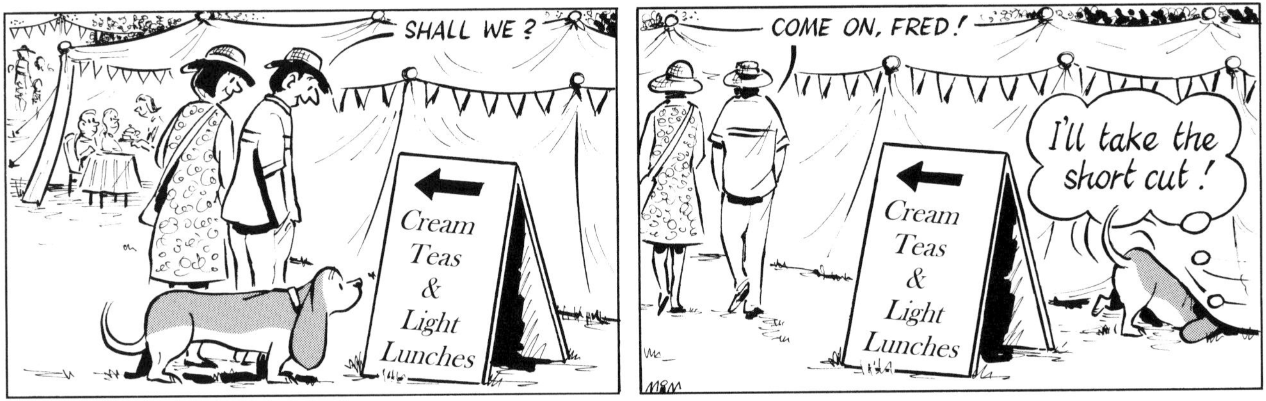
SHALL WE ?
Cream Teas & Light Lunches
COME ON, FRED!
Cream Teas & Light Lunches
I'll take the short cut!
M&M

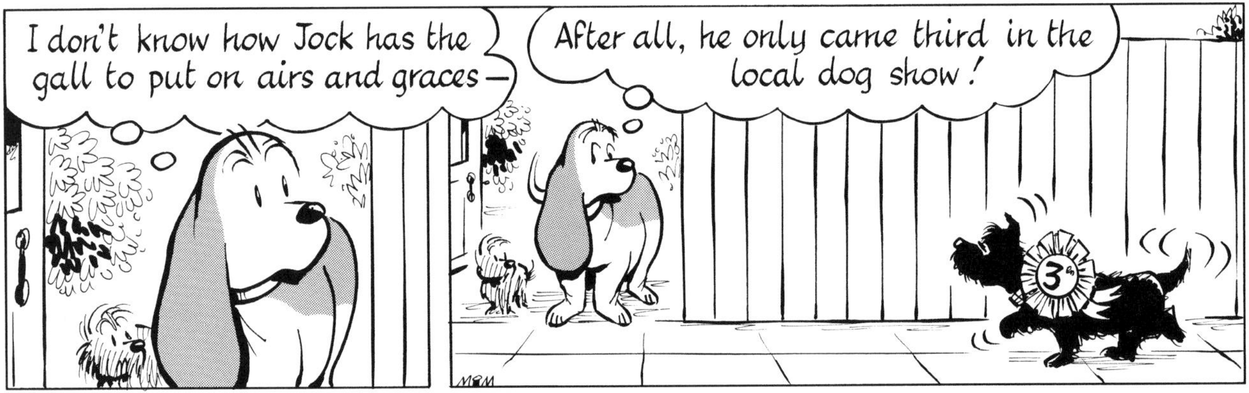
I don't know how Jock has the gall to put on airs and graces —
After all, he only came third in the local dog show!
3rd
M&M

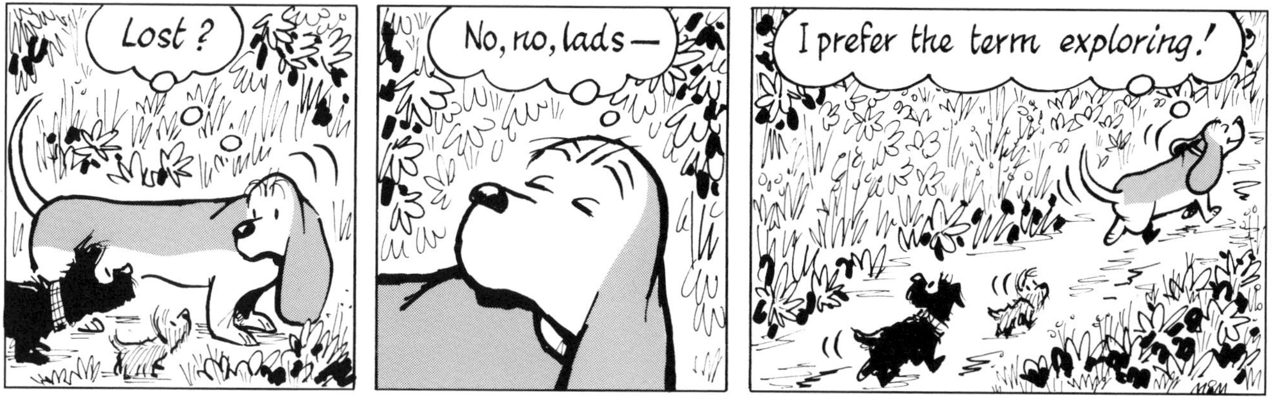
Lost ?
No, no, lads —
I prefer the term exploring!
M&M

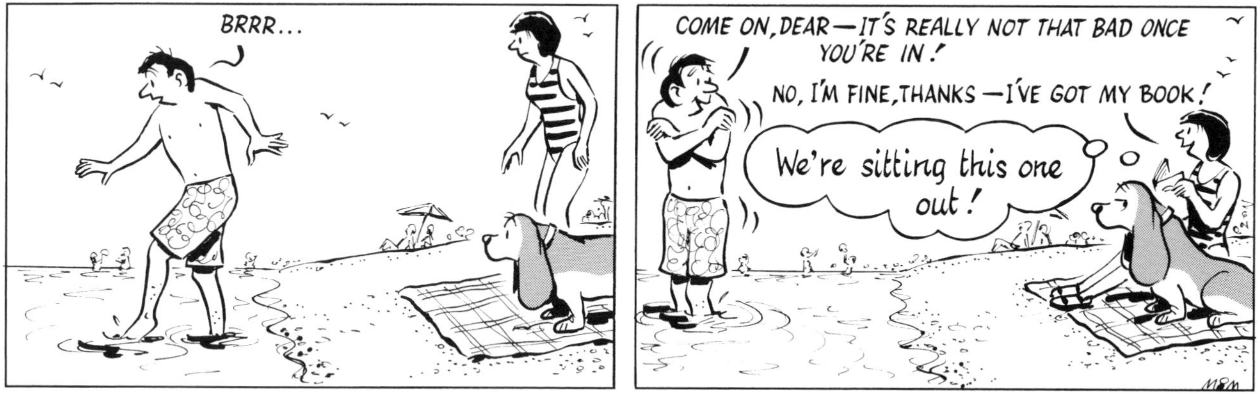
BRRR...
COME ON, DEAR — IT'S REALLY NOT THAT BAD ONCE YOU'RE IN!
NO, I'M FINE, THANKS — I'VE GOT MY BOOK!
We're sitting this one out!
M&M

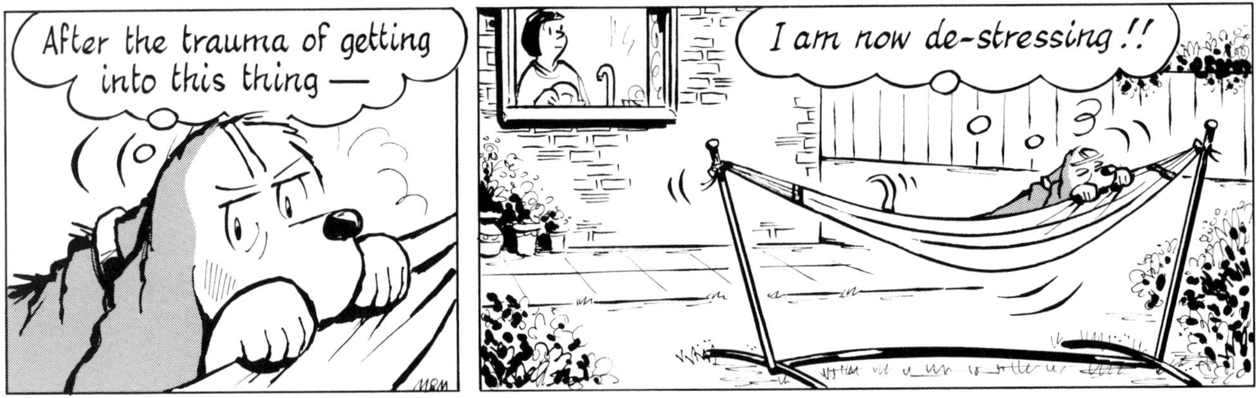
After the trauma of getting into this thing —
I am now de-stressing!!

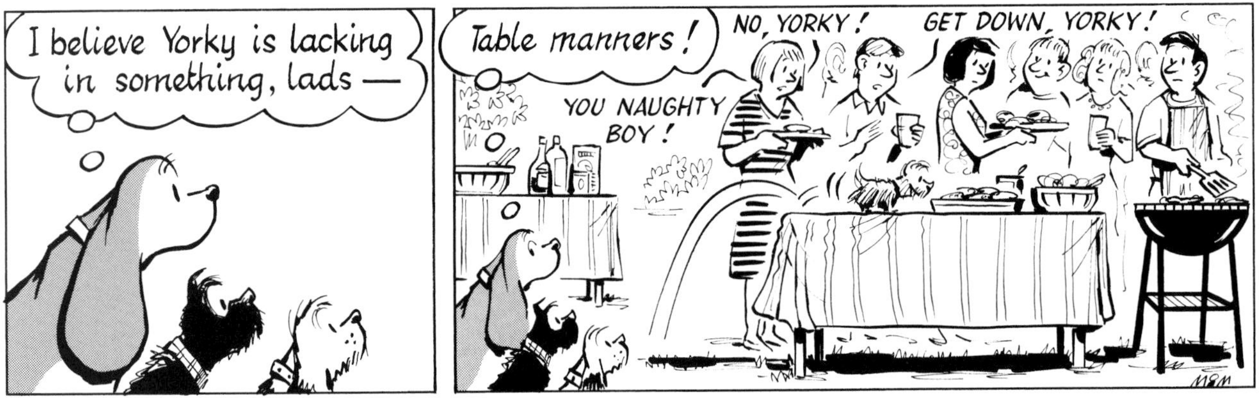
I believe Yorky is lacking in something, lads —
Table manners!
NO, YORKY!
GET DOWN, YORKY!
YOU NAUGHTY BOY!

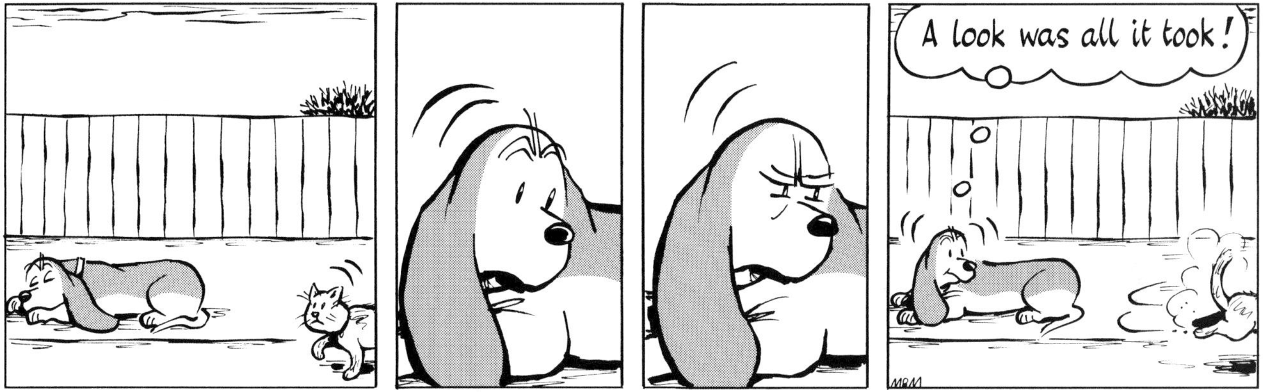
A look was all it took!

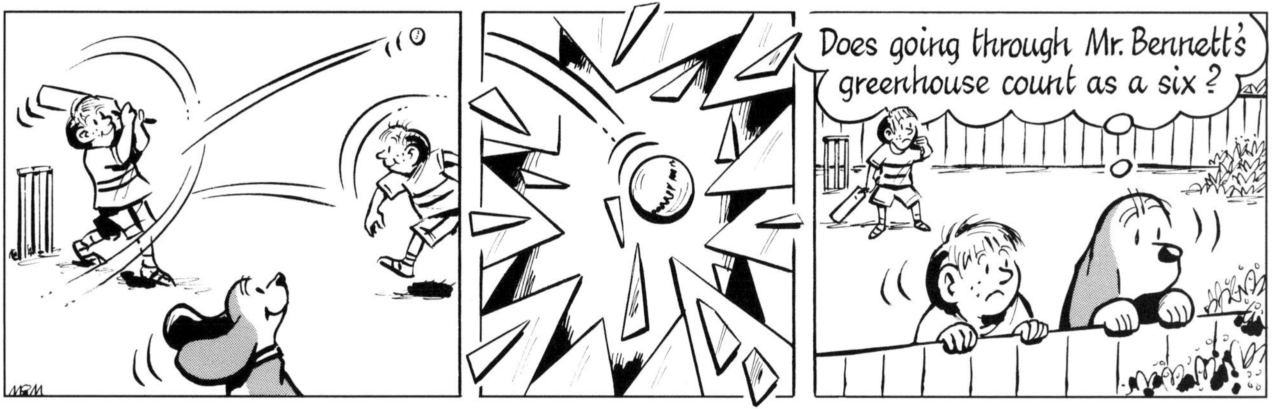
Does going through Mr. Bennett's greenhouse count as a six?

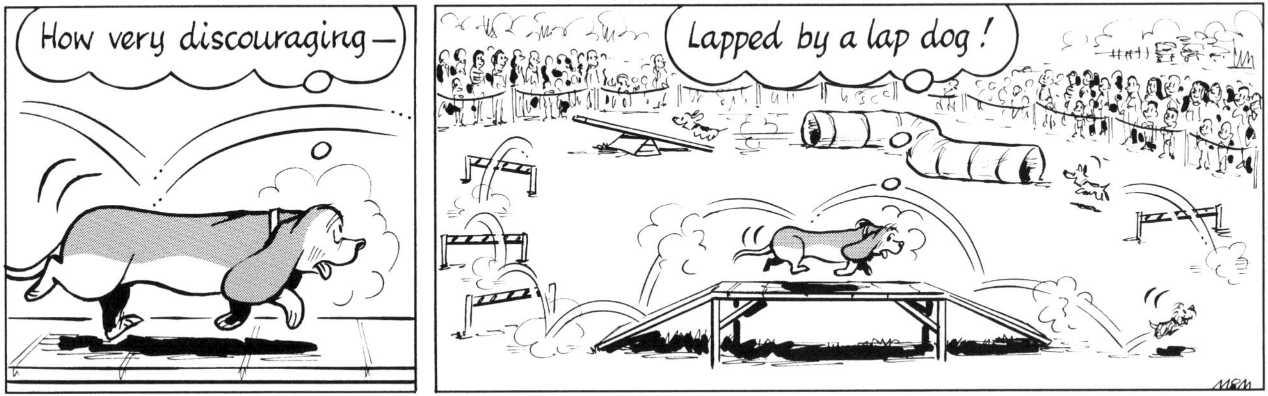
How very discouraging –
Lapped by a lap dog !

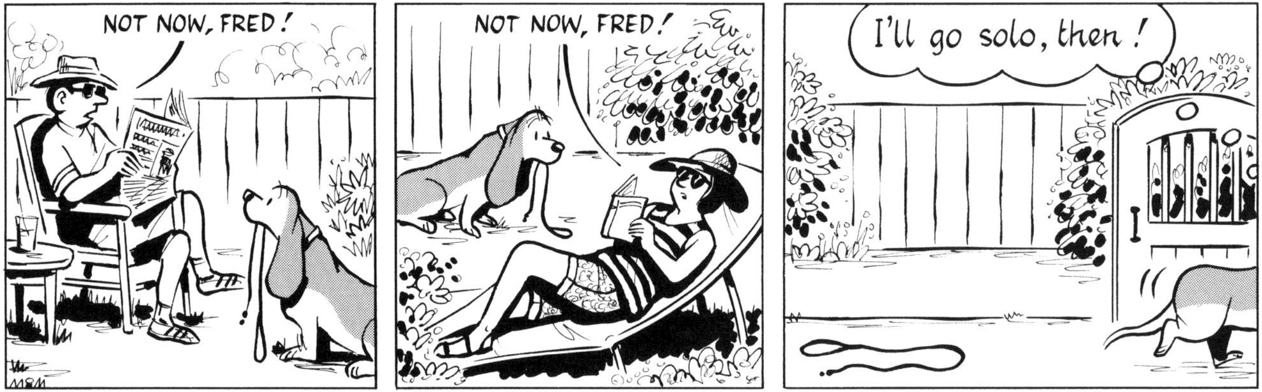
NOT NOW, FRED !
NOT NOW, FRED !
I'll go solo, then !

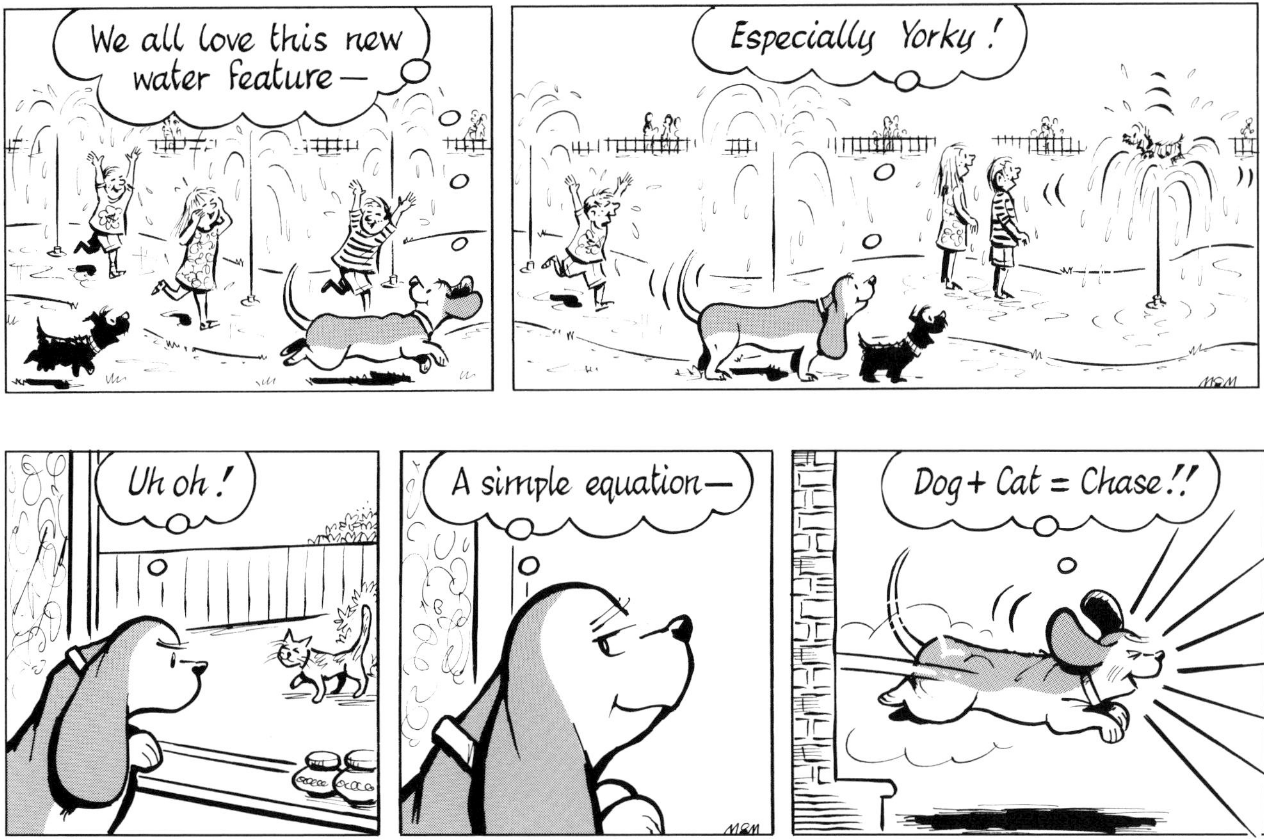
We all love this new water feature—
Especially Yorky!
Uh oh!
A simple equation—
Dog + Cat = Chase!!

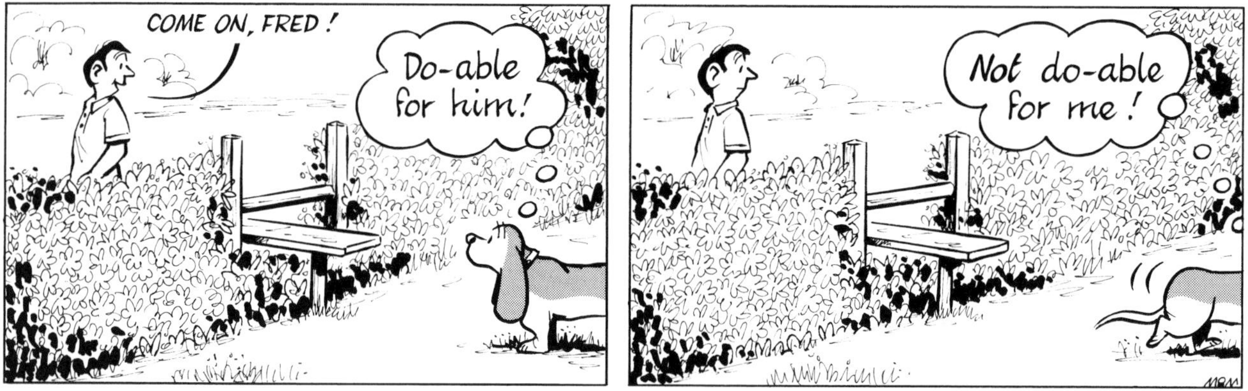
COME ON, FRED!
Do-able for him!
Not do-able for me!

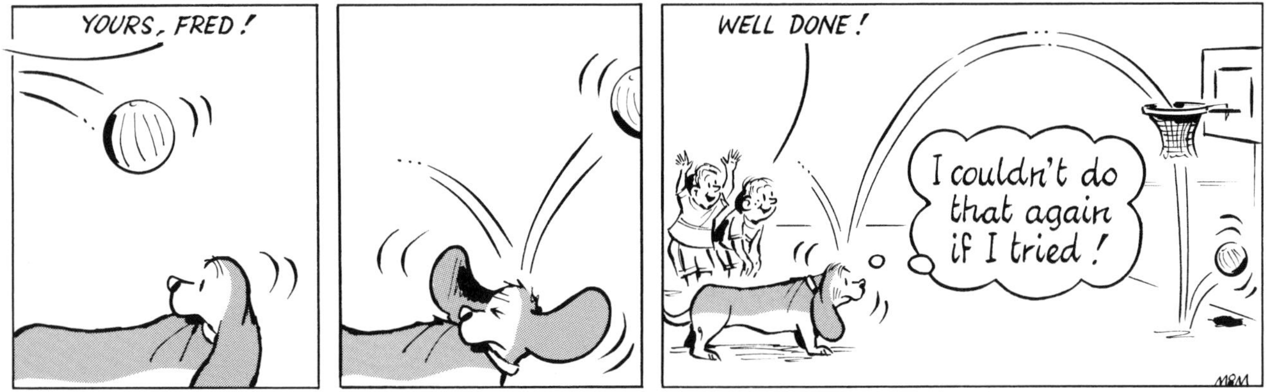
YOURS, FRED!
WELL DONE!
I couldn't do that again if I tried!

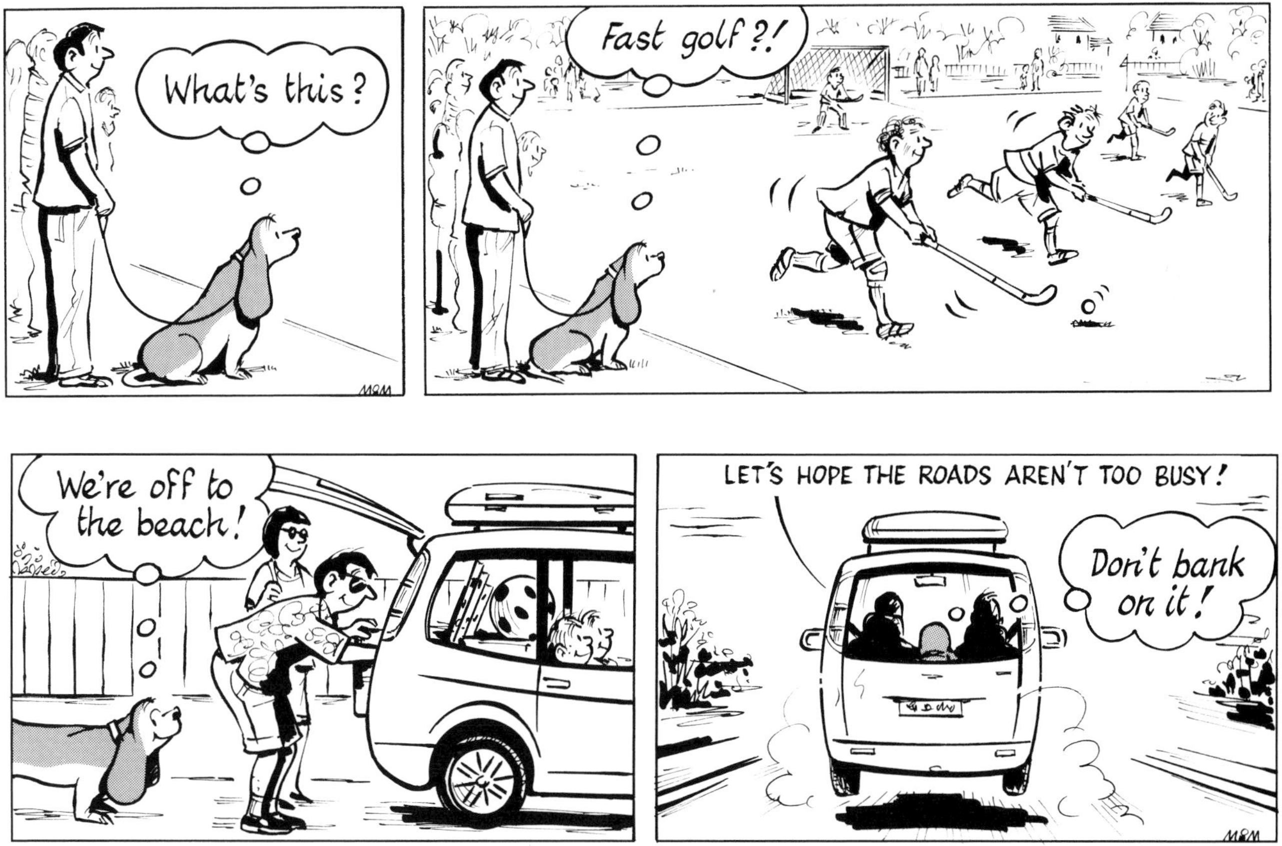
What's this?
Fast golf?!
We're off to the beach!
LET'S HOPE THE ROADS AREN'T TOO BUSY!
Don't bank on it!

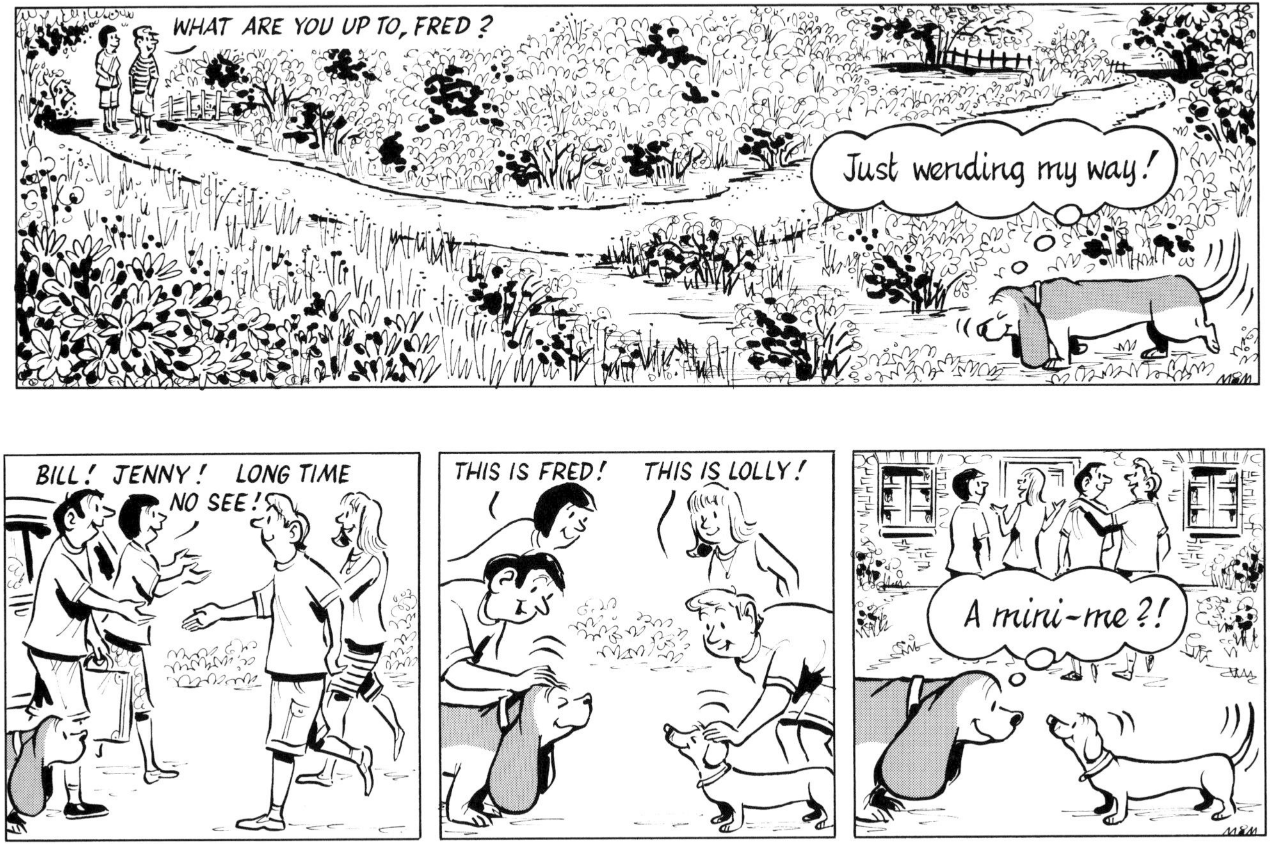
WHAT ARE YOU UP TO, FRED ?
Just wending my way!
BILL! JENNY! LONG TIME NO SEE!
THIS IS FRED!
THIS IS LOLLY!
A mini-me ?!

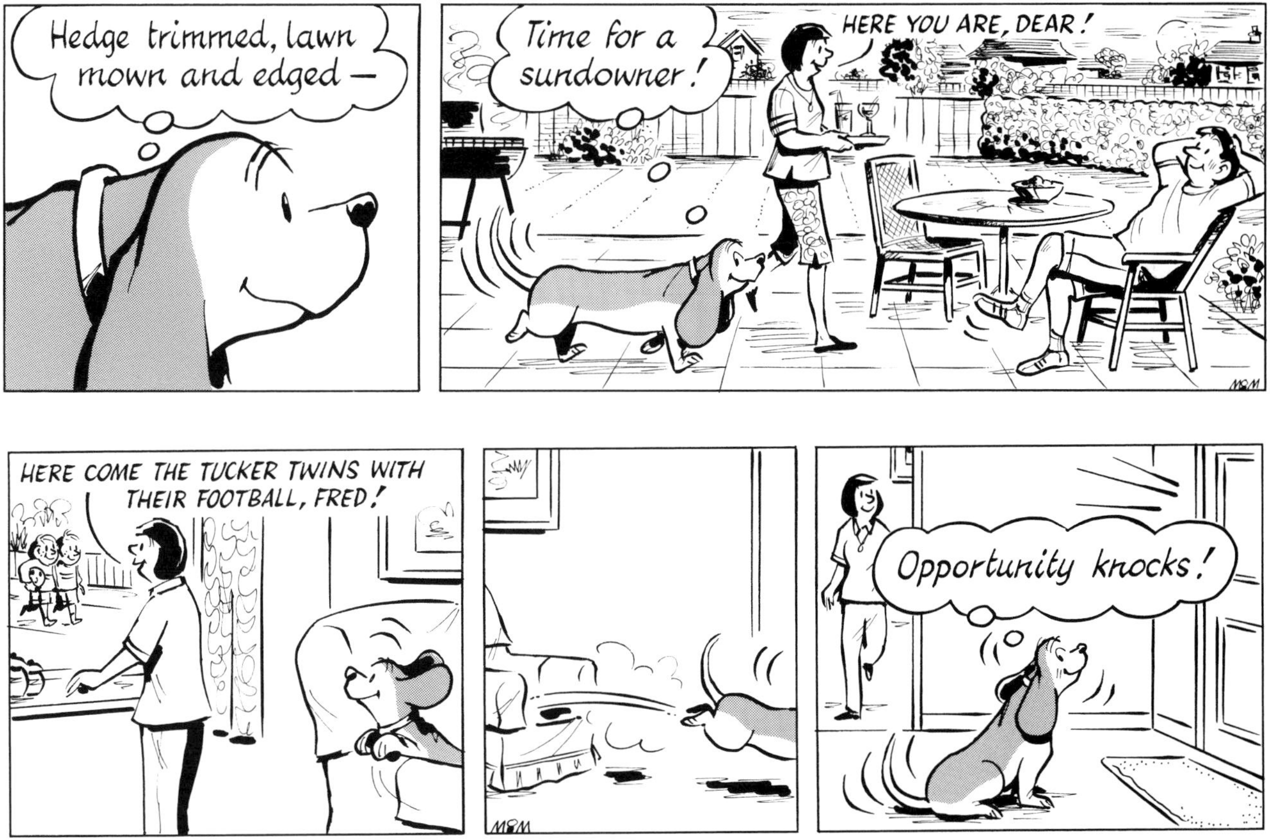
Hedge trimmed, lawn mown and edged –
Time for a sundowner!
HERE YOU ARE, DEAR!
M&M
HERE COME THE TUCKER TWINS WITH THEIR FOOTBALL, FRED!
M&M
Opportunity knocks!

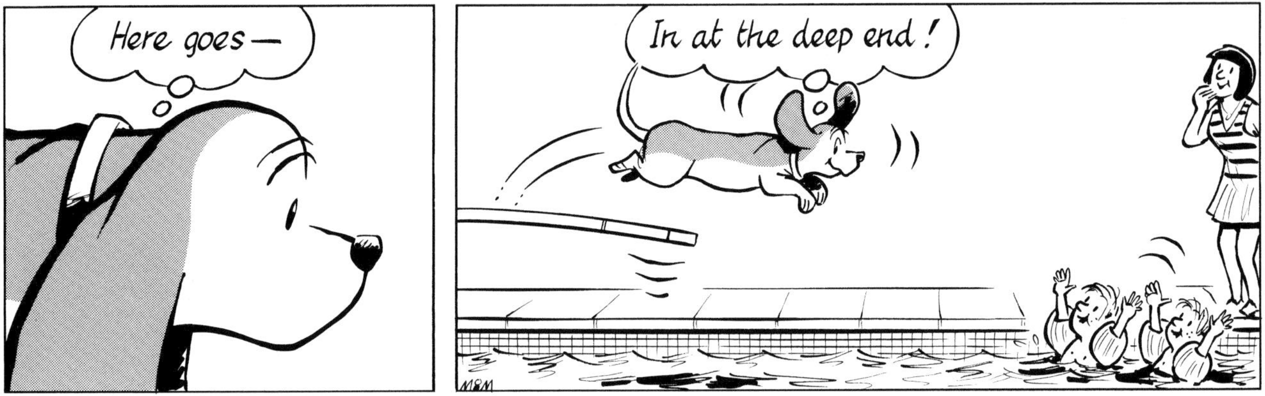
Here goes —
In at the deep end!

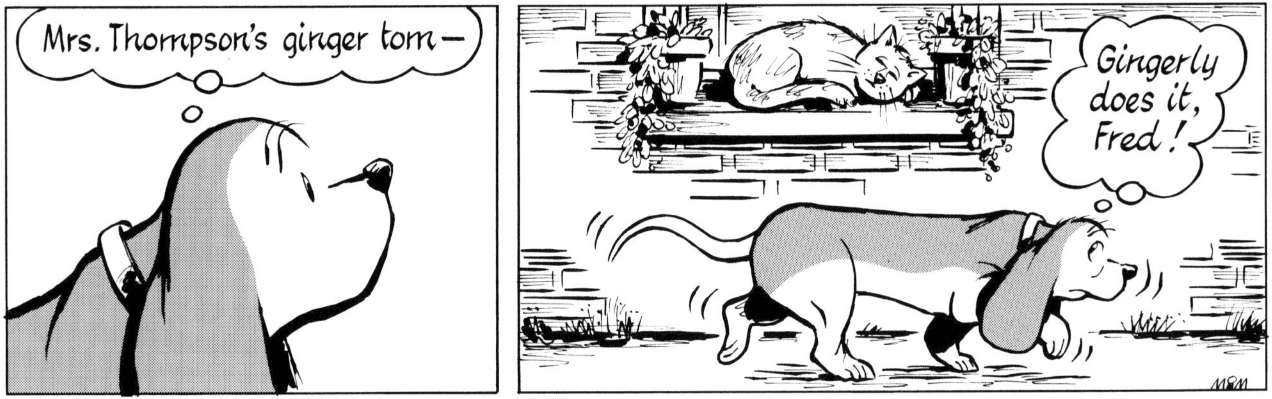
Mrs. Thompson's ginger tom —
Gingerly does it, Fred!

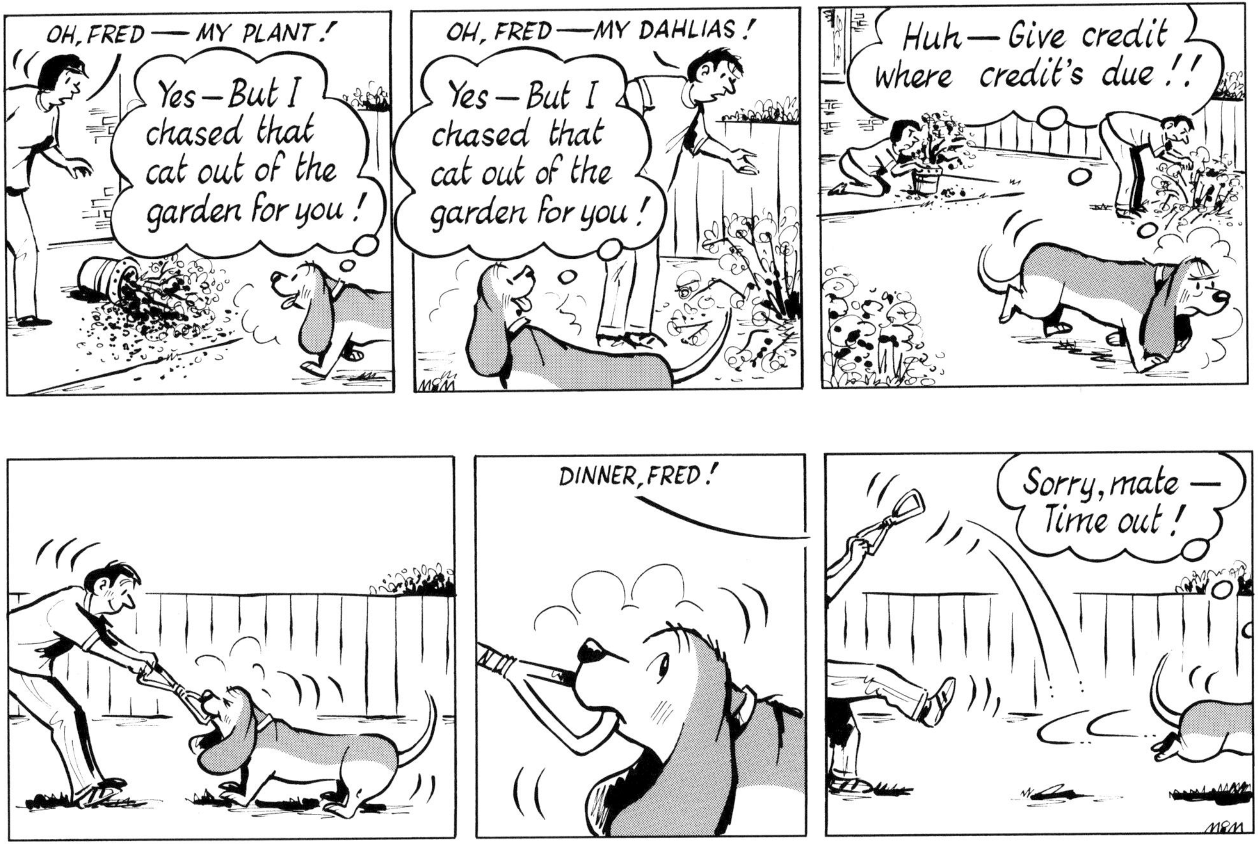
OH, FRED — MY PLANT!
Yes — But I chased that cat out of the garden for you!
OH, FRED — MY DAHLIAS!
Yes — But I chased that cat out of the garden for you!
Huh — Give credit where credit's due!!
DINNER, FRED!
Sorry, mate — Time out!

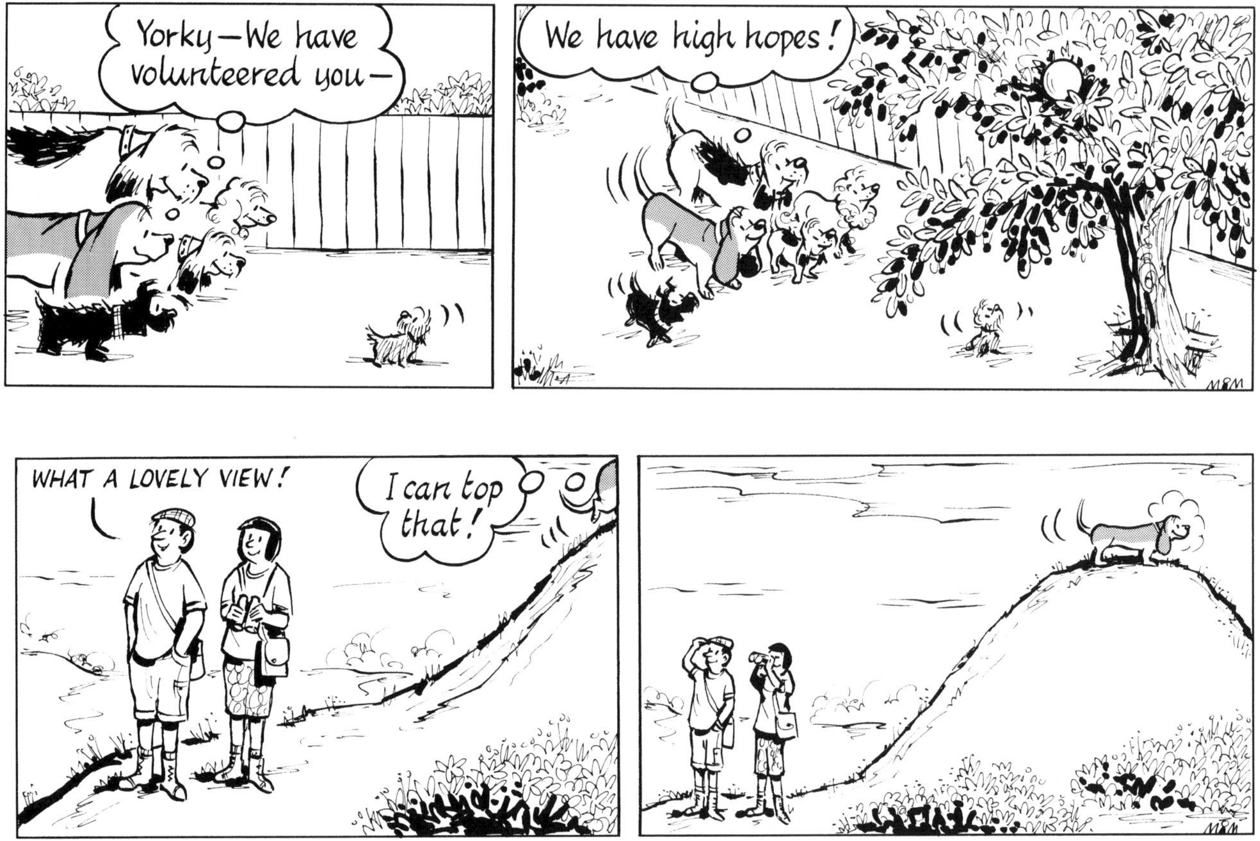
Yorky—We have volunteered you—
We have high hopes!
WHAT A LOVELY VIEW!
I can top that!

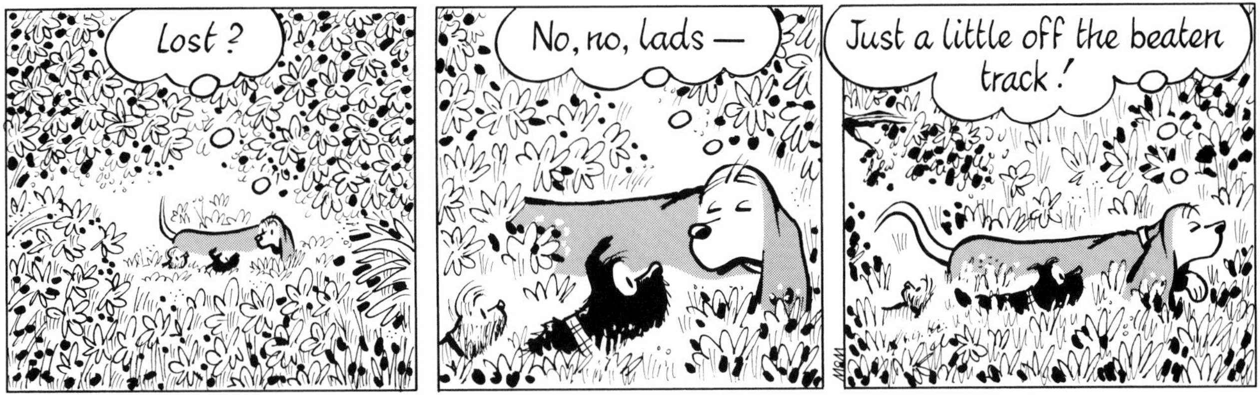
Lost?
No, no, lads —
Just a little off the beaten track!

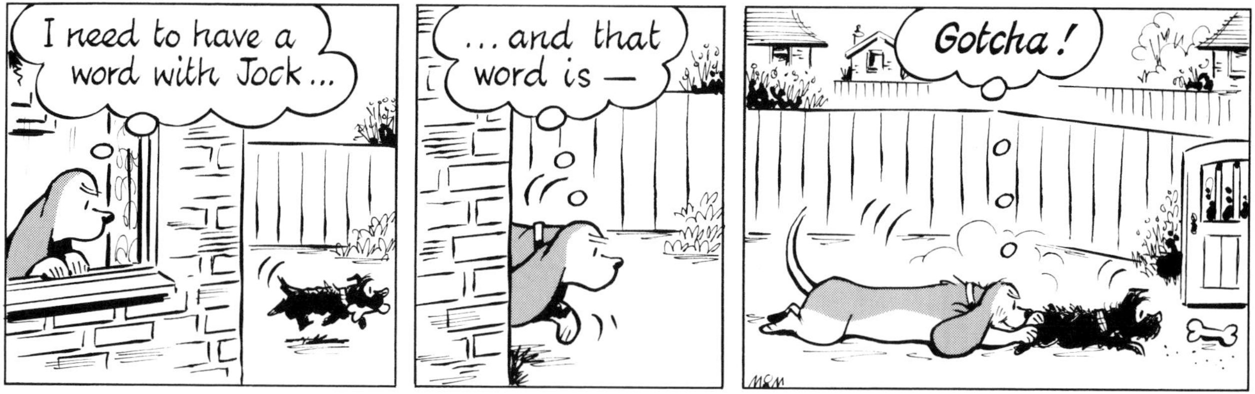
I need to have a word with Jock...
... and that word is —
Gotcha!

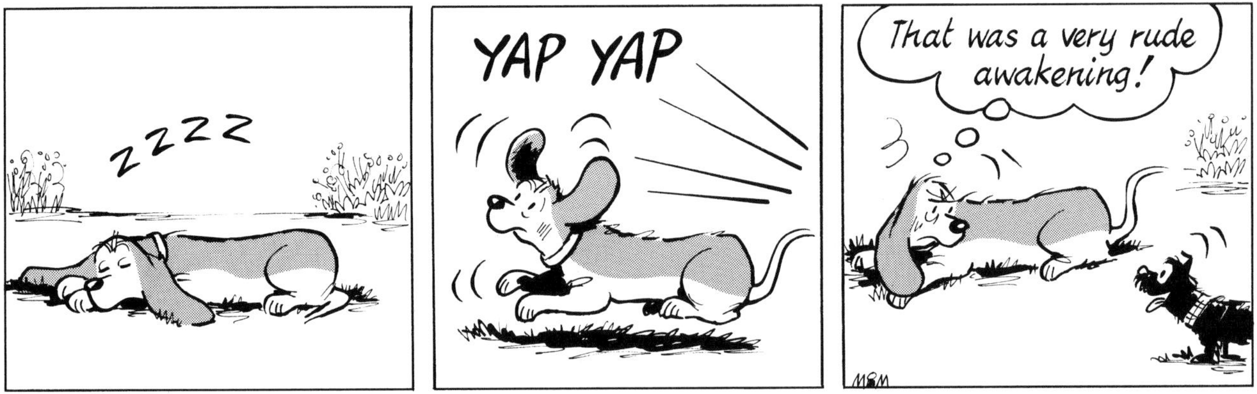
ZZZZ
YAP YAP
That was a very rude awakening!
MBM

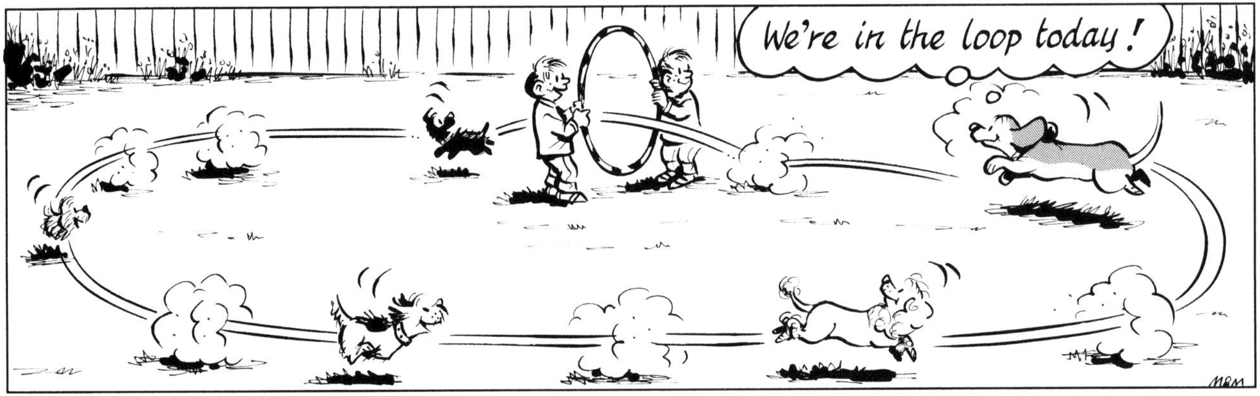
We're in the loop today!
MBM

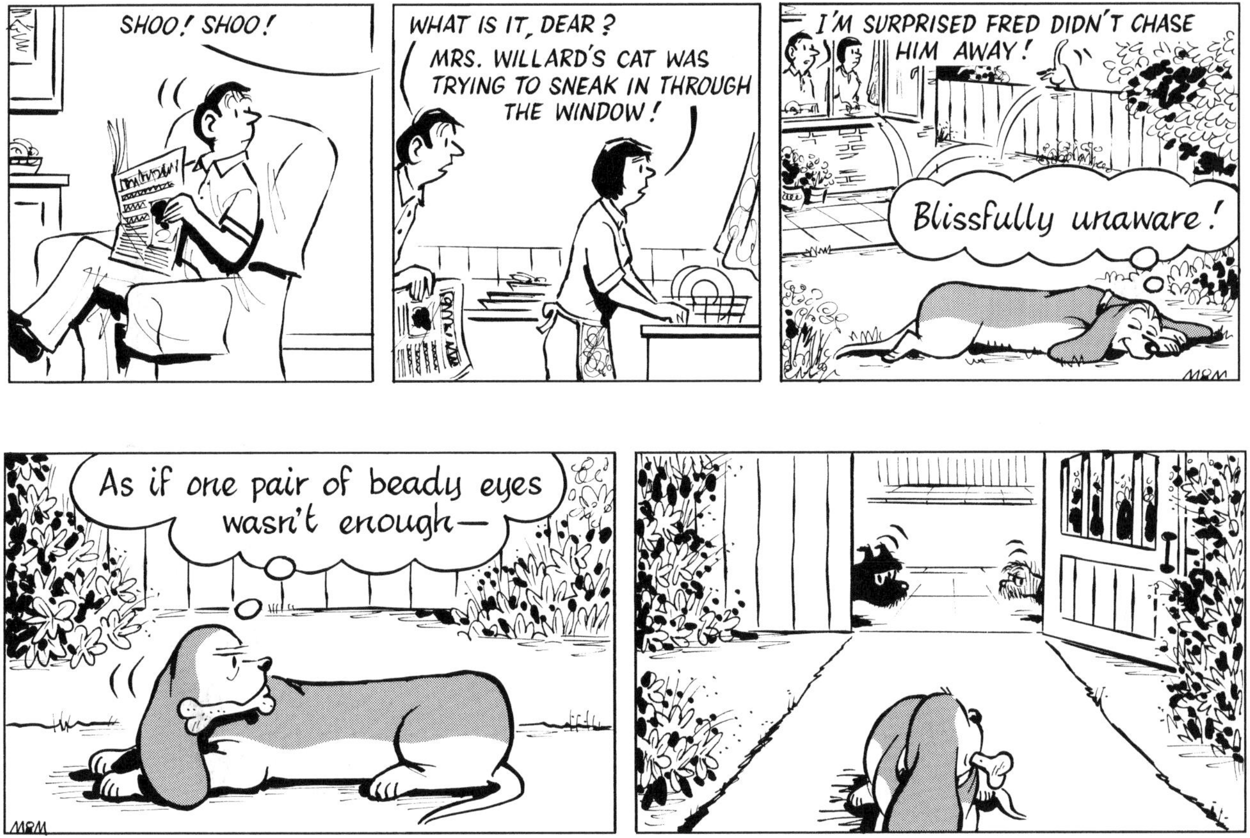
SHOO! SHOO!
WHAT IS IT, DEAR?
MRS. WILLARD'S CAT WAS TRYING TO SNEAK IN THROUGH THE WINDOW!
I'M SURPRISED FRED DIDN'T CHASE HIM AWAY!
Blissfully unaware!
MRM
As if one pair of beady eyes wasn't enough—
MRM

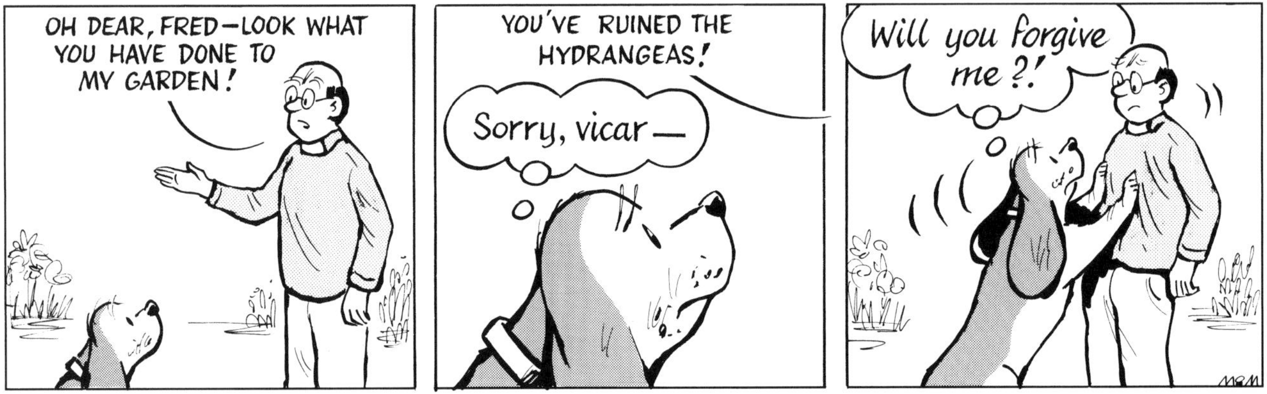

OH DEAR, FRED—LOOK WHAT YOU HAVE DONE TO MY GARDEN!
Sorry, vicar—
YOU'VE RUINED THE HYDRANGEAS!
Will you forgive me?!

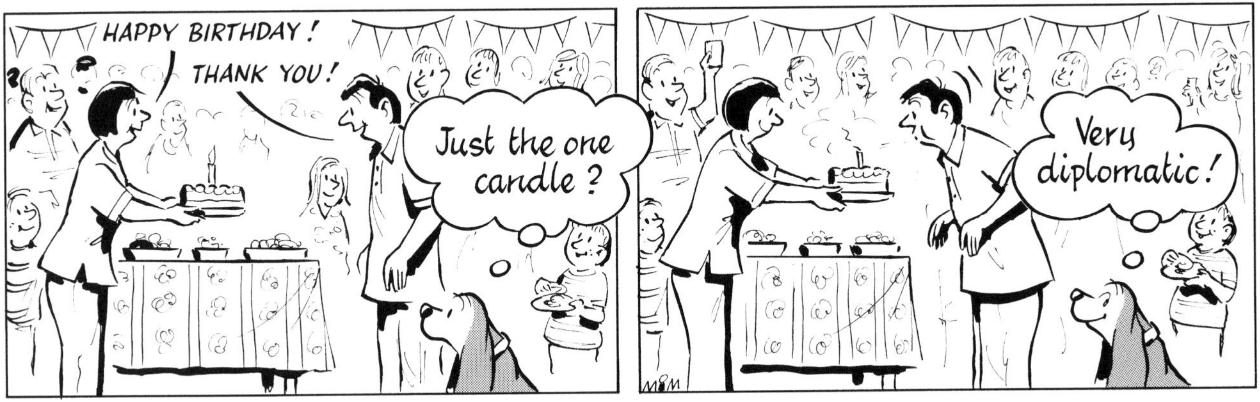

HAPPY BIRTHDAY!
THANK YOU!
Just the one candle?
Very diplomatic!

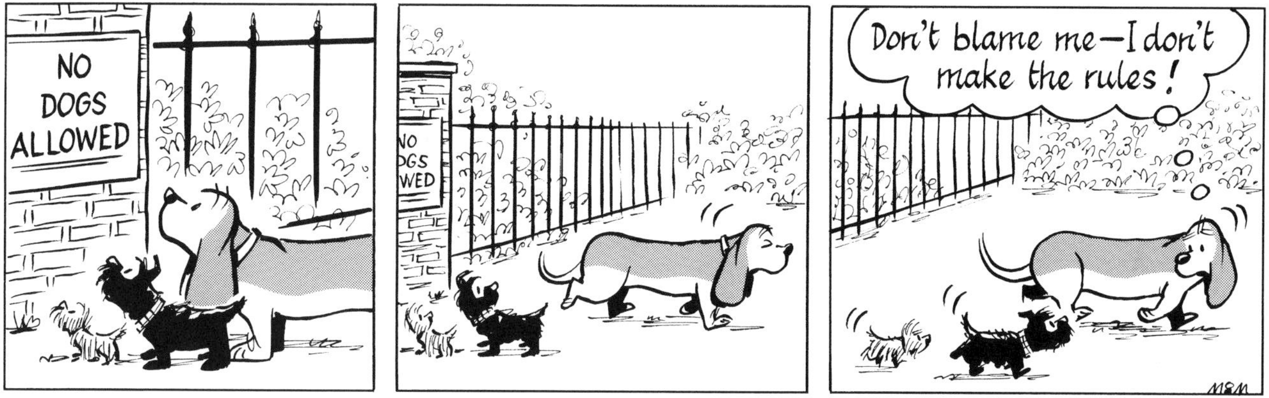
NO DOGS ALLOWED
Don't blame me—I don't make the rules!

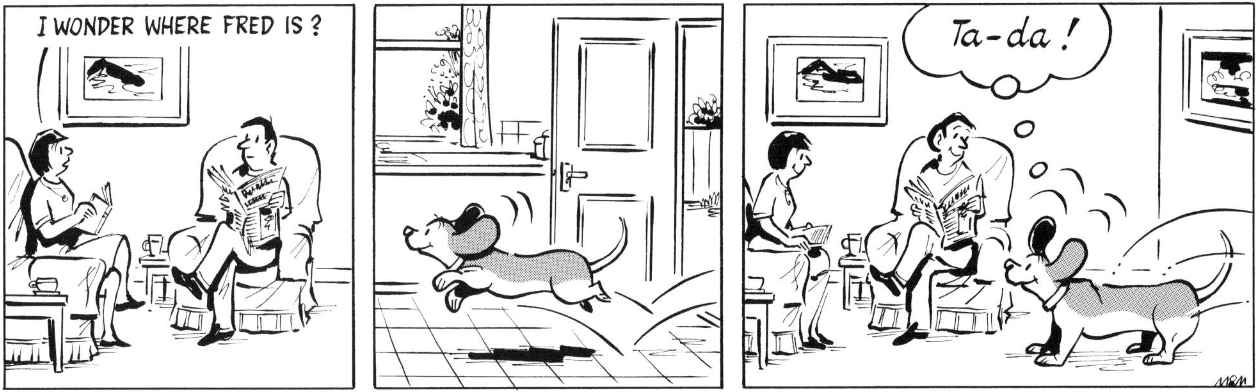
I WONDER WHERE FRED IS ?
Ta-da !

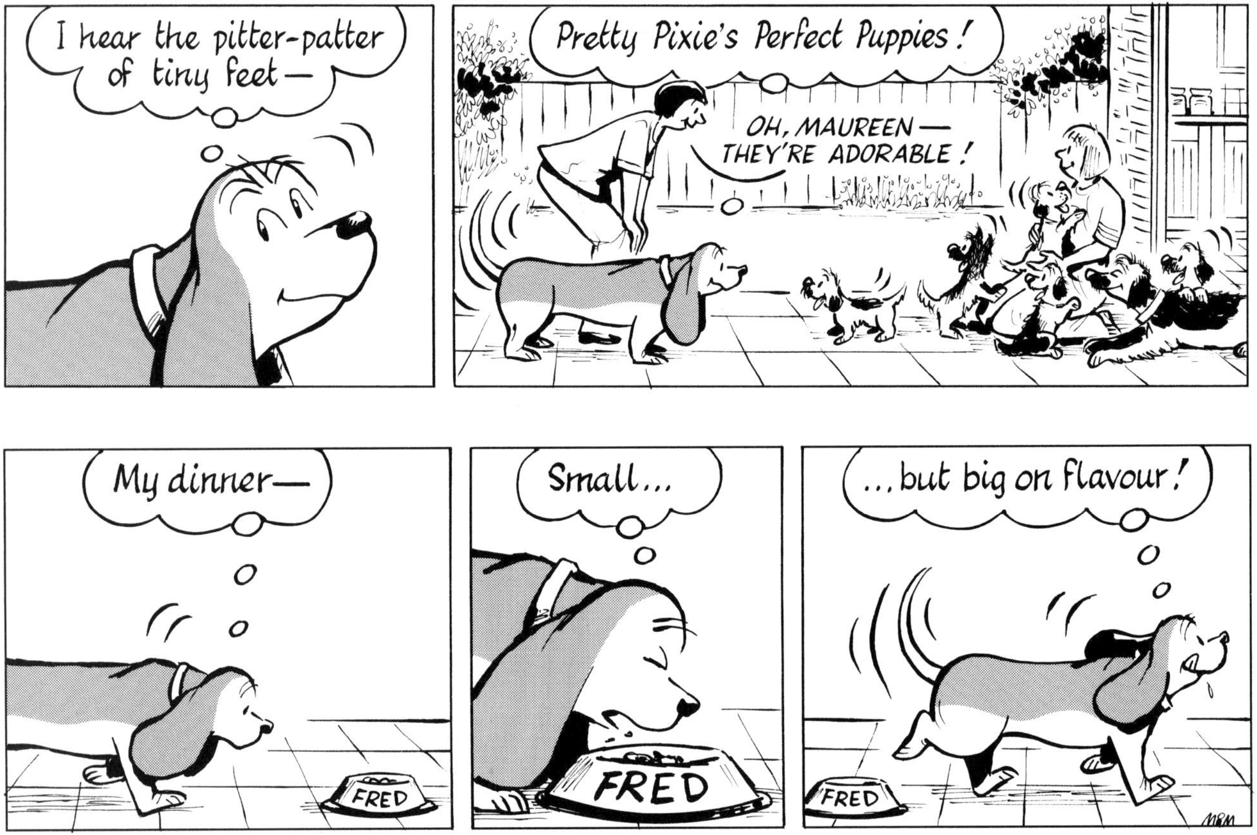
I hear the pitter-patter of tiny feet—
Pretty Pixie's Perfect Puppies!
OH, MAUREEN— THEY'RE ADORABLE!
My dinner—
Small...
FRED
...but big on flavour!
FRED
FRED
MBM

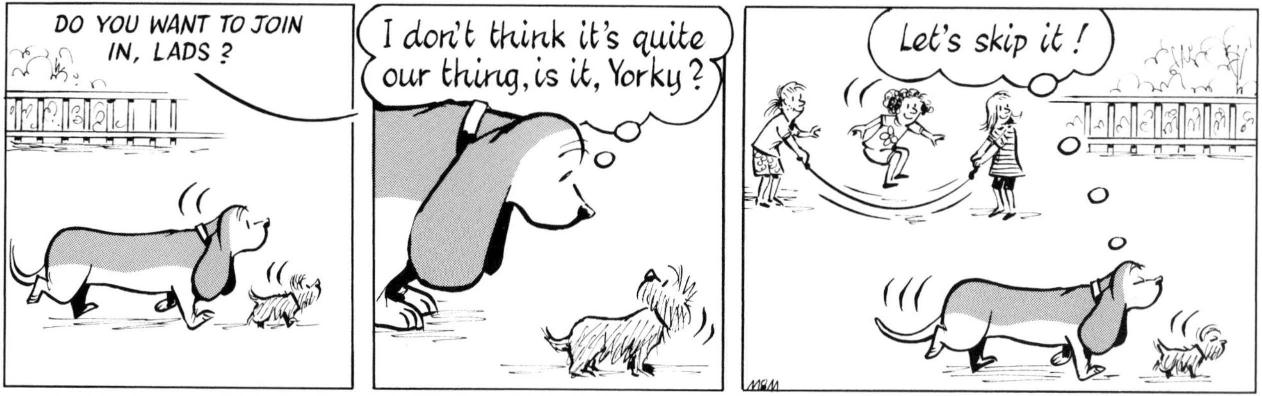
DO YOU WANT TO JOIN IN, LADS ?
I don't think it's quite our thing, is it, Yorky ?
Let's skip it !

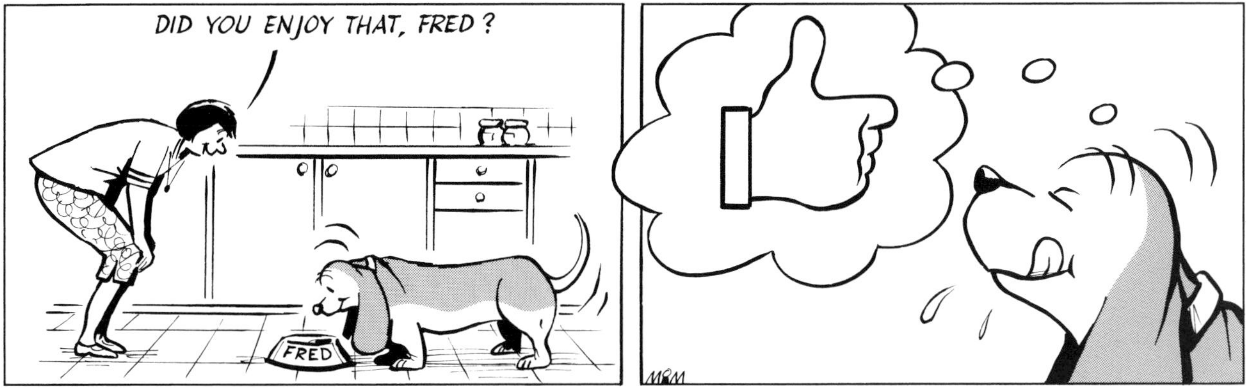
DID YOU ENJOY THAT, FRED ?
FRED

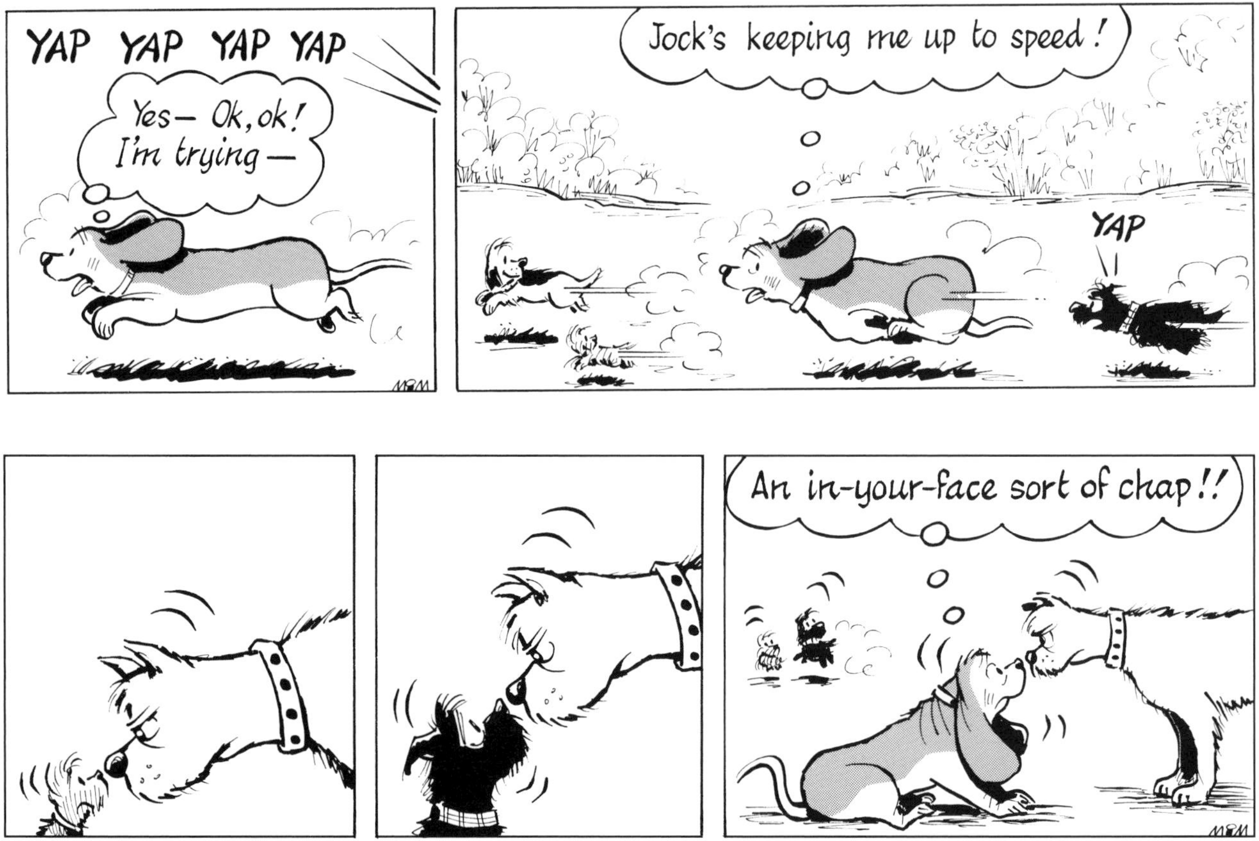
YAP YAP YAP YAP
Yes— Ok, ok! I'm trying —
Jock's keeping me up to speed!
YAP
An in-your-face sort of chap!!

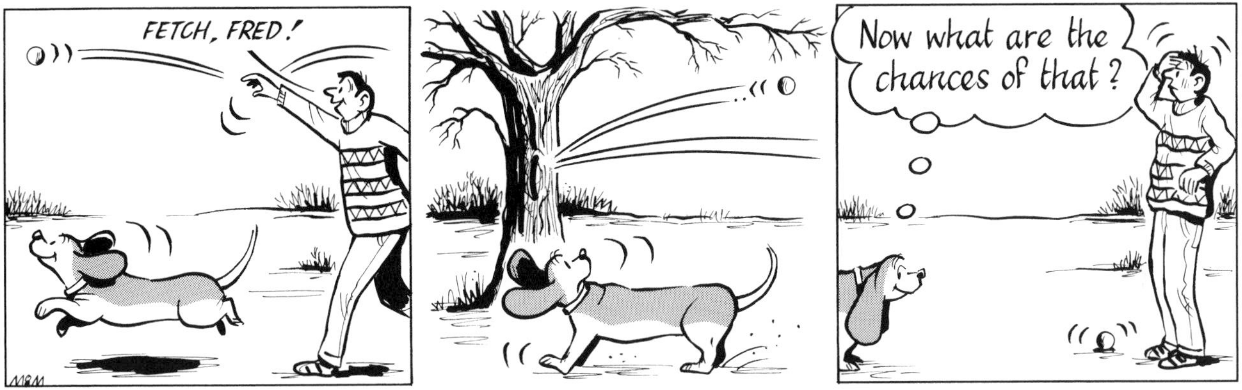
FETCH, FRED!
Now what are the chances of that?
MGM

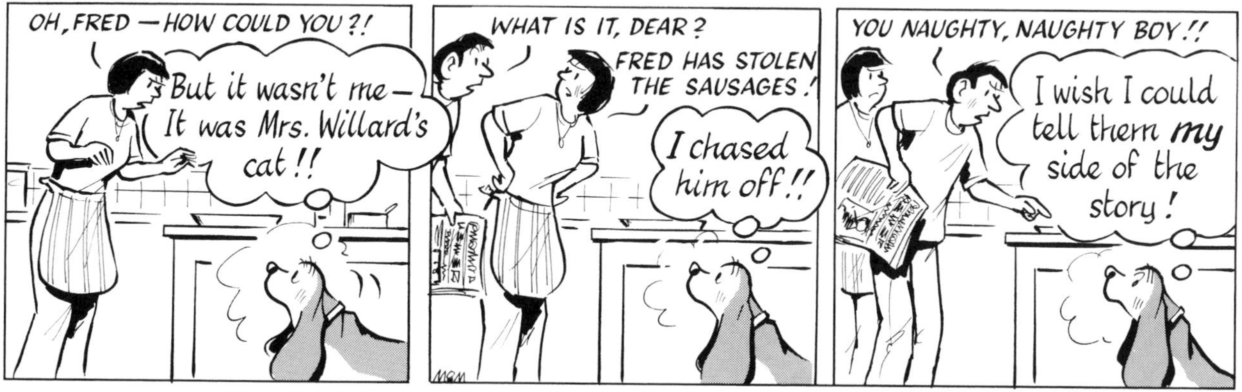
OH, FRED — HOW COULD YOU?!
But it wasn't me — It was Mrs. Willard's cat!!
WHAT IS IT, DEAR?
FRED HAS STOLEN THE SAUSAGES!
I chased him off!!
MGM
YOU NAUGHTY, NAUGHTY BOY!!
I wish I could tell them *my* side of the story!

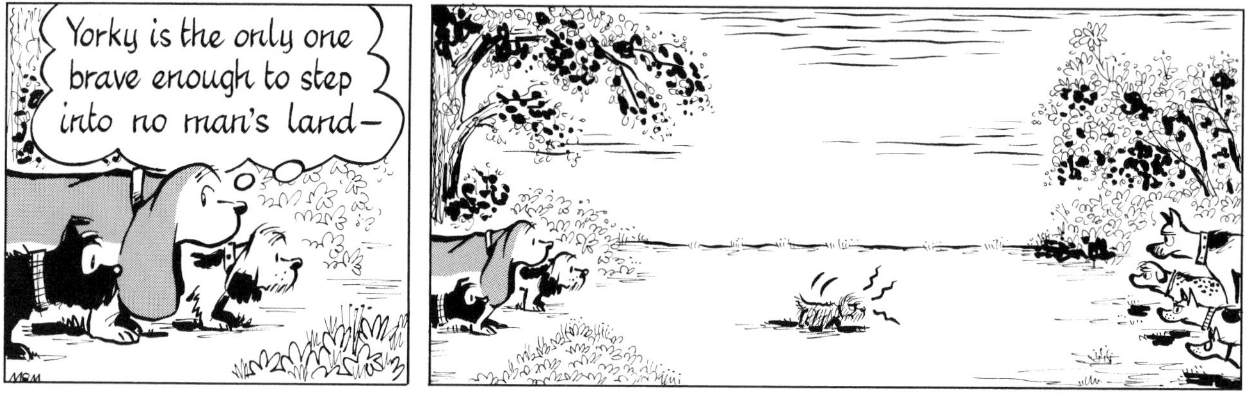
Yorky is the only one brave enough to step into no man's land–

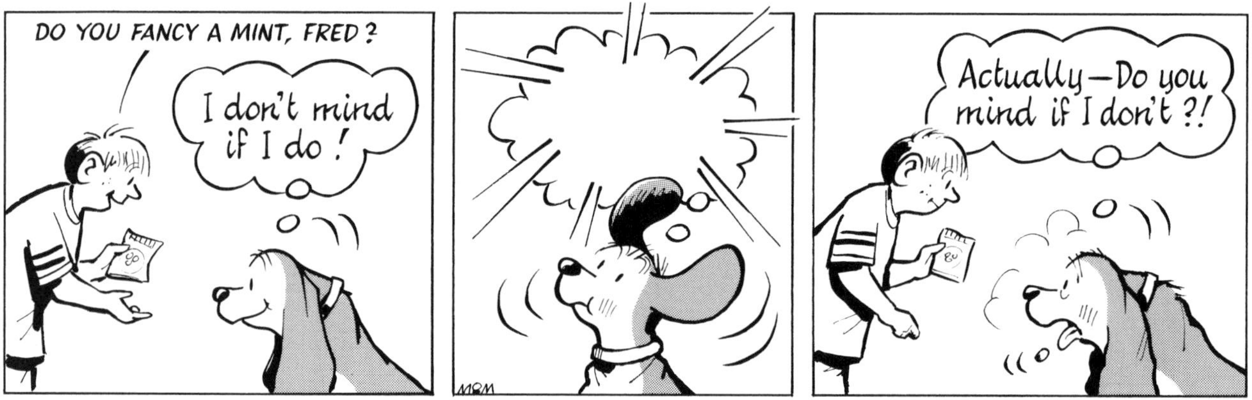
DO YOU FANCY A MINT, FRED?
I don't mind if I do!
Actually–Do you mind if I don't?!

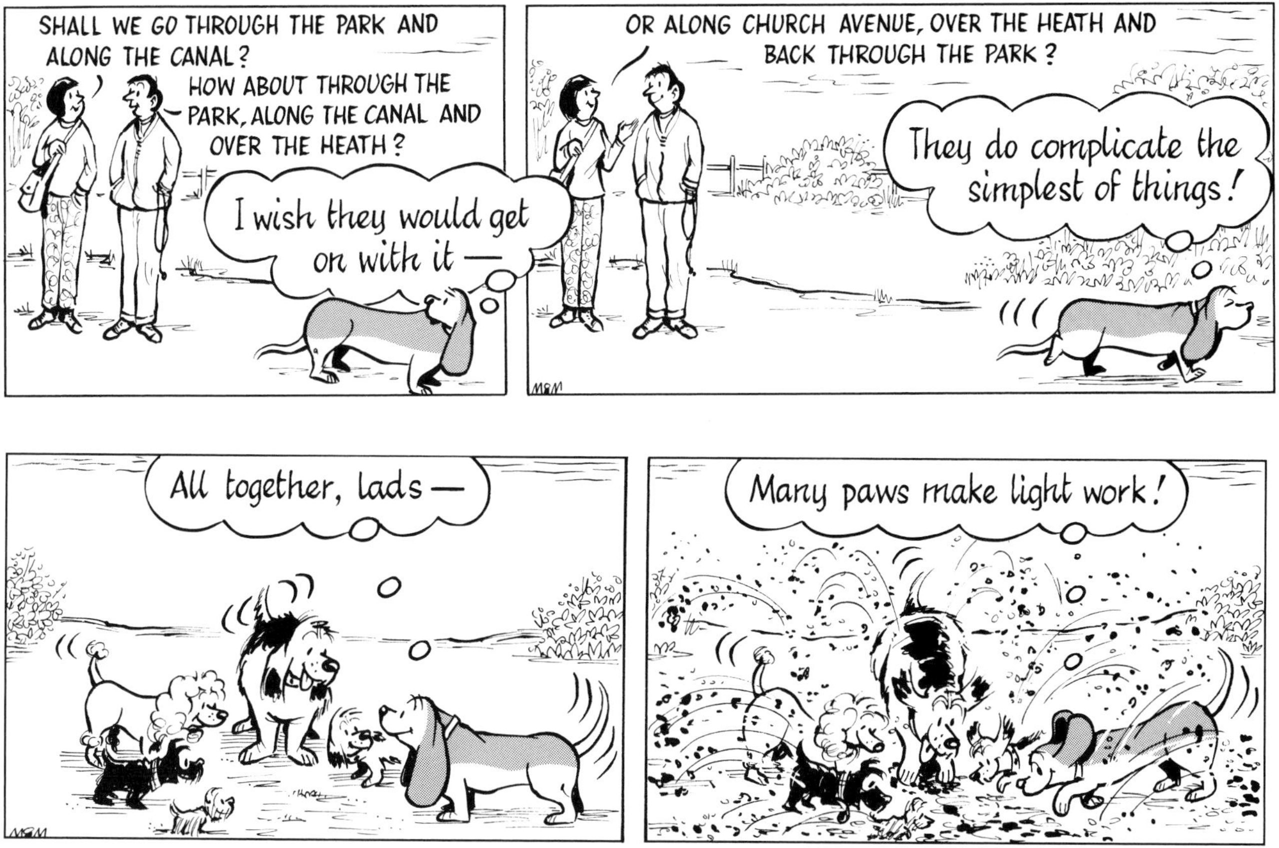
SHALL WE GO THROUGH THE PARK AND ALONG THE CANAL?
HOW ABOUT THROUGH THE PARK, ALONG THE CANAL AND OVER THE HEATH?
I wish they would get on with it —
OR ALONG CHURCH AVENUE, OVER THE HEATH AND BACK THROUGH THE PARK?
They do complicate the simplest of things!
MSM
All together, lads —
MSM
Many paws make light work!

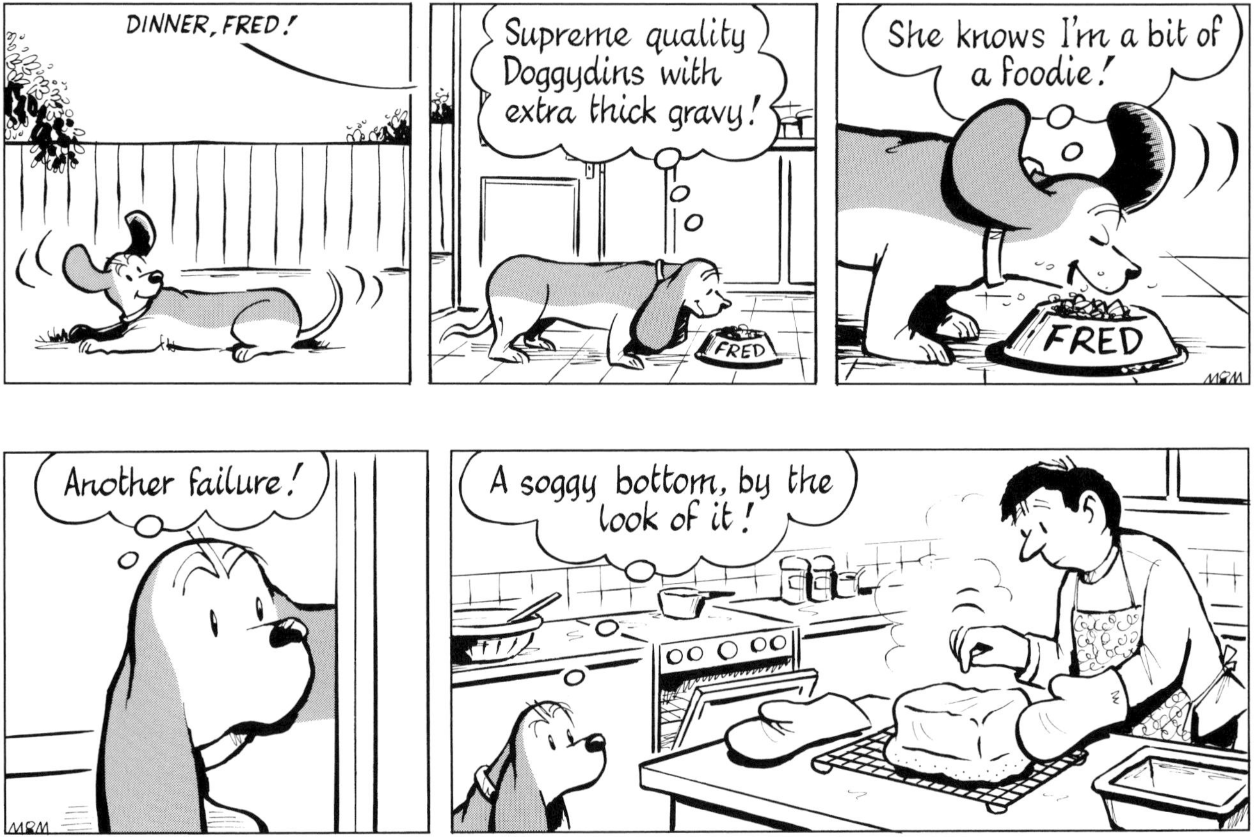
DINNER, FRED!
Supreme quality Doggydins with extra thick gravy!
FRED
She knows I'm a bit of a foodie!
FRED
Another failure!
A soggy bottom, by the look of it!

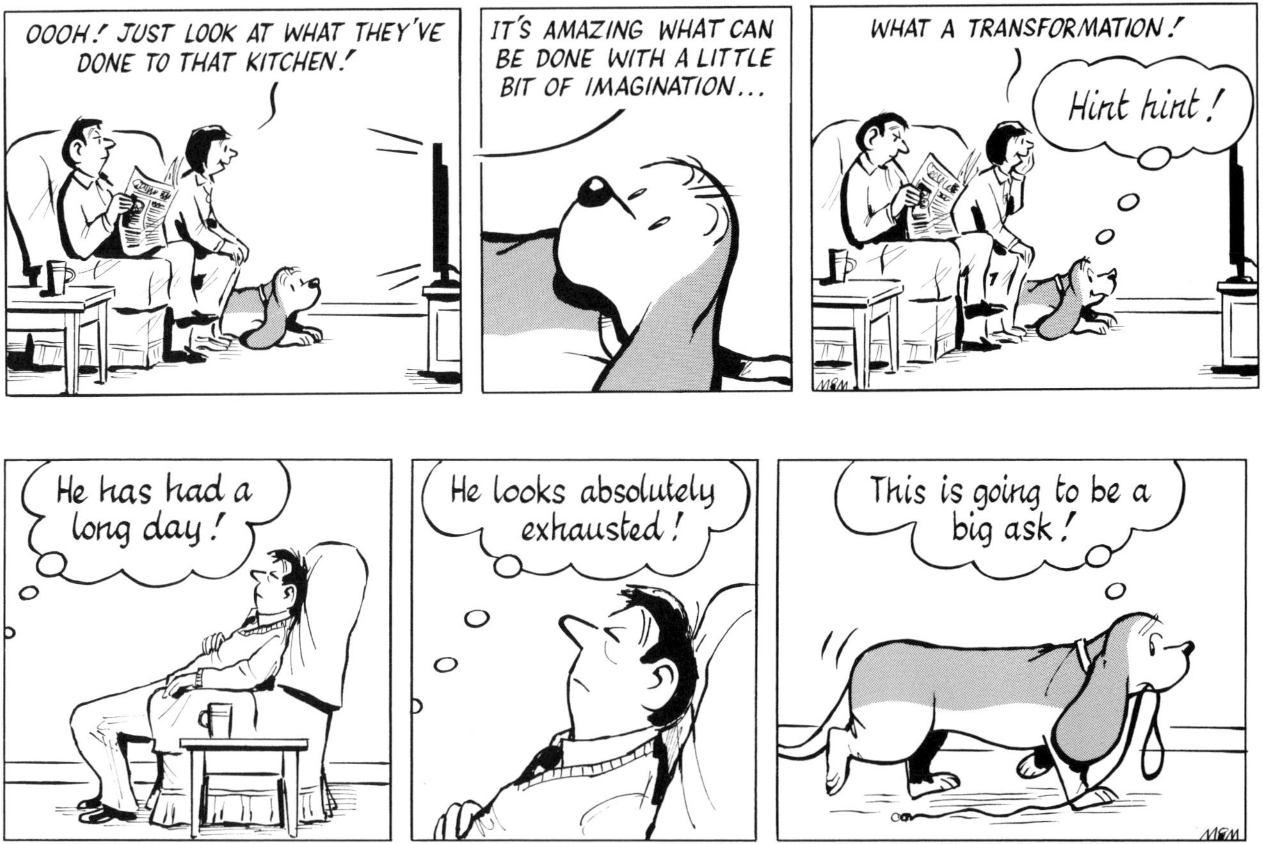
OOOH! JUST LOOK AT WHAT THEY'VE DONE TO THAT KITCHEN!
IT'S AMAZING WHAT CAN BE DONE WITH A LITTLE BIT OF IMAGINATION...
WHAT A TRANSFORMATION!
Hint hint!
He has had a long day!
He looks absolutely exhausted!
This is going to be a big ask!
MGM
MGM

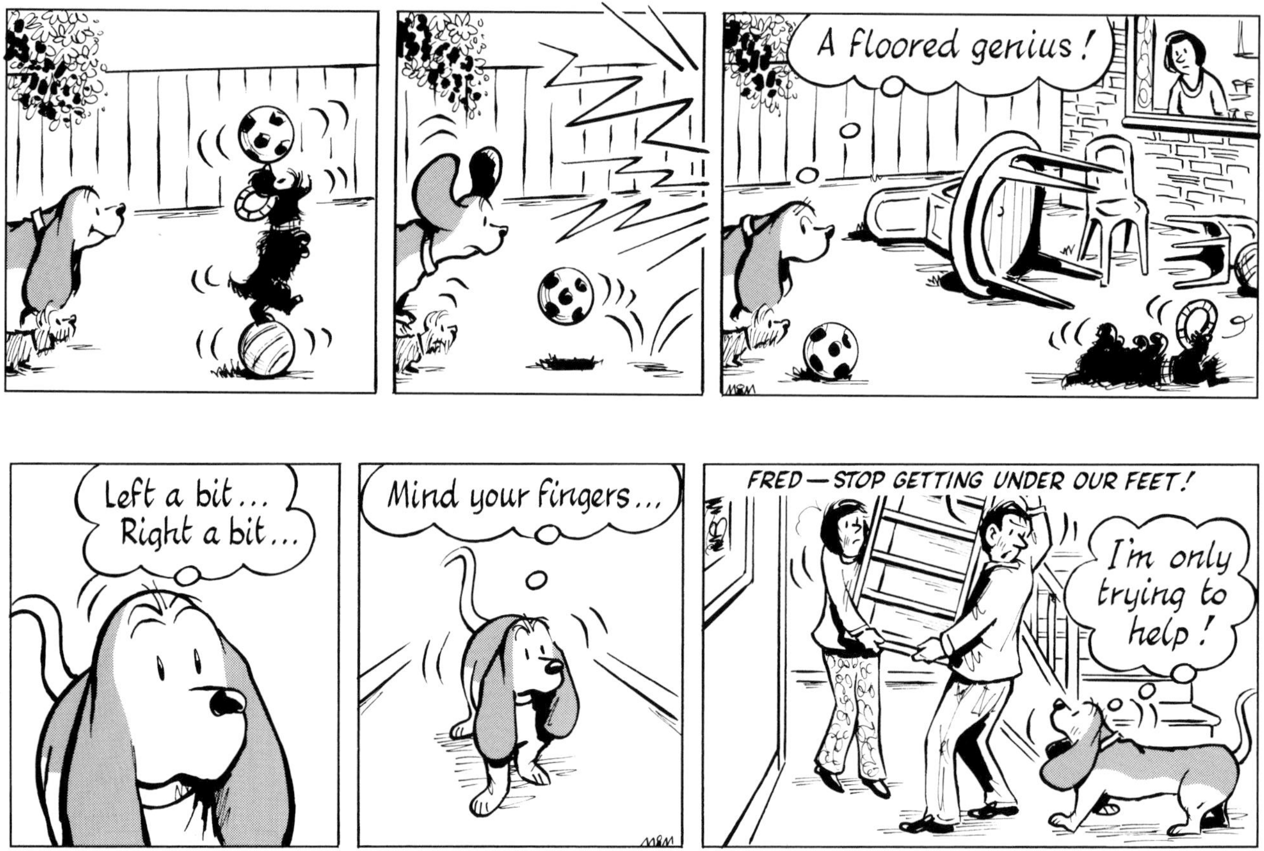
A floored genius!
Left a bit... Right a bit...
Mind your fingers...
FRED—STOP GETTING UNDER OUR FEET!
I'm only trying to help!

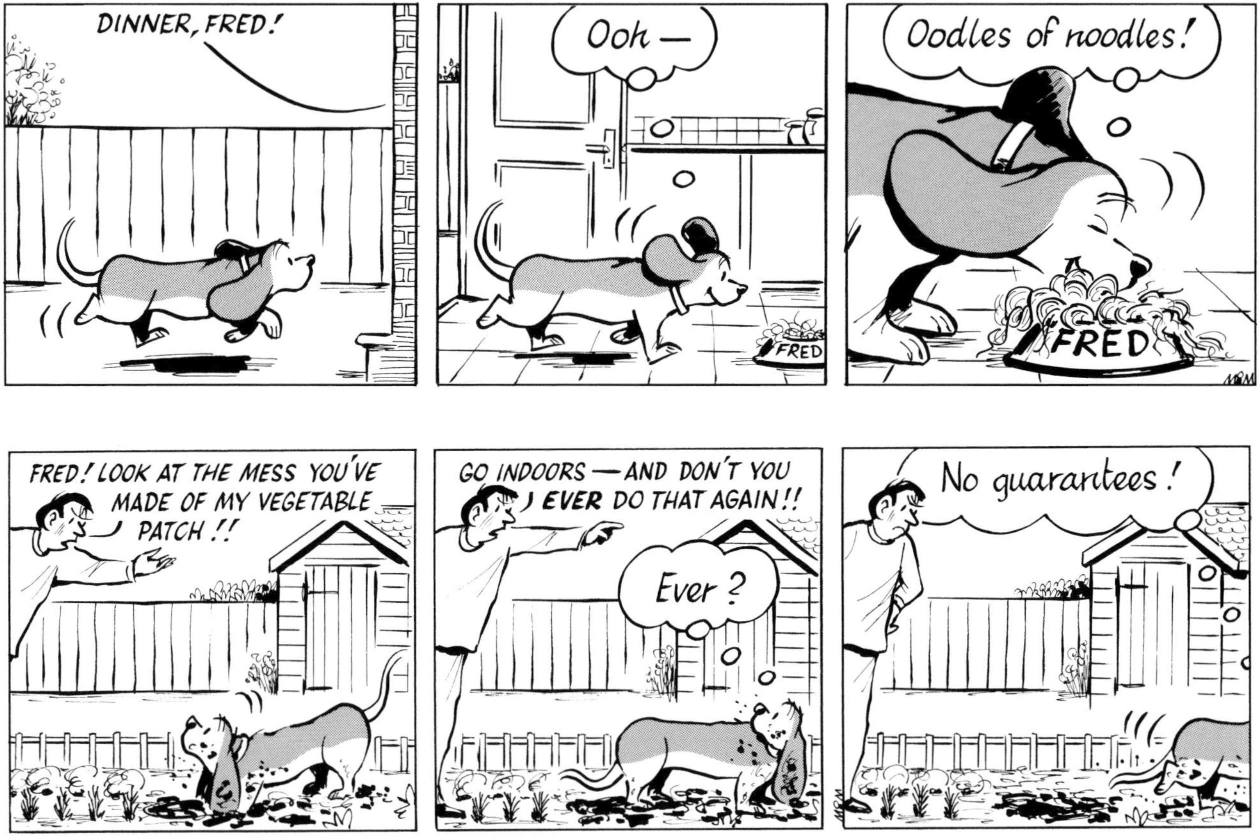
DINNER, FRED!
Ooh —
FRED
Oodles of noodles!
FRED
FRED! LOOK AT THE MESS YOU'VE MADE OF MY VEGETABLE PATCH!!
GO INDOORS — AND DON'T YOU EVER DO THAT AGAIN!!
Ever?
No guarantees!

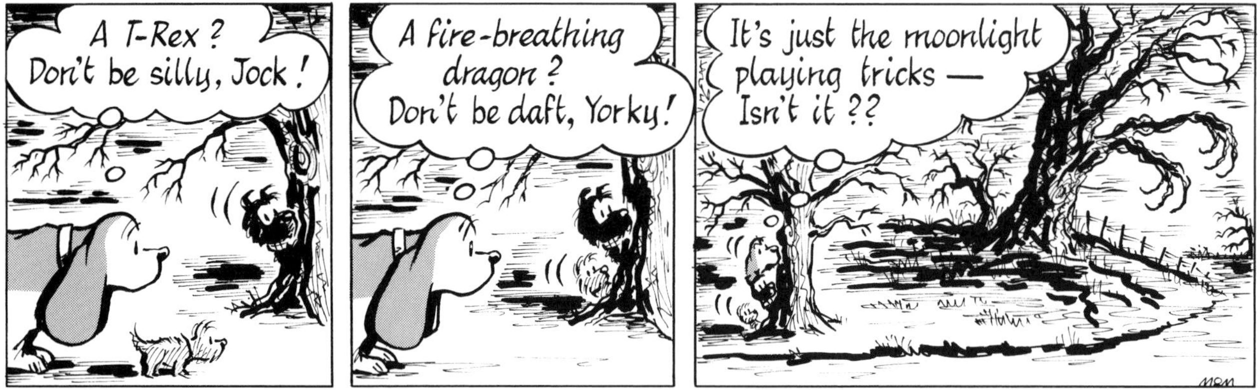
A T-Rex? Don't be silly, Jock!
A fire-breathing dragon? Don't be daft, Yorky!
It's just the moonlight playing tricks — Isn't it??
MGM

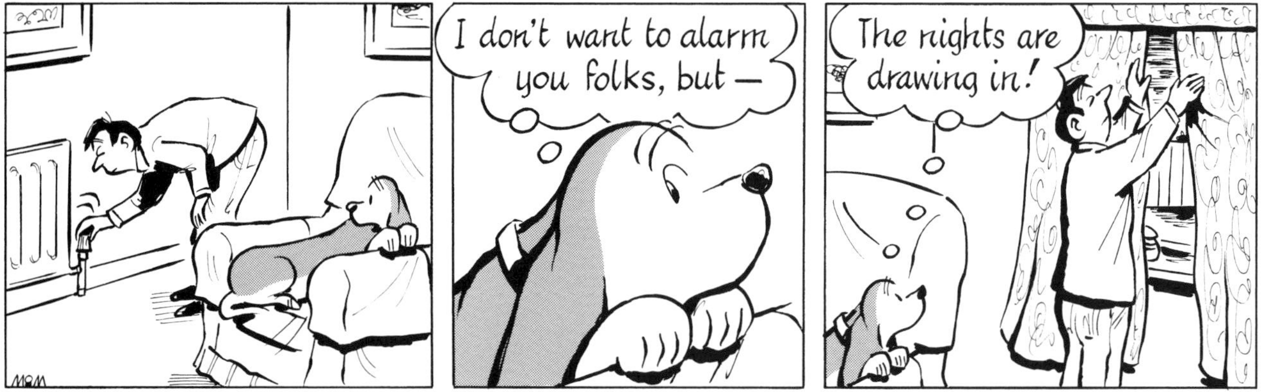
MGM
I don't want to alarm you folks, but —
The nights are drawing in!

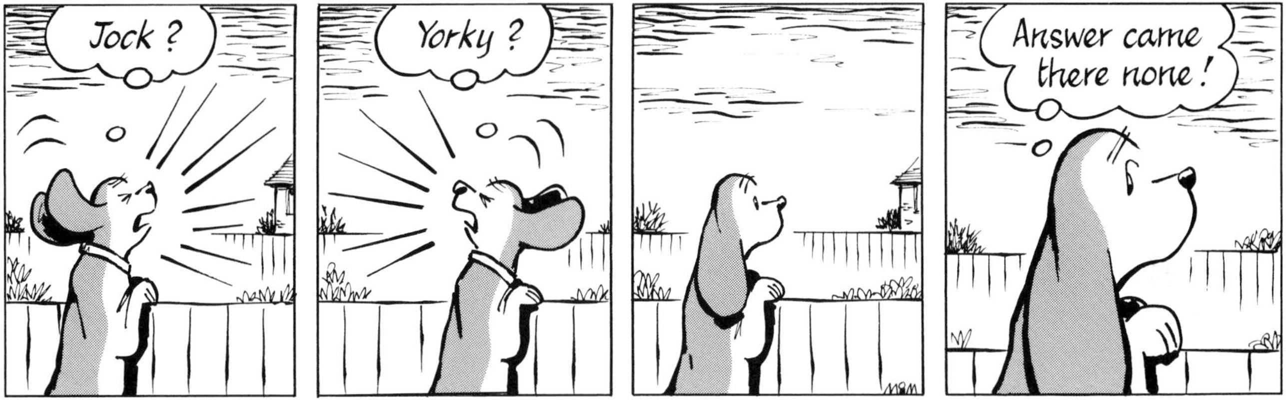
Jock ?
Yorky ?
Answer came there none !

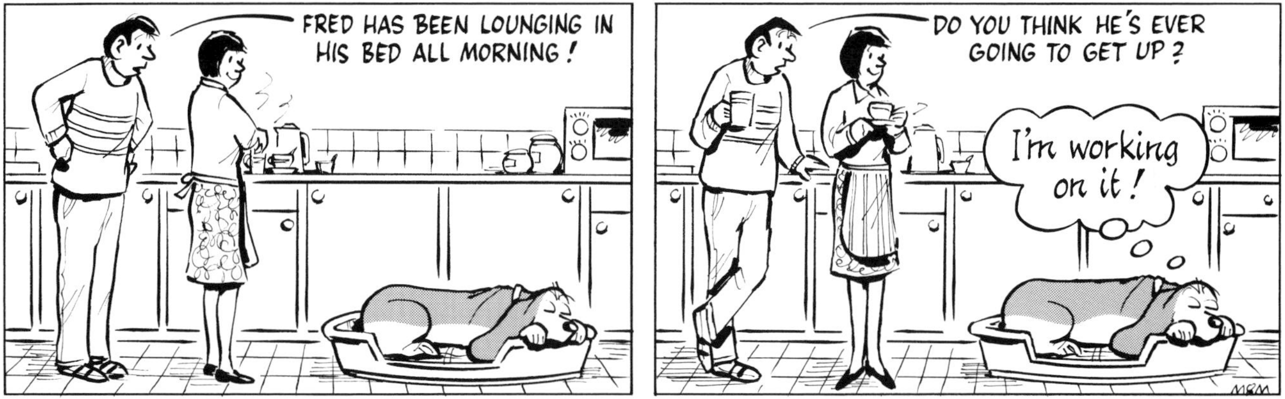
FRED HAS BEEN LOUNGING IN HIS BED ALL MORNING !
DO YOU THINK HE'S EVER GOING TO GET UP ?
I'm working on it !

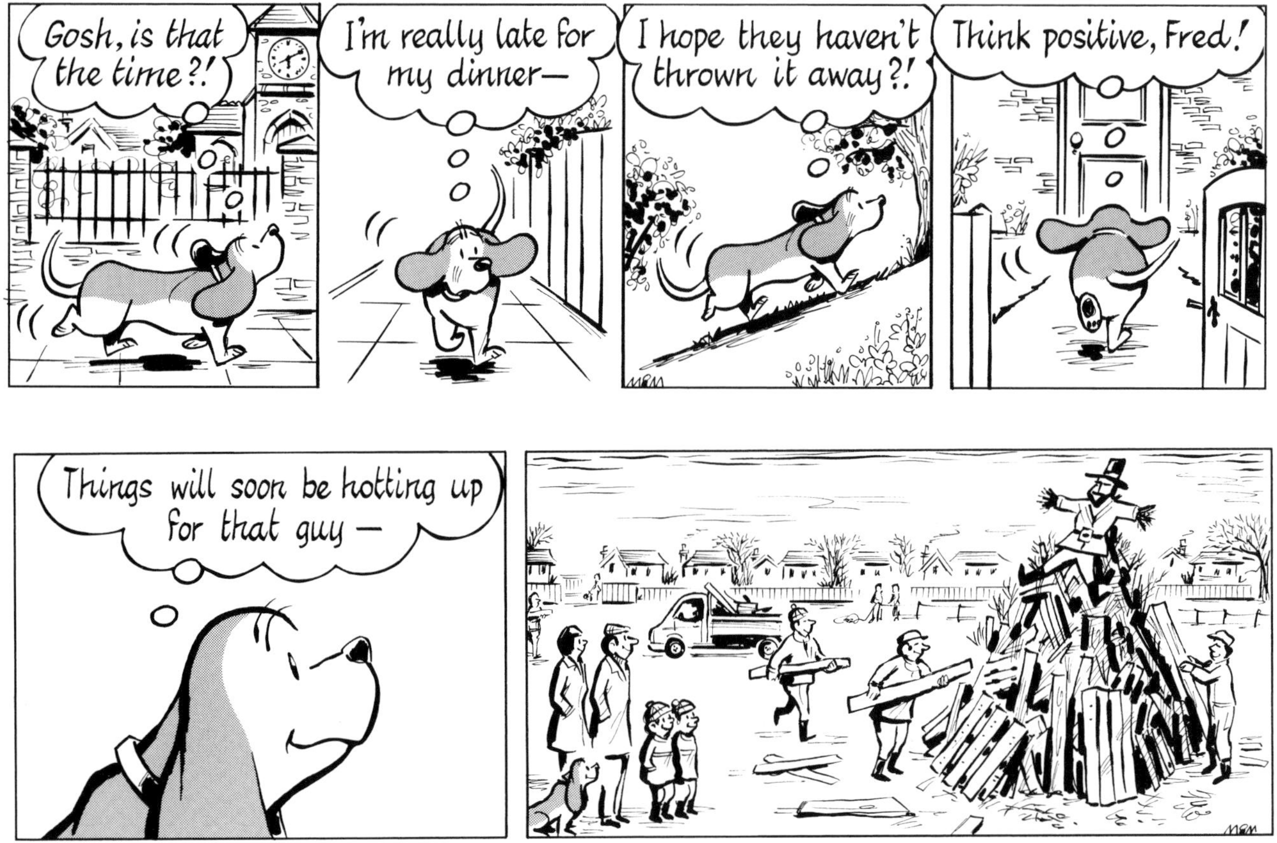
Gosh, is that the time?!
I'm really late for my dinner—
I hope they haven't thrown it away?!
Think positive, Fred!
Things will soon be hotting up for that guy –

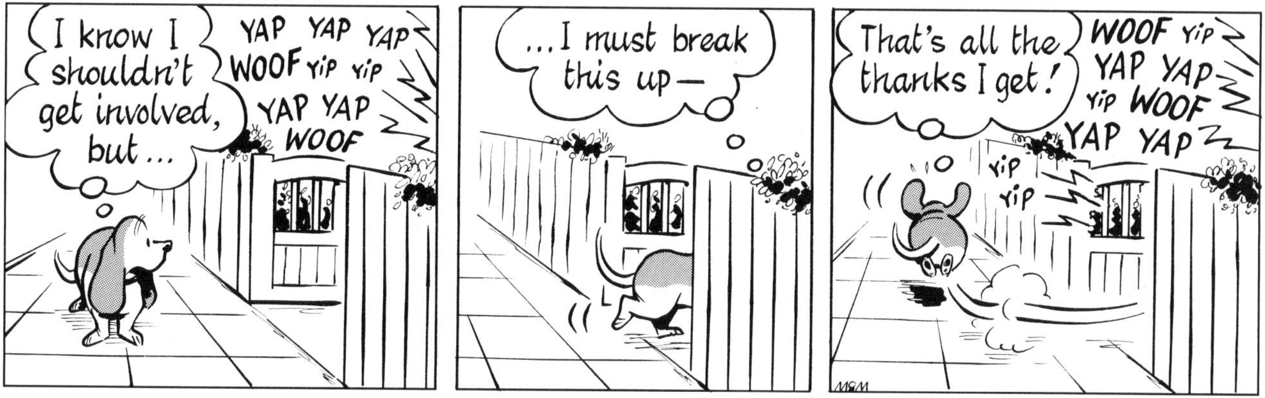
I know I shouldn't get involved, but ...
YAP YAP YAP
WOOF Yip Yip
YAP YAP
WOOF
... I must break this up—
That's all the thanks I get!
WOOF Yip
YAP YAP
Yip WOOF
YAP YAP
Yip
Yip
M&M

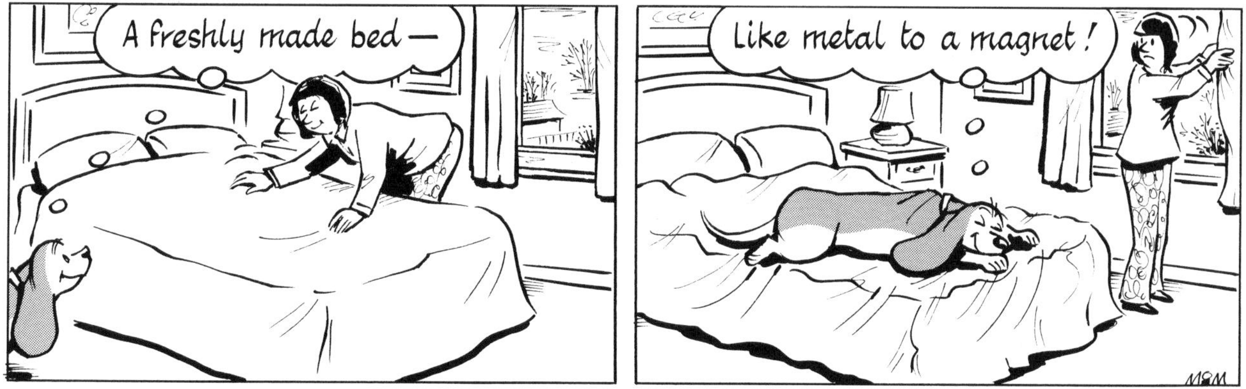
A freshly made bed—
Like metal to a magnet!
M&M

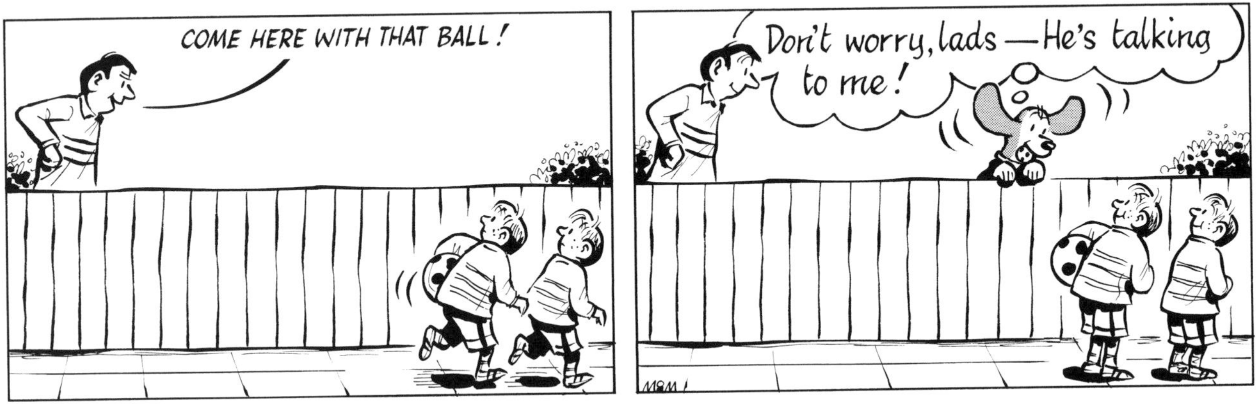
COME HERE WITH THAT BALL!
Don't worry, lads — He's talking to me!

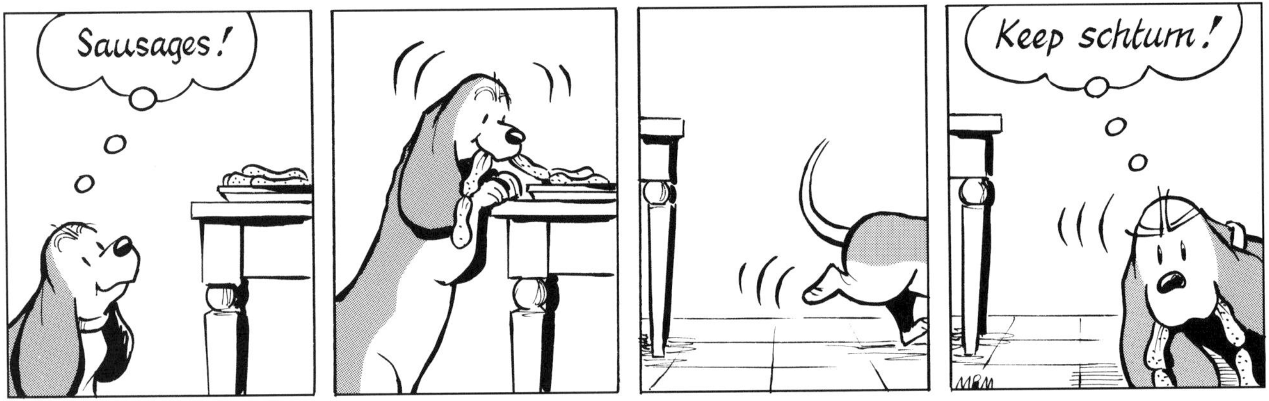
Sausages!
Keep schtum!

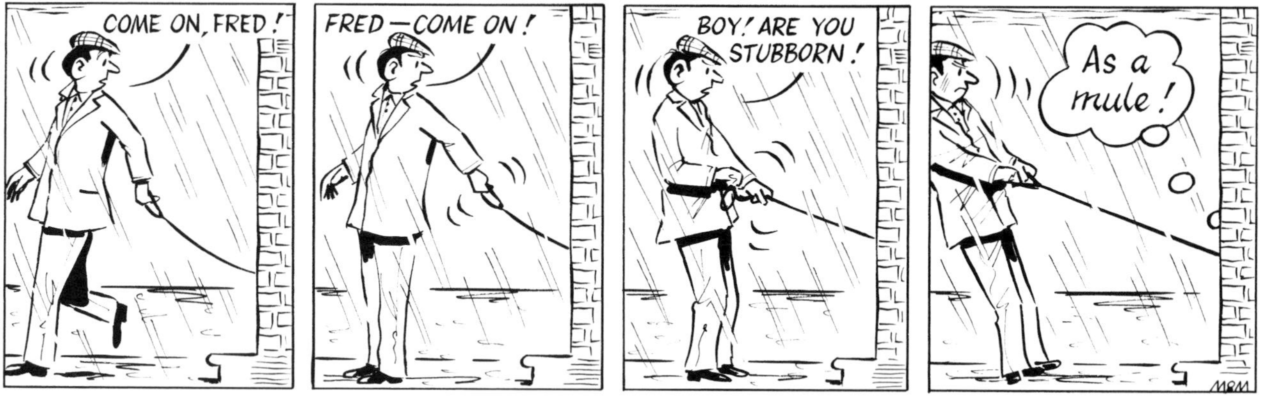
COME ON, FRED!
FRED—COME ON!
BOY! ARE YOU STUBBORN!
As a mule!
M&M

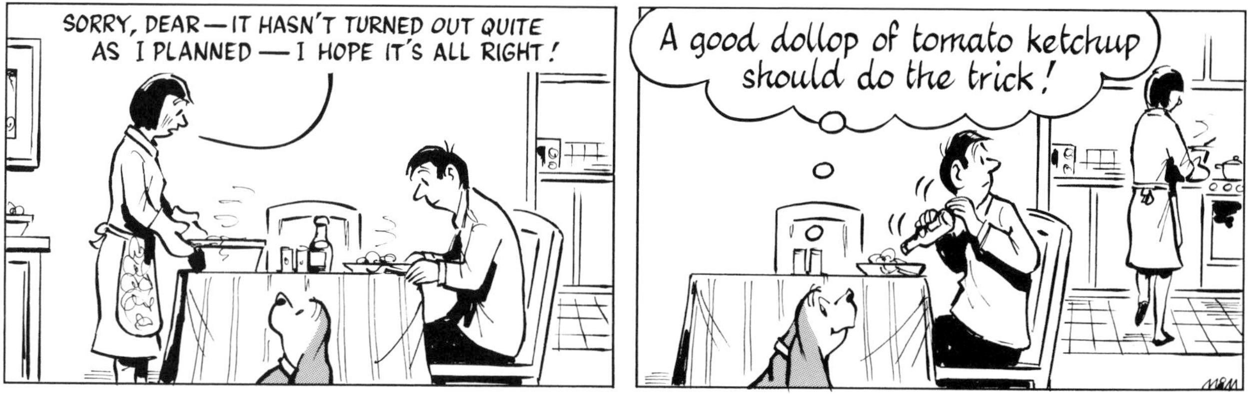
SORRY, DEAR—IT HASN'T TURNED OUT QUITE AS I PLANNED—I HOPE IT'S ALL RIGHT!
A good dollop of tomato ketchup should do the trick!
M&M

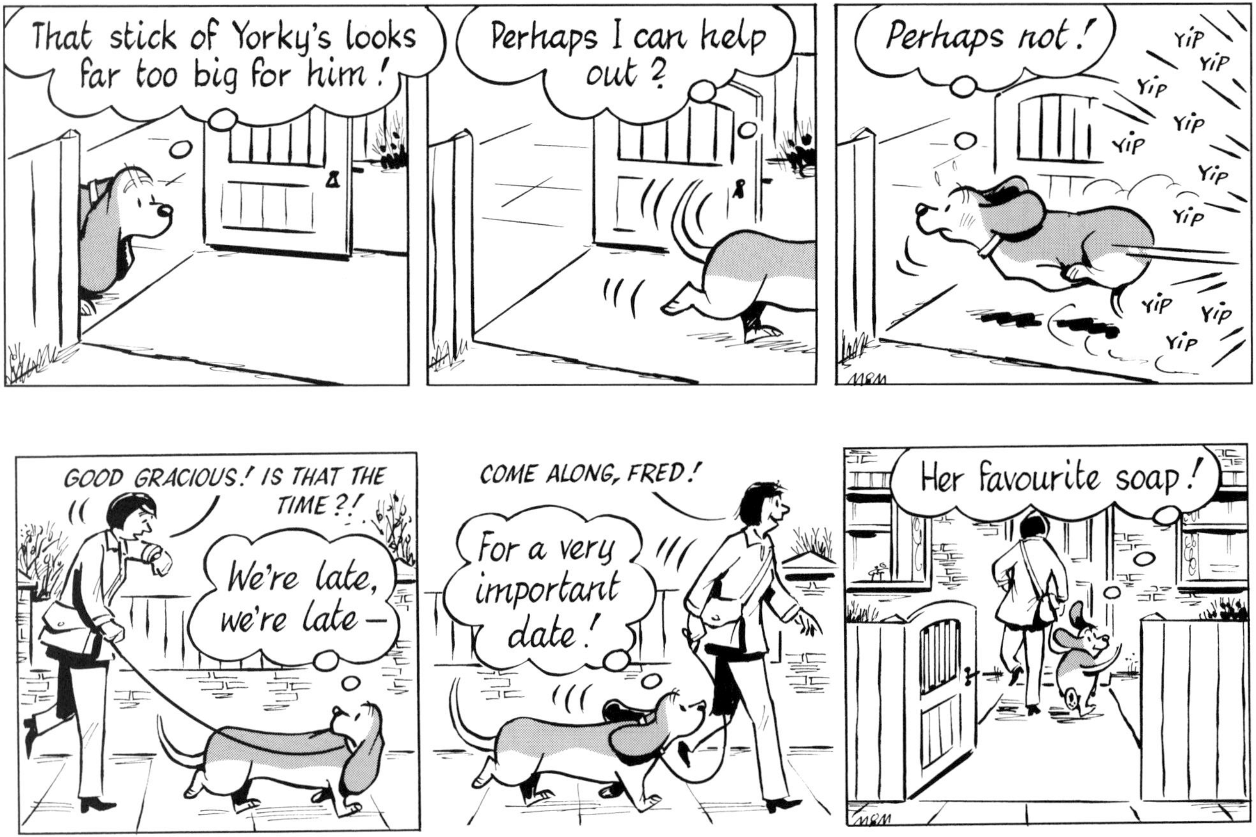
That stick of Yorky's looks far too big for him!
Perhaps I can help out?
Perhaps not!
YIP YIP YIP YIP YIP YIP YIP YIP YIP YIP
GOOD GRACIOUS! IS THAT THE TIME?!
We're late, we're late –
COME ALONG, FRED!
For a very important date!
Her favourite soap!

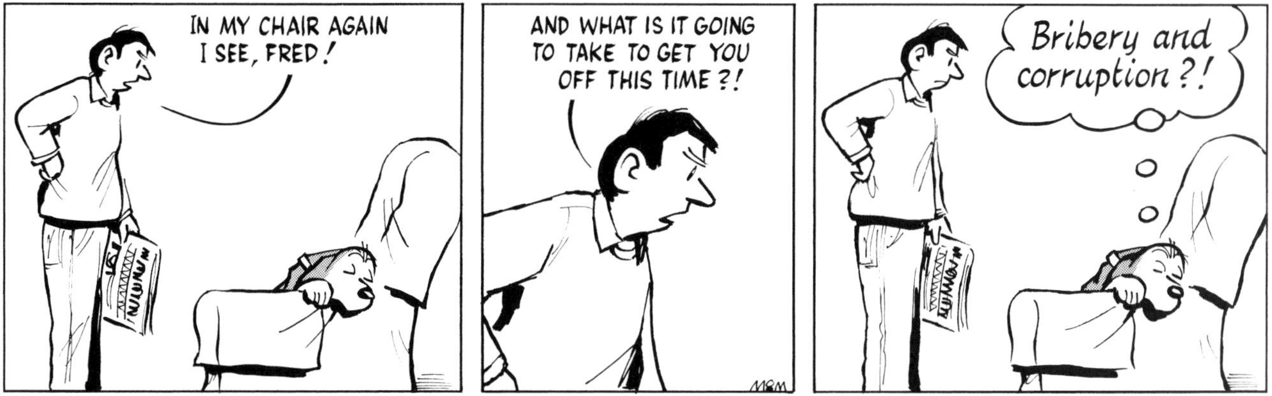
IN MY CHAIR AGAIN I SEE, FRED!
AND WHAT IS IT GOING TO TAKE TO GET YOU OFF THIS TIME ?!
Bribery and corruption ?!

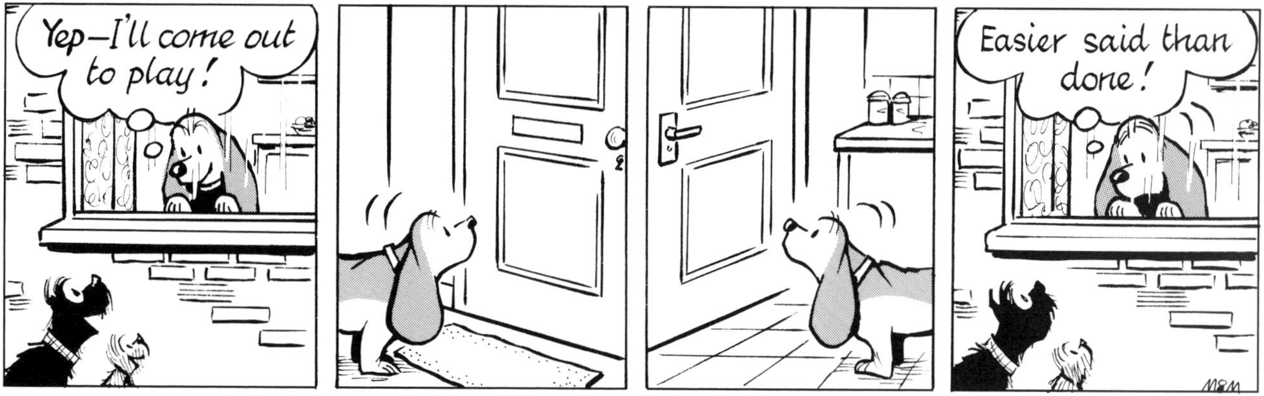
Yep—I'll come out to play!
Easier said than done!

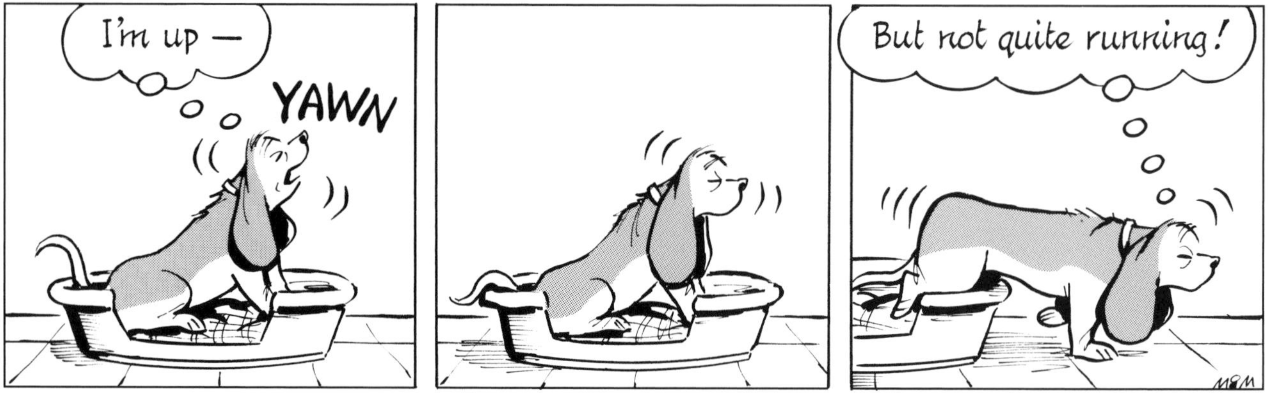
I'm up —
YAWN
But not quite running!
M&M

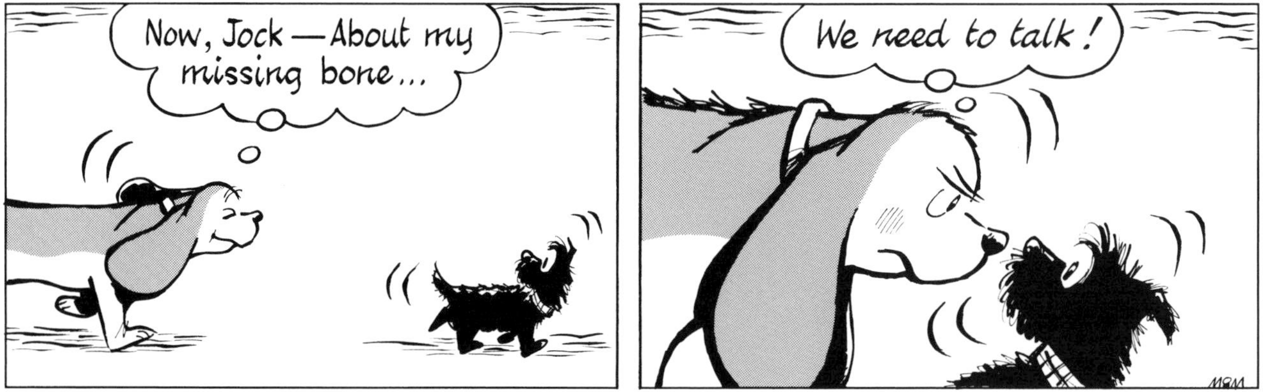
Now, Jock — About my missing bone...
We need to talk!
M&M

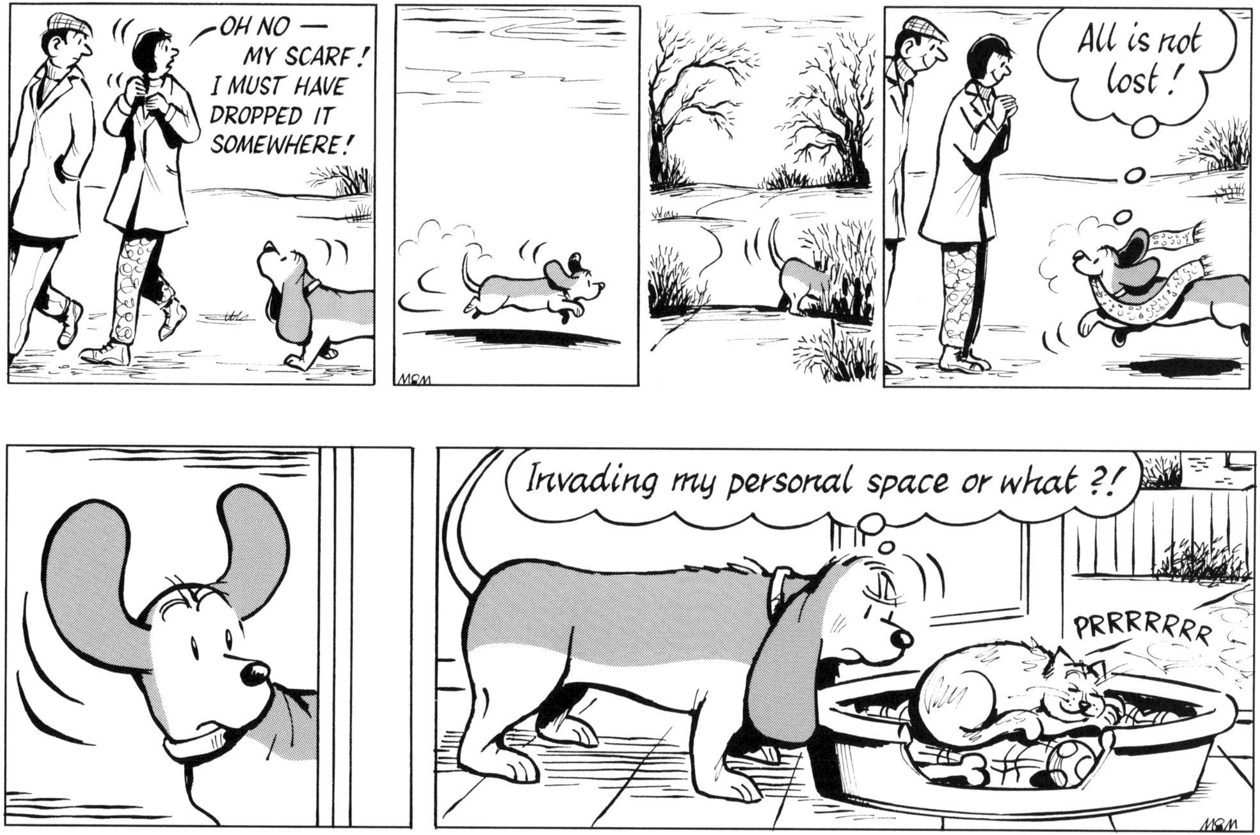
OH NO — MY SCARF! I MUST HAVE DROPPED IT SOMEWHERE!
MSM
All is not lost!
Invading my personal space or what?!
PRRRRRRR
MSM

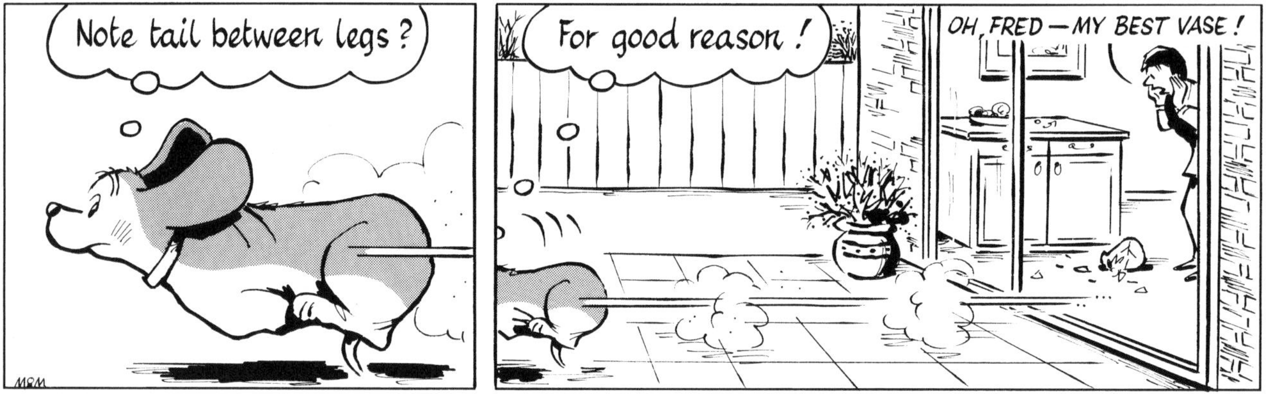
Note tail between legs?
For good reason!
OH, FRED—MY BEST VASE!

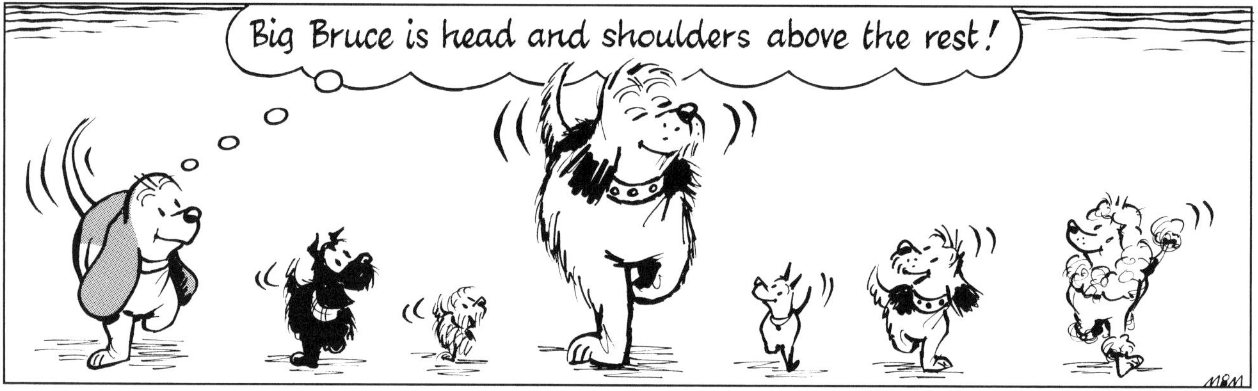
Big Bruce is head and shoulders above the rest!

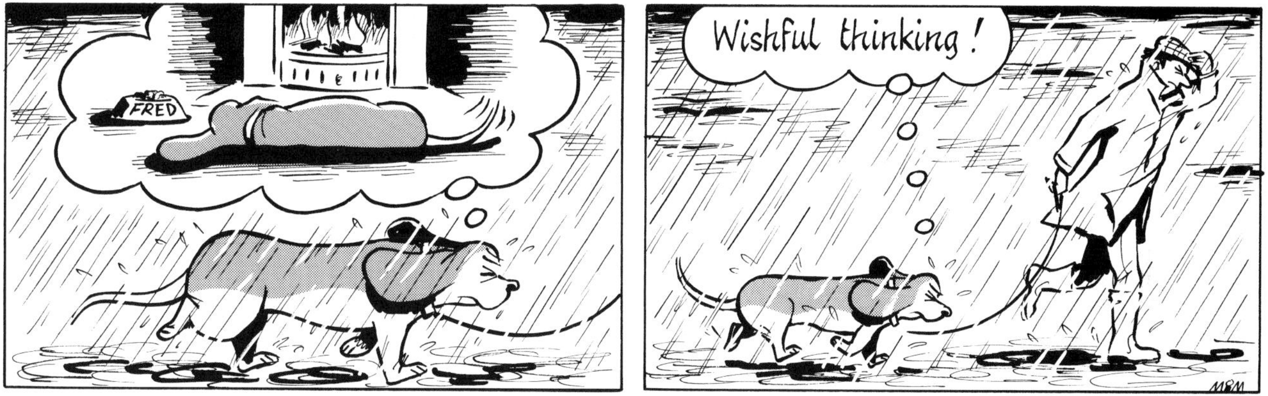
FRED
Wishful thinking!

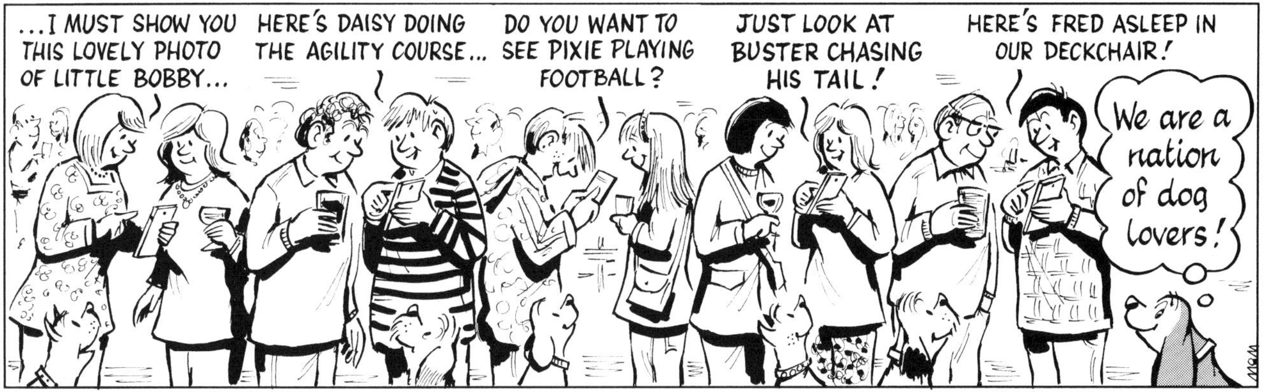
...I MUST SHOW YOU THIS LOVELY PHOTO OF LITTLE BOBBY...
HERE'S DAISY DOING THE AGILITY COURSE...
DO YOU WANT TO SEE PIXIE PLAYING FOOTBALL?
JUST LOOK AT BUSTER CHASING HIS TAIL!
HERE'S FRED ASLEEP IN OUR DECKCHAIR!
We are a nation of dog lovers!

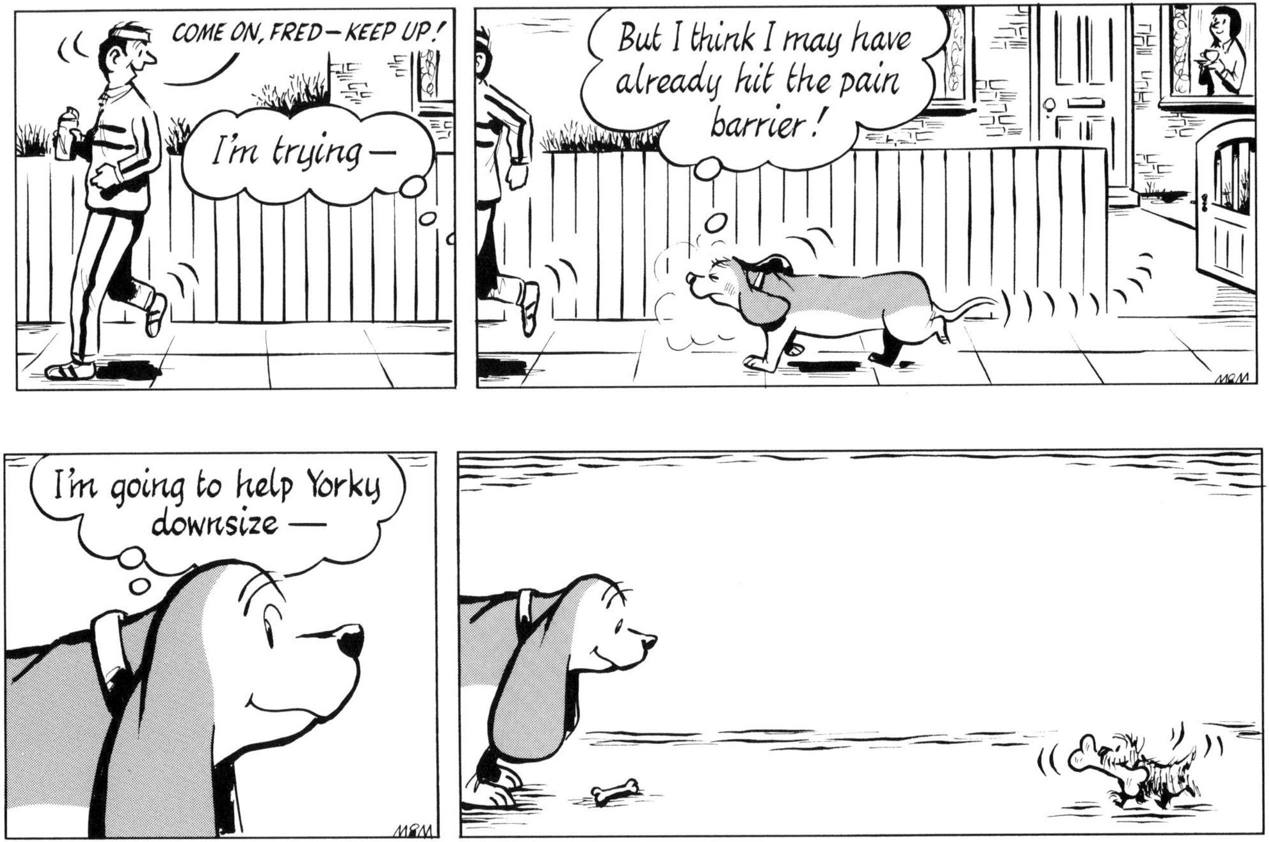
COME ON, FRED—KEEP UP!
I'm trying—
But I think I may have already hit the pain barrier!
I'm going to help Yorky downsize—

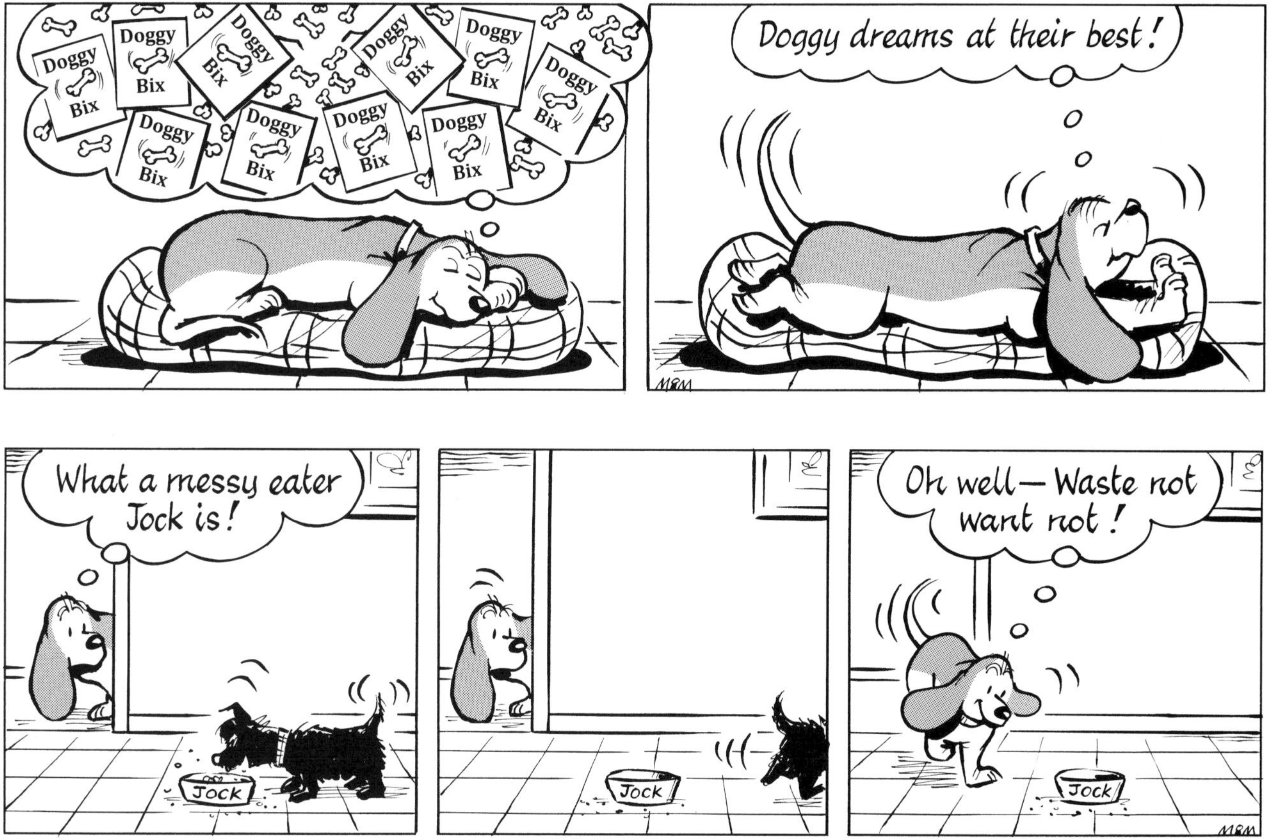
Doggy Bix
Doggy dreams at their best!
MBM
What a messy eater Jock is!
JOCK
JOCK
Oh well— Waste not want not!
JOCK
MBM

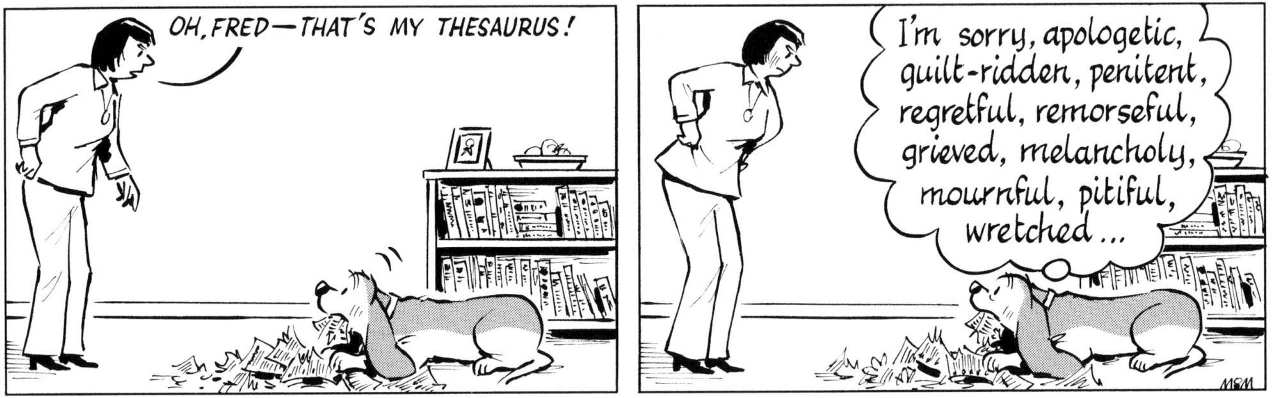
OH, FRED—THAT'S MY THESAURUS!
I'm sorry, apologetic, guilt-ridden, penitent, regretful, remorseful, grieved, melancholy, mournful, pitiful, wretched ...

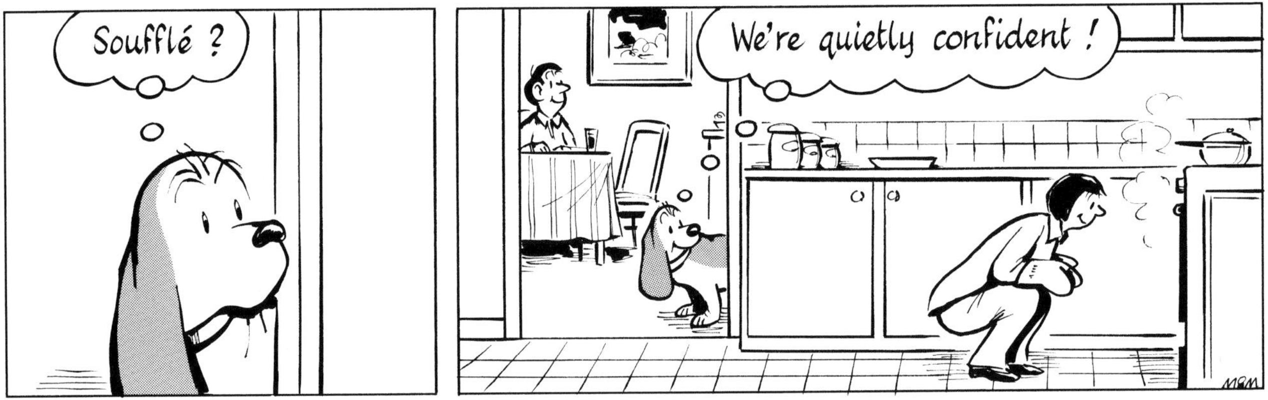
Soufflé ?
We're quietly confident !

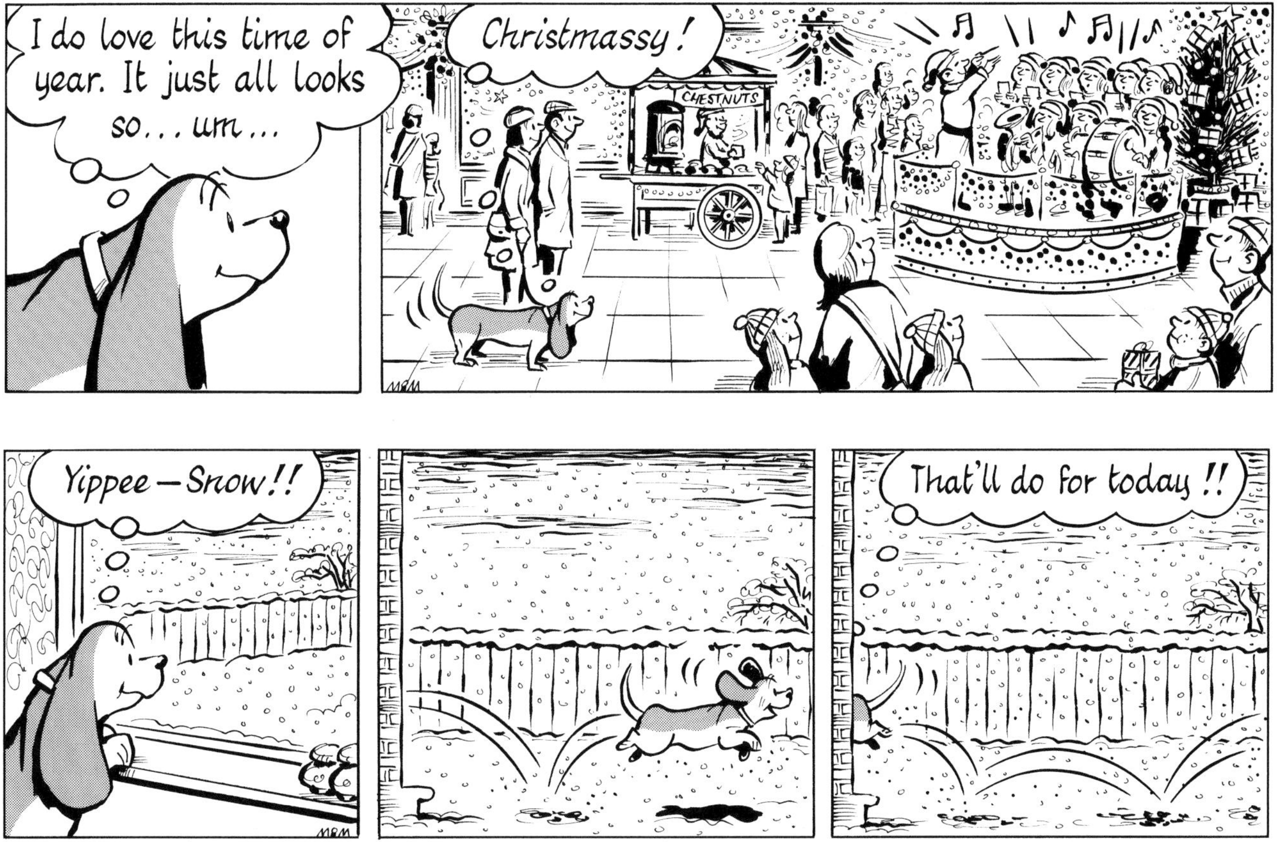
I do love this time of year. It just all looks so... um...
Christmassy!
CHESTNUTS
MBM
Yippee—Snow!!
MBM
That'll do for today!!

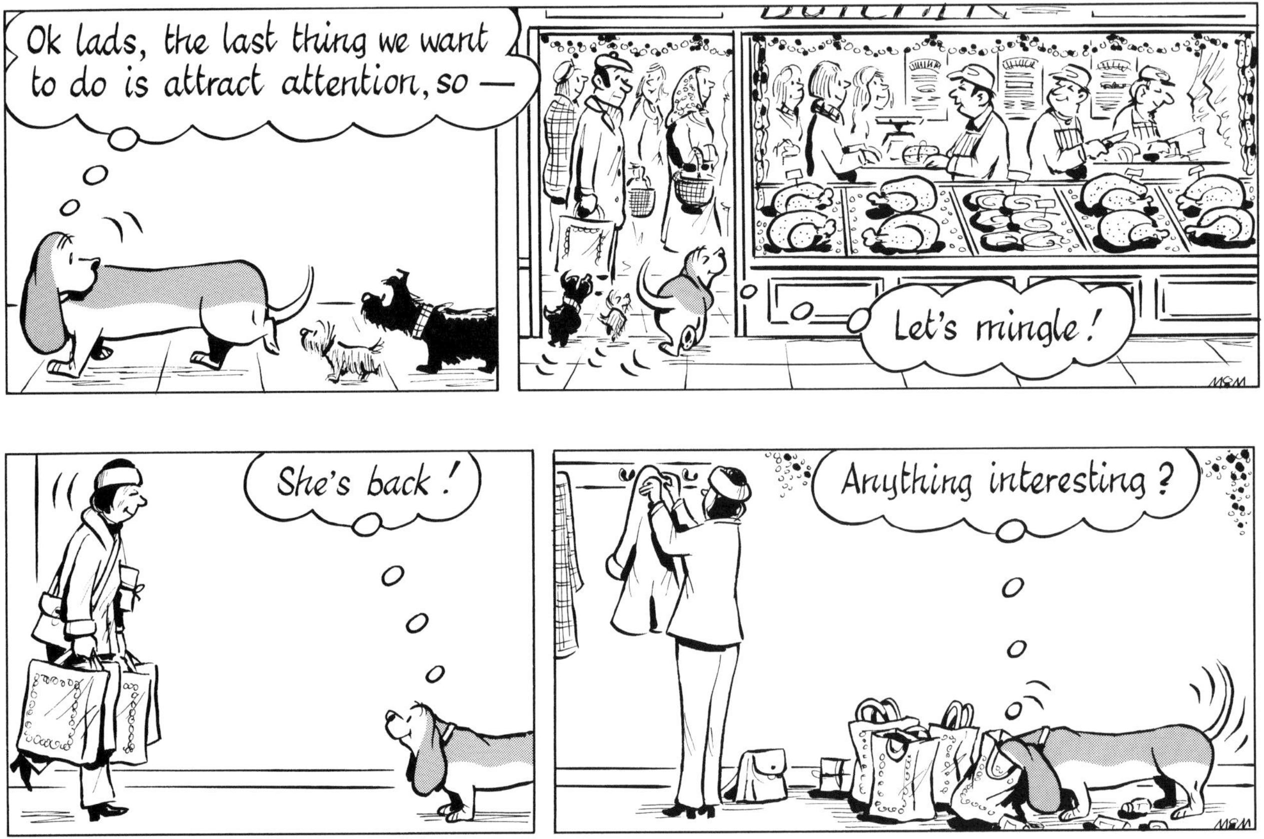
Ok lads, the last thing we want to do is attract attention, so —
Let's mingle!
She's back!
Anything interesting?

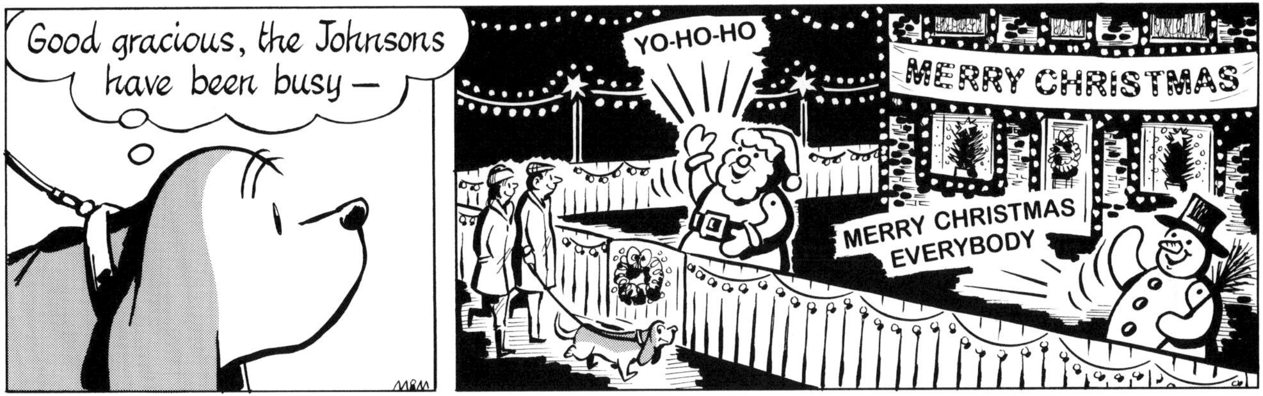
Good gracious, the Johnsons have been busy –
YO-HO-HO
MERRY CHRISTMAS
MERRY CHRISTMAS EVERYBODY

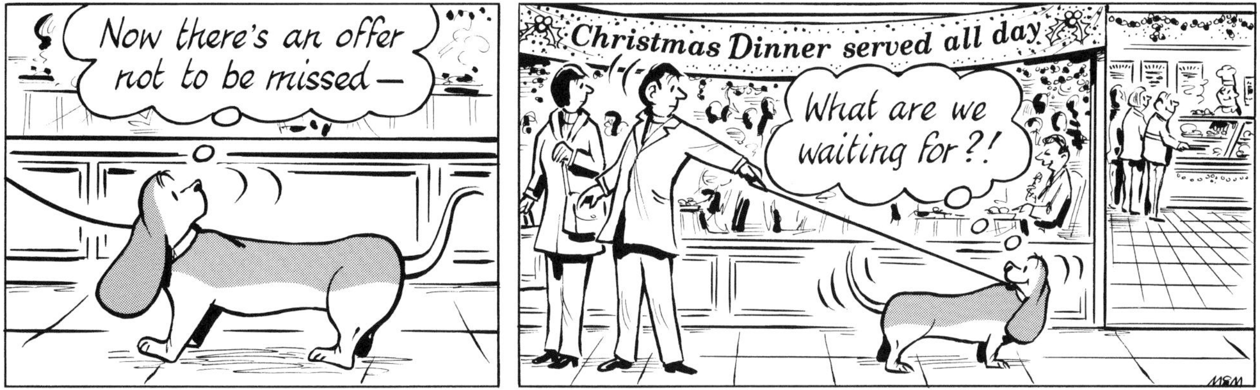
Now there's an offer not to be missed –
Christmas Dinner served all day
What are we waiting for?!

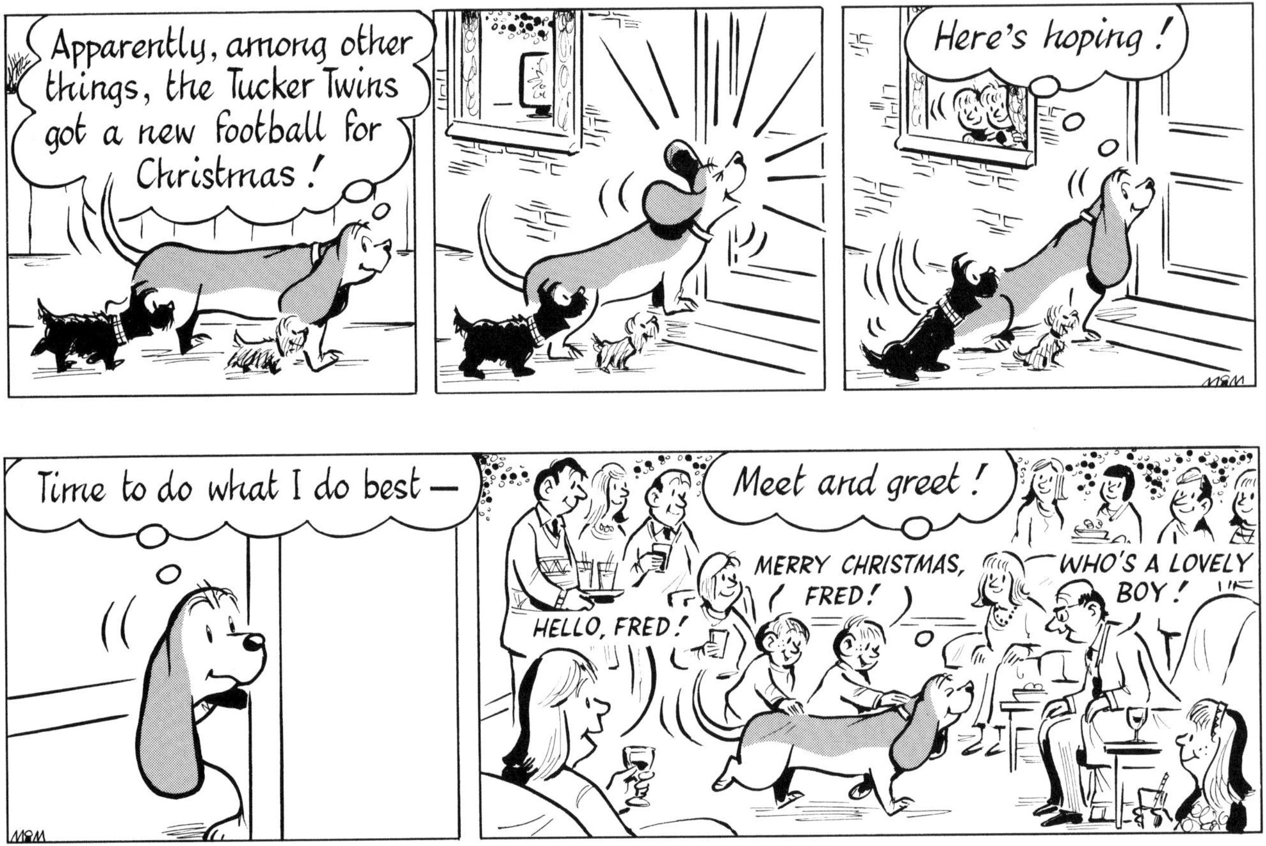
Apparently, among other things, the Tucker Twins got a new football for Christmas!
Here's hoping!
Time to do what I do best —
Meet and greet!
HELLO, FRED!
MERRY CHRISTMAS, FRED!
WHO'S A LOVELY BOY!